MW01295232

SHOOT FOR THE STAR

SHOOT FOR THE STAR version 3

Copyright 1993, 1996, 2011 by William F. Bates. All rights reserved. No portion of this book may be reproduced without the written permission of the publisher.
Published in the United States of America. Original ISBN 0-8499-3986-0.

If you are interested in having Bill Bates speak at your church, organization or special event, please contact him direct at bill@billbates.com

To Graham, Brianna, Hunter, Tanner and Dillon, my children...Shoot for your Own Star.

And to my father Dan Bates and my Uncle John Graham, whose lives shone like the brightest Star.

Acknowledgments

All of my life, all I have ever asked for has been an opportunity to prove myself. So I would like to thank those people who gave me the opportunity to write this book, thus fulfilling another dream.

Above all others, thanks to my wife Denise. She is the light of my life and has endured through thick and thin to be at my side with great love and mothering our beautiful children.

Thanks to Ron Cook for encouraging me to begin this project. Thanks to Bill Butterworth for putting my thoughts on paper and becoming a good friend.

Thanks to my Mother Peggy and Katherine, my wife's mother, for their unending dedication to our wonderful family.

Finally, thanks to Bob Davidson, another family man, for reviving and updating this book.

SHOOT FOR THE STAR

Version 3

Copyright 1993, 1996, 2011 by William F. Bates. All rights reserved. No portion of this book may be reproduced without the written permission of the publisher.

Published in the United States of America. Original ISBN 0-8499-3986-0

Vince Lombardi Trophies in Bill Bates office

"If we had 11 players on the field that played as hard as Bill Bates does and did their homework like he does, we'd be almost impossible to beat. Bill Bates and Cliff Harris are the greatest hitters I ever saw." – Tom Landry

"Bill Bates has covered kicks better, with more enthusiasm, and for more seasons than any other player I've ever seen. Every game starts with a kick, but when Bates is on the field, every game begins with a Bang!"
-John Madden

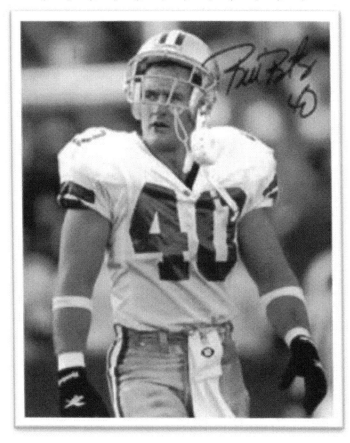

"You give yourself up. You do the things that you weren't made to do. Those are the kind of things our fans think of when they think of Bill Bates. He's a big part of the tradition of the Dallas Cowboys."
-Jerry Jones

Table of Contents

Prologue — 9
1 - "We Want the Ball!" — 17
2 - "Hit Someone as Hard as You Can!" — 25
3 - "Dream and Shoot for the Stars!" — 37
4 - "Trust in the Lord" — 45
5 - "We Are Counting on Bill at Tennessee" — 55
6 - "Winners Never Quit and Quitters Never Win!" — 65
7 - "What More Do You Want from Me?" — 79
8 - "Denise Can't See You Right Now!" — 89
9 - "It's Thursday Before the Last Saturday Preseason Game!" — 97
10 - "You'd Be the 13th Pick of the Dallas Cowboys!" — 113
11 - "He's what Defense is All About, Mean and Onery!" — 127
12 - "He Reminds Me of Me" — 139
13 - "The Greatest Hitter I Ever Saw" — 147
14 - "Turn Off That Machine!" — 153
15 - "Don't Mess Up the Hair" — 165
16 - "Call Me and Tell Me How Many There Are!" — 179
17 - "I'm Not Bullet-proof for a Reason" — 185
18 - "There's a Lot of Tape Left-You Can Still Tape Me!" — 197
19 - What Are Your Training Methods? — 211
20 - "Once I Make That First Hit, I'm Back!" — 225
21 - "Can We Repeat?" — 231
22 - "Put It In Three-inch Letters-We Will Win The Game!" — 239
23 - "Who's Gonna Win the Super Bowl? Daddy Is!" — 249
24 – Epilogue — 257
25 - Living the Dream — 263
26 - Super Bowl XXX — 275
27 - The Show goes on — 289
28 - After All the Years — 293
29 - Dan Bates — 313
30 - New Stars — 317
31 - Miracles & Family — 329
Biography — 343

Prologue – The first time I saw Bill Bates
by Bob Davidson

I was new to the area and looking to take in some great football. I walked swiftly across the parking lot toward the large stadium in the distance, late for the game. Hopefully I could find my seat before the end of the first quarter. The roaring crowd told me the action was already taking place on the field.

Entering the turnstiles, the stadium announcer's deep bass voice broadcast that the Eagles were set to punt. Good, that meant I would see the first drive of the championship home team with their all-star quarterback, running back and receivers. The articles in the newspaper all touted how great this team was. It was said that it was probably the best in their history.

I found the tunnel out to the seats. A tall police officer in high black boots was standing beside the usher and neither noticed me because they were focused on the action on the field. The Eagles had already punted and the teams were lined up for the play.

Looking back, it wasn't a complicated play or one that much could be written about, just a short slant caught in full stride by a split receiver, who then outran the defense to the end zone. The crowd reacted with everyone standing and screaming a deafening roar. The hometown team had taken the lead. I stood and watched the extra point before starting my climb to the highest part of the stadium.

The kick-off team ran onto the field as I turned to make my climb up the steep steps and was marching up when the ball was kicked. Everyone was on their feet and I was still climbing, then I heard the distinctive sound of pads and helmets hitting.

It was the sound that everyone in the stadium had come to the game to hear. It is the sound of the ultimate football hit; one that feeds the crowd. It is the type of hit that ignites a team and makes the team jump in the air and scream at the top of their lungs. It is the sound made when two opponents, travelling at their top speed, putting all of their year round training on the line in a single man on man moment.

One would be the victor, the other would fall. Both had put their all into that split second. It is the super hit the crowd craves, what the coaches crave and mostly, what the players crave.

That hit meant that two players believed in themselves and were willing to lay it on the line for their team. Hit's like this make men out of boys. Hits like this turn a game around and make a team a champion. Everyone in the stadium could feel that hit!

I spun around at the sound of the impact to see one player flat on his back, the other player several yards beyond him still in motion. The football was bouncing right in front of him and even though the hit had slowed him down, his momentum was still carrying him awkwardly with flailing arms and legs toward the fumbled ball of his opponent. Scooping it in as he fell, he curled tightly around the ball to insure no-one else could hit it loose.

The Announcer came off his seat and boomed in his deep bass voice "TACKLE AND RECOVERY BY BATES!" The crowd roared.

I saw Bates on the ball, curled up tight. The whistles had blown and he was still holding tight to that ball. He only let it go when the referee reached down to pick it up. The crowd was still screaming at the top of their lungs welcoming Bates back across the field to the sideline.

I finally made it up to my seat and getting my money's worth was easy as the All-Star quarterback showed why he had led the team to championships by scoring on the very next play. This time he dropped back out of the shotgun and put the ball into a high arc down the sideline. The nose of the ball turned down, spinning in a perfect spiral to the outstretched hands of his favorite receiver. The crowd roared again, the home team up by two scores in the first quarter.

The kick returner who had a slobber-knocker put on him by Bates was nowhere to be found. The Eagles Head Coach was relieved to see the ensuing kick-off go through the end zone. He and his coaches had watched plenty of film and had planned on running away from Bates on kickoff returns but it seemed that he was everywhere.

Now, they would get another chance to run their own highly touted offense. Both teams had some of the best players in the league and had won the right to be in this round of the playoffs.

Bates stayed on the field, lining up as a leader in his defensive backfield. On the first play he broke up a pass over the middle and on then third down he met a running back, who outweighed him by thirty pounds, in the offensive backfield. The back had a full head of steam and was just making the corner when Bates slid between his blockers and like a bullet shot out of a gun, launched himself into the oncoming path of the back. It was another slobber-knocker. This time the back took a little longer getting up but Bates was back in the huddle getting slaps and high fives.

"BATES ON THE TACKLE!" the bass voice boomed again to the roar of the crowd. It was easy to see why this team was so loved by their fans. And from the looks of the play on the field, the players loved their fans.

After the unsuccessful sweep, the Eagles punted. There was Bates again, catching the punt! The high arching ball drove him back ten yards where he cleanly caught it with soft hands. He then turned toward the sideline. Making the corner, he turned up field, a wall of blockers in front of him. He raced swiftly and smoothly up the field, tight roping the sideline for over forty yards. An Eagle player got a piece of him causing him to step on the line or he would have taken it all the way to the bank.

I had barely been in my seat for 2 minutes, yet I had already seen some incredible play on the field. I didn't know who this Bates guy was, other than reading a few short articles about the team. I was there to see the Championship team from the year before.

Having forgotten my glasses in the car it was hard to see all of the action on the field. As the game progressed it was apparent that this Bates guy was the real deal. Looking back it seemed that the announcer was

11

crediting him up with at least every other tackle if not more. How could one guy be all over the place like Bates? The announcer continued to call his name over and again all night.

The fans in the stadium were loud and cheered every play. It was soon apparent that I would not need the seat very often during this game. Everyone stayed standing and during the plays they were yelling out encouragement. They weren't just yelling, it was more like the scream of a jet engine around me. They were seasoned fans who had perfected the art of cheering at the right time and keeping quiet when it was an advantage to their team.

A couple of rows in front of me sat two attractive blondes. One had a cowbell that never seemed to stop ringing except when she was taking pictures. The other, who was clearly her sister, yelled extra loud and was totally focused on the action on the field. They knew their football. It was hard not to notice them.

Everybody around could see that they were leading the cheers from our section. Whenever the announcer reported another first down for the team they would start pointing in the direction of the end zone and yelling "Move those chains, move those chains, move those chains!" Whenever Bates made a play they would give each other a hug and high-five all those around them. The cowbell seldom stopped except for pictures, hugs and high fives! Watching the game was fun but seeing these two blondes bounce around with so much energy increased the entertainment value.

Turning to the man sitting beside me I pointed to the two blondes and commented "they sure are having fun."

"That's Bill Bates wife. They've got a lot to cheer for" he said over the roar of another "Tackle by Bates!"

I was getting my fill of good football that night as the home team took it to the Eagles. Late in the game I was looking down on the sideline when I finally found Bill Bates standing, feet apart, arms crossed and looking intently out onto the field at the offense running the clock down towards the end of the game.

The coaches were making sure that all the reserves had gotten into the game and it would only be a matter of minutes before the celebrations started in the middle of the field.

That was the first time I saw Bill Bates in person. It wasn't in a Stadium in Dallas and Bill Bates wasn't wearing number 40. He was standing on the sidelines helping coach the Nease High School Panthers.

The Bates that I kept hearing announced over and over on the PA system were his two sons, Graham and Hunter. His two younger sons were on the sidelines as ball boys, and were taking in the action on the field. The man beside me explained that everywhere you look you would find a Bates. He even pointed at another beautiful blonde down front who was a triplet to the boys playing on the field.

Hunter Bates has since gone on to play defensive back for Northwestern University while Graham Bates plays defensive back for Arkansas State. Of course they both make their marks on special teams. Tanner Bates was a standout cornerback for Ponte Vedra High School and a stalwart in their start up football program. He is now starting a career in the entertainment industry when he finishes his fast track degree at Full Sail University.

The youngest Bates boy, Dillon now plays for Ponte Vedra High School and has started since his freshman year at linebacker. He hasn't stopped growing but it is already apparent that he will be the biggest Bates boy yet. Just like his daddy and big brothers he knows how to deliver a slobber-knocker and recorded over 100 tackles in his sophomore year alone.

Amongst all this testosterone in the Bates family is Brianna. As a triplet she learned to fend for herself. Adding two more boys to the family, it must've seemed unfair to her growing up. Instead she has used it to her advantage and is studying English at Florida University. She is a beautiful young lady with the smile of her mother and no doubt the toughness of her daddy.

Denise Bates is contagious. As Mama Bates she heads the household. She is her children's biggest fan and the head cheerleader in the stands. Her sidekick at every game is the woman who I thought was her sister. No, she is not her sister, she is her mother Katherine. The two of them never miss a game unless schedules conflict, which they often do with two Division I football players and a rising high school STAR.

What I mean about contagious is her smile and love for life. She is genuine and happy and with that combination, it is easy to see why she is admired and emulated. To ask her, she is unaware of the people who watch her cheering in the stands as the announcer once again says "Bates on the tackle!" She doesn't realize other parents' admiration when she cheers for every one of their sons. She knows it takes a team to win a championship.

The All-Star Quarterback on the field that night has gone on to win a Heisman Trophy, National Championships at Florida and a NFL first round draft pick for the Denver Broncos. He has really touched the hearts of many and a wonderful young man. His name is Tim Tebow.

13

Bill Bates didn't become an NFL player by himself. His strong Christian faiths, strong will, the strength of his family and Denise, the love of his life are the blocks in the foundation that formed his career. The coaches from his earliest days forward are looked back upon as helping form the character that has sustained Bill throughout his professional career and it continues today as he sets the right example of being a champion to young men and women.

Bill, with Bill Butterworth, wrote Shoot for the STAR in 1994 to Chronicle his story in football from his earliest beginning as a player in the Mullins Methodist Church league in Germantown, Tennessee and up until that point in his NFL Career.

Since its original release Bill went on to win Super Bowl XXX with the Cowboys, coach in the NFL, started numerous successful businesses and now continues to coach his sons and their teammates. He sets a great example of leading a good life.

In 2011 Bill is still winning football awards. If you look Bill up in Wikipedia you will find that Tom Landry once said, "If we had 11 players on the field that played as hard as Bill Bates does and did their homework like he does, we'd be almost impossible to beat". In 2011 Bill won the Tom Landry Legend Award.

After reading Shoot for the STAR, I had to have more. My son Tyler Davidson plays on the Ponte Vedra Sharks with Dillon Bates. This has allowed me to get to know Bill and his family. The Ponte Vedra Sharks football program is only a few years old and with the leadership of Head Coach Michael Loyd and the inspiration of a group of some of the finest assistant coaches in the State of Florida, including Bill, they have won a District Championship and two rounds of State Playoff games in just their fourth year as a football program.

Bill finally agreed to continue his writing, not to just get me off his back, but to update a wonderful story about his life and the family that he and Denise are raising.

Dallas Cowboys fans will be treated to stories about their glorious past and additional stories about Super Bowl XXX where Bill won his third Super Bowl ring. He updates you about what has taken place in his life since his retirement from the NFL. You will find out about his family and how he has stayed connected with football as both a coach and with his business enterprises.

Finally you will see Denise Bates's Family photo album throughout the book. She is known in the family as the *Mamarazzi* because she takes so many pictures to preserve the family's history. This is no ordinary family album. You will be treated to never before published private photographs of some of the Cowboys legends, Bill as a player, Awards, Super Bowl Rings and memories. You will be treated with pictures of the Bates boys and the championship teams they have played success they are having. The Bates family is special and through Denise's lens you will see how true Champions live, love and play.

Bill continues to give inspirational speeches today. Normally he will end every speech with the same short poem. After reading this book you will see how Bill has lived out his faith in his life and the rewards he has received. The end of the poem says "Count on God, instead of yourself."

To Bill it is not about the glory but the journey every day. Sure, he likes the sweet taste of victory and has learned to savor it. Throughout his career he never knew from one day to the next if he would be cut from the team. He always gave them a reason to keep him. Bill could never let down his physical training or mental attitude. It caused him to give thanks for every day he was wearing the STAR on his helmet and now the diamond encrusted rings on his hand.

It is my honor to call him a friend.

-Bob Davidson

Super Bowl XXVII, XXVIII and XXX

"We Want the Ball!"

"This one's for you, Bill."

The slap on the back and those words of encouragement came from my teammate, Emmitt Smith. I was sitting in front of my locker in the dressing room deep inside the belly of the Georgia Dome. Emmitt was not alone in his sentiment.

Several other Cowboys had made their feelings clear to me in a similar way. It's an humbling feeling to hear your teammates say to you, "We're gonna win this game for you, Bill Bates!" But then again, that's what makes this Cowboy team so great.

There's real comradery and respect.

"Thanks, man," is about all I could muster up. My heart was full. This was no ordinary game the guys were talking about. It was January 30, 1994 in Atlanta, Georgia.

It was the Super Bowl.

As far back as I can remember, I had hoped one day to play in this game.

Our head coach, Jimmy Johnson, had gone to great pains during the week before this game to point out how important this game would be. For the second year in a row the Dallas Cowboys would represent the NFC in the World's Championship. Coach didn't want the second time to throw anybody off. "Sure, we were here last year. Sure, we won. Sure, we got Super Bowl rings. We achieved the ultimate in our professional careers. It's true that that's the case for a lot of you guys."

"But that's not true for everyone," Coach continued.

"Bernie Kosar (our backup quarterback) wasn't here last year.

"You don't have a Super Bowl ring, do you, Bernie?"

"No, sir, I don't," Bernie replied.

"Do you want a Super Bowl ring, Bernie?" "Yes, sir, I do!"

"So, you see, guys? You're playing for Bernie Kosar out there! Eddie Murray (our kicker), do you have a Super Bowl ring?"

"No, I don't, sir."

"Do you want a Super Bowl ring?"

"Yes, sir! I've waited for this opportunity my whole life!" "So guys, you're playing for Eddie Murray out there!"

(This was especially meaningful to our team, since Eddie was thirty-nine years old-a real veteran.) I didn't fall into the same category as these two guys, but there was a similar feeling in the air. The truth was-I did have a Super Bowl ring from our victory in Pasadena.

But I never left the sideline.

I remember January 1993 very clearly. I was rehabilitating from a horrible knee injury. I could not play in that Super Bowl. I didn't even dress.

The day before I was out on the links at beautiful Bel Air Country Club in southern California, playing golf with Jack Wagner, the actor. The twosome behind us caught my attention. It was Dan Marino and John Elway, two of the most famous quarterbacks in the game. I've always thought of them as two of the best, both playing for teams that are always strong. They caught up with us at one point and we began to small-talk. They sensed how hard it was for me to sit the Super Bowl out.

"I wish I was playing," I lamented. "I wish I could be a part of it."

"You are a part of it!" they both replied quickly. "Enjoy it! We just wish we were in your shoes-even injured- just to be there. You are a part of it because you are part of the team!"

I remember being encouraged by their words. I did everything I could to be helpful on the sidelines. I was part of the *team*. But this year was different. This year I could play.

We had been in Atlanta for several days before the game. The media hype was colossal and there were people everywhere! We couldn't take one step without being accosted by a hoard of reporters. Sure, it was exciting, but it was also a royal pain! Therefore, Saturday night before the game, Coach Johnson thought it best to move us to another hotel, where we could enjoy a little quiet and solitude in an otherwise hectic week.

The next day we rode buses to the stadium after chapel and our pregame meal. Since we changed hotels, it was a longer bus ride than usual because we were further way from the Georgia Dome. I guess what I'm saying is the bus ride gave me a good chance to think. The bus ride is usually pretty quiet. Most guys are either reading or listening to tapes on a Walkman. Quiet tells the coaches that you are serious about the game that's ahead. The coaches like that. As highway whizzed by, my mind traveled to the chapel service that morning. Coach Johnson had invited a priest, Father Leo, to speak to us, and his comments were very meaningful to me. "How fortunate you are to be in this situation," the Father commented. "So few ever get here. Give thanks to God for this wonderful opportunity."

"Remember your parents today. They put you in this position. Think of their sacrifices so that you could be here. How proud your parents must be as they sit in the stands, watching their sons play in the biggest game in all of professional sports. Think of all their flashbacks in this great moment. Remember your teachers and your coaches, all who contributed to you being here today."

Father Leo then led our Catholic teammates in mass, while all the Protestants moved to another room, circled up, held hands, and prayed together. There were about fifteen of us who talked to our heavenly Father. It was a very moving experience as each of us, one by one, prayed out loud to the Lord.

On the bus, I continued to determine that I was going to take it all in. I thought back to all the people who had been a part of my life who would not be in the stadium, but would see the game on television. My heart was filled with gratitude for a long list of fine folks.

The bus arrived, and the routine of dressing for the game began. When you include the taping of ankles and other individual preparations, it can take more than an hour to get fully dressed. I tried hard to go through my routine, attempting to treat this one like any other game. It wasn't easy. A game like this one really tests your ability to focus. Adrenaline runs high, so it is vitally important to keep every- thing in its proper perspective.

Once dressed, I joined my teammates out on the field for warm-ups. I wanted to go through my normal routine out on the field as well, but I was aware of the unusual amount of adrenaline in my system, so I was cautious. When a person carries a large amount of adrenaline in their system, even jogging can bring on fatigue. I also noticed the air in the fully enclosed Georgia Dome. It was very thick. That alerted me to the possibility of a loss of a lot of water weight, which could lead to cramps. This type of air could also cause hyper- ventilating. So what does a player on the field think about during pregame warm-ups? Well, this player was silently asking God, "Please don't let me hyperventilate on the field, okay? Please? Don't let me pass out, okay?"

We left the field and returned to the dressing room. Shortly it would be time for Coach Johnson's pregame talk. But before that meeting, we participated in another kind of meeting that had become a standard ritual for many of us Cowboys.

At this point we met with our team chaplain, John Weber, for prayer. The whole team is invited but, of course, it is voluntary. Most of the team participates but, even so, we try to be sensitive to the rest of the team by not making a big deal out of it in front of everyone. For that reason, we go off to pray in a more private spot. For our team, that spot happens to be the showers! It's quite a sight to see a bunch of grown men in football uniforms, each down on one knee, earnestly praying in the shower! As strange as it may look, it's incredibly meaningful for us to focus in on God's grace in our lives.

Once again my mind flashed back to Pasadena ... the year before. During our prayer I remember being grateful to God for allowing me to be a part of this amazing event. I was truly thankful. But I also remember telling the Lord I'd sure be grateful if we could come back to the Super Bowl next year so I could play in it, instead of just watching! God heard my words and smiled down on me because-sure enough-here we were again.

John led us in prayer and then we quickly moved back into the locker room for Coach Johnson's remarks. This coach is a motivator. He wanted his remarks to inspire and relax us so we could play at our full potential. "This is a big game-it is the Super Bowl," Coach began. "But it's also just another game. We need to play our game out there. And, remember, we are a four-quarter team. We will win this game in the fourth quarter. If we blow 'em out right away, that's fine. But if we don't-if we get behind-remember, that's okay, because we'll get them in the fourth quarter." Coach got us all pumped up. We left the lockers and headed up to the tunnel.

Fortunately, I had the presence of mind to enjoy this moment in the tunnel. The introductions of the players take place here. You wait in the tunnel, they announce your name, and you run onto the field. I found myself thinking, so this is what it's like to run out of the tunnel for the Super Bowl!

Since we were the visiting team, we were introduced first.

Then we stood on the sidelines as our opponents, the Buffalo Bills, were introduced. It was almost time!

Natalie Cole stepped to the microphone at midfield and sang the national anthem beautifully. But I have to admit, as is usually the case during "The Star-Spangled Banner," my mind was someplace else. My mind was with my family. My thoughts are always with them, so for that reason, I don't make a conscious effort to locate them in the stands during the game.

I thought about Denise and what a great wife she is to me.

I silently thanked God for her and our four kids, Brianna, Graham, Hunter, and Tanner. I knew Denise was in the stands with my parents, Dan and Peggy, as well as my two sisters, Rosemary and Rachel. Also in the Bates' family section were Denise's mom, Katherine, her stepdad, Jerry, my

Uncle Jim, Cousin Jay, and a host of others who came to be supportive. Emotion was running high!

At the end of the anthem, I continued my routine by running around and stretching a little to stay loose. I put my right leg over the bench and did my right hamstring stretch, then my left hamstring stretch. Then I switched by putting my left leg over the bench and did the same thing. Physically, I was ready.

It was time for the coin toss.

Each week Coach Johnson announces the captains for that particular game. We would have six players as captains: two from offense, two from defense, and two from special teams. The captains chosen for the Super Bowl from the Dallas Cowboys were Michael Irvin and Kevin Gogan from the offense, Ken Norton and Jim Jeffcoat from the defense, and from special teams, Eddie Murray and Bill Bates.

As we walked from the sideline to the center of the field, we tried to ease our nerves by joking about how much money had been bet on this game-even how much money had been bet on this coin toss!

At midfield we met the officials who introduced us to the Bills' captains. We shook hands with Jim Kelly, Kent Hull, Andre Reed, Darrell Talley, Mark Kelso, and Steve Tasker. Then the referee produced the specially minted coin that commemorated this occasion. As he showed us which side was heads and which side was tails, Ken Norton preserved the true dignity of this moment by saying, "Wow, that's a really nice coin! Can I get one of those from you?" We all laughed and, in doing so, released a little of our nervous energy.

The referee then handed the coin to the other person who accompanied us to the center of the field. It was Joe Namath, Hall of Fame quarterback from the New York Jets. This particular Super Bowl was celebrating the AFC's first win, back in the time when Namath's gutsy prediction of a victory was the stuff of headlines.

In the NFL, the visiting team always makes the call.

Tradition had the AFC as visitors on odd-numbered years and NFC as visitors on even-numbered years. The referee, Bob McElwee, explained to the crowd: "Dallas, you are the visiting team, so you will be making the call. Who will make the call from your team?"

I raised my hand.

"Captain Bates, you will make the call."

The year 1994 was our year and I wanted to make the right call! As a matter of fact, earlier in the week I had been discussing the coin toss with Denise.

"What do you think I should call?" I asked her.

"What do you usually call?" she replied.

"I usually call tails."

"Well, whatever you usually call loses ... so if I were you, I think I'd call something different for a change." We both looked at each other and laughed. Yet, as much as I love to listen to Denise and as much respect as I have for her judgment, something in my gut said, Stick with tails!

So as Joe Namath wished us good luck, he flipped the coin in the air. I blurted out as loud as I could, "TAILS!"

When the coin landed, it didn't land flat but, rather, began rolling around on the ground. Actually, those of us around the midfield had to back away in order to see the coin in its final resting place. My stomach tightened as I looked on in curious anticipation.

"Captain Bates, it's tails!" The official made a good call.

I was totally pumped up with an electric emotion beyond description. I bellowed out the four words I had hoped I could offer: "We want the ball! We want the ball! We want the ball!" Okay, so I turned four words into twelve words, but I was so excited! Looking back, I'm certain the official heard me the first time, but I was so into it, I couldn't restrain myself!

Dick Enberg, broadcasting the game to millions over NBC, echoed my words: "You can hear Bill Bates, one of the captains of the Cowboys, saying, 'We want the ball!' So they'll be on offense."

As I ran off the field with my fellow captains, I thought back to Father Leo's words: "Remember your parents . . . remember their sacrifice ... remember your teachers ... your coaches ... give thanks to God for them ... give thanks to God for this opportunity so few get ... how fortunate you are ... remember .... Remember .... "

"Hit Someone as Hard as You Can!"

"Billy, slow down before you break something!"

I remember all the energy I had growing up. If it had been a different place and time, people would have described my boundless energy with other words. I was most likely a borderline hyperactive child, as well as possibly suffering from Attention Deficit Disorder. All I know is, I could really tear up the house. In my earliest recollections of growing up, I was the proverbial "bull in a china shop," running through our house, knocking over lamps, and breaking dishes.

I was born June 6, 1961, outside Knoxville, Tennessee. My parents, Dan and Peggy Bates, were back then-and still are today-a very strong influence in my life. Dad worked as a field sales manager for Exxon, so he put in lots of extra hours to provide for us financially. I guess you'd call us a comfortable, upper-middle-class family. Mom opted to stay home to raise her children. Their first child came in 1958-my sister Rosemary. I arrived three years later, and then my sister Rachel was born ten years after me.

We moved around a little bit during the early years of my life. We lived in Knoxville until I was eight months old. Then we moved to Alabama for the next seven years, living in Birmingham and Prattville. I don't recall a great deal about those years in Alabama, with the exception of a story my mother loves to tell.

It seems that when I was in second grade, I was quite the ladies' man. To hear my Mom tell it, all the girls in my class had crushes on me. Well, on this particular day our teacher gave us an in-class assignment and thought it would be safe to slip out of the classroom for just a minute or two. While the teacher was gone, the little girl who sat in front of me turned around and decided to demonstrate her undying affection for me. She did this by taking out her pair of round-edged scissors and cutting off generous portions of the hair on my head. To finish the job, she also cut off my eyebrows and trimmed my eyelashes! What could be worse?

I'll tell you what's worse-the next day was the day we had our school pictures taken. Everyone in my grade has a permanent reminder of my fate. So much for being a ladies' man!

When I was eight, we moved back to Tennessee, but this time to the Memphis area, where we stayed for the next four years. My parents decided to get me into organized sports at a young age. It was one of their most significant accomplishments. Not only did it set me on a path that I would follow for the rest of my life, but it also saved our house from total destruction by my unharnessed energy!

I participated in every sport I could sign up for. I played Little League baseball. I played in a children's golf program (by the way, golf is the secret love of my life, but I'm getting ahead of myself), and, of course, I played football.

I was eight years old when Mom and Dad signed me up to play football as part of the Mullins Methodist Church league in Germantown, Tennessee, right outside Memphis. My mom recalls a neighbor, a former football coach, telling her, "I've been watching your son play ball here in the neighborhood. He sure handles a football well. If I were you, I'd get him in a league. He could turn out to be a real good player." That was all she needed to hear.

Even though I was not one of the bigger kids, I was assigned the position of offensive guard. We were quite a sight, I'm sure. Since we were only eight-year-olds, we were easily distracted. I remember my dad standing on the sidelines, getting frustrated over our lack of respect for our coach. Dad pulled me over to the side once, early in the season, and told me in no uncertain terms,

"Billy, if you want to play football, get over there and pay attention to your coach!" I've continued to follow that advice throughout my entire sports career.

It was my first taste of organized football but, beyond that, it was not really memorable to me. I can't even remember the name of the team! My recollection focuses around one key phrase: We were terrible.

How terrible? So terrible that the last game of the season found the coach using this type of pregame motivation:

"Okay, so we haven't won a game all season-that's true. But you can change that by what you do today. I want you to go out there and play tough. Do you hear me? I said play tough. If you do, this game could mean as much as winning them all."

We went out on the field and played as hard as our little eight-year-old bodies would allow. And we won ... by one point!

I loved how I felt on the football field. After having so much energy bound up inside me, it was such a thrill to be able to expend that energy without getting in trouble for it.

Years later someone asked one of my grade-school teachers to describe the way I was back then, and she said, "I don't remember a great deal, but what I do recall was that Billy was quite the bully of the playground." I was a troublemaker. I would go out and pick fights, relying on my boundless energy to get me through. I was far from the perfect little boy. I was a handful. My parents knew how I liked to get into scuffles, so my mom used to suggest that I go out, collect sticks and twigs, and use them to hit on a big tree. Anything to keep me out of fighting!

The summer of '69 was meaningful for me, not only because of the football league, but because of another family that was intimately woven into the fabric of my life.

They were the McCrary family. The dad, Conrad Senior, always coached the championship team in our league (which obviously was not the team I was on that first year). He was known for picking the kids who would win. Conrad Senior had two sons-Conrad Junior and Brian. Conrad was a year older than me, and Brian was a year younger.

One summer day the "bully" of the playground decided he needed to defend his turf. Since I loved to pick fights, I got into a big one with one of the McCrary boys. As playground fights go, this was a humdinger. I'll never forget it. I fought my hardest-which was usually enough to win. But that day was different.

I lost.

Not only did I lose, but I lost to Brian-the kid who was a year younger than me.

I can still see it in my mind, Conrad standing off to the side, ready to rescue his kid brother if necessary. How embarrassing-it wasn't necessary! Here I was the bully, and I got beat.

Now, don't get me wrong-I'm not advocating bullies or fights, but I am saying that I learned a valuable lesson that day. I left the playground muttering under my breath, "This won't happen to me again!"

It was a significant day for me in that it signaled the beginning of taking care of my body. I wanted to be proud of my body. I wanted to "bring it under control," as it says in the Bible. I didn't want to be looked on without favor. It started me on a quest of all-out strengthening and conditioning that is still a part of my life to this day. The competition provided by the McCrarys was a positive addition to my life. They helped push me toward the goal of achieving my personal best.

So I was grateful to Conrad and Brian for the contributions they made to my life by beating me up that day. And just to show my gratitude, the three of us became best friends.

The next year I was placed on a football team that seemed to have greater potential. I still wasn't on McCrary's team, but it appeared that our team would be McCrary's toughest competition. I was moved from offensive guard to linebacker and running back.

When the practices began, our coach, B. R. Pruett, told us we needed to choose a name and an appropriate symbol for our uniforms. Like most kids that age, we looked in starry- eyed awe at the horseshoe of the Baltimore Colts or the star of the Dallas Cowboys as symbols of greatness. But our coach had different ideas.

"I want us to choose a name especially for us, so I've come up with a name and a symbol." We all waited in curious expectation to hear his next words.

"We're going to be called the Headhunters," he continued. "Our symbol is a skull." And with that, he showed us our helmets. Sure enough, on each side was an ugly, black skull, the perfect symbol to appeal to a nine-year-old's sense of competition. The coach went on to explain to us a clever piece of motivational strategy.

"Not only will the skull be displayed on the sides of our helmets, but each of you will have the word 'Headhunters' printed on the front of your jerseys. But," he added, "The only way to get 'Headhunters' written on your jerseys is to earn it."

"Coach, what do we have to do to earn it!" we all asked in anxious anticipation.

"It's very simple," Coach replied. "The only way to truly become a Headhunter is to go out on the field and hit someone as hard as you can." We looked at each other and smiled.

"When I see you hit someone as hard as you can, then you'll get 'Headhunters' printed on the front of your jersey. So, go out there and do it!"

That was all I needed to hear. Our first game was an exciting one for me. All of us were out there with numbers on our jerseys, but no name. I wanted to change that. I wanted to be the first guy to have 'Headhunter' on his chest.

I was playing linebacker on defense. Our opposition had a quick little running back that wasn't all that easy to catch. But I kept seeing the word "Headhunter" on my jersey and decided to go for it.

Early in the game, I hit him for a tackle. It was one of those hits where everything was wrong for the running back and everything was right for the linebacker. I hit him square and put him on his back. It didn't go unnoticed by the coach, either! I was the only guy to get "Headhunter" on his jersey that first game.

Games were enjoyable for me up to that point. But on that day something else was added to it-I realized what this game was all about for a guy like me. I got a taste for the thrill of competing in the context of an event we called football. I really believe that was the day I got hooked on not only the game, but the coach's philosophy: Hit someone as hard as you can. That went along just fine with who I was.

It was a pretty good season for us. We played each team in our league twice. As was expected, the real competition was McCrary's team, the Blue Devils. At our first meeting with them, they beat us by one point. The second time would be for the championship.

Coach Pruett really wanted the victory over the Blue Devils, or "The Baby Blues," as he began to refer to them. He did something so time consuming and so "all-out" that it still amazes me to this day.

We played our games on Sunday afternoons. The Sunday evening before the championship game with the Blue Devils, Coach Pruett began sending us motivational letters, one for every day of the week-to keep our minds in focus for this final game. These letters were so foundational in setting up the basics of motivation in my mind that I have kept every letter after all these years. Each one was pounded out on an old typewriter ... each filled with love and enthusiasm.

Sunday night he wrote:

Dear Headhunter:

Isn't it great to be a winner!

As Coach "Bear" Bryant (Alabama) says, "Winning isn't everything, but it sure beats anything that comes in second." I couldn't agree more. You guys played a tremendous game today, and I'm so proud to be associated with you that I could just "bust." You beat a really good team today, a team that fought all the way and never gave up. I respect them for the way they competed, but I respect you more because you competed and won! This may sound harsh, but it is nonetheless true-the world loves and remembers the winners!

I think it is important to consider how you won the game today. There were no outstanding stars. There is no one or two guys you can point to and say that they are responsible for the Victory. It was a team victory. We won because every- one played at his best. I think you will agree that football, more than any other sport, is a team sport. If just one guy breaks down on just one play, it can cost you a touchdown and the game. We won today because we didn't have any breakdowns. Everyone did his best on every play. That's what it takes when you're playing a good team.

And that's what it's going to take next week! It's going to take your best effort. You know as well as I do that the Baby Blue team is a good team. But you also know as well as I do that we're a better team. The only way they can beat us is for us not to make an all-out effort ... for us to beat ourselves. And that just isn't going to happen again! They've gotten their gift win off us for the year. This time they had better have their pointed tails and horns taped on, because the Headhunters are going after their heads.

Revenge is the theme for this week! Revenge, revenge, revenge. And it's going to be oh so sweet. Dedicate yourself to a Headhunter victory Sunday ... and to revenge. Be willing and determined to settle for nothing less. I don't know about you, but I wish the game were tomorrow so we could take their heads that much sooner! I almost feel sorry for the Blue Devils Sunday because they're going to run into the most ferocious band of Headhunters they've ever seen. (Almost, but not quite.)

Let's take home some heads Sunday, Headhunters.

B. R. Pruett

"Head" Headhunter

He put those letters in the mail on Monday morning and everyone on the team received a copy in his mailbox on Tuesday. My nine-year-old mind was completely captivated by Coach's all-out determination. I read and reread the statements, determining to do my best.

Wednesday, another letter was waiting for each team member when we arrived home from school.

Dear Headhunter:

As you know I've been reading Coach "Bear" Bryant's excellent football book, Building a Championship Football Team, and I'm very impressed by some of the things he says. At one point he says, "Quitting comes easy for many people. Many do not want to pay the price to be a winner. It requires little effort to be a loser-and anyone who tries can be most successful." Champions, though, are willing to pay the price and develop that will to win that cannot be put down. Champions always reach back and get that little extra, show their true colors, and rise to the challenge.

Wishers are dreamers. There's nothing wrong with dreaming-in fact, it's a good thing to have a dream. But the champion is the one willing to back up his dream! You've got to dream, yes-but more important, you've got to have a will that makes the thing come to pass.

Coach Bryant includes a poem in his book that I think says an awful lot. I'd like for you to read it. If you're not much on poems yet, you might like to have your parents read this with you.

IT's ALL IN A STATE OF MIND

If you think you are beaten, you are.

31

If you think you dare not, you won't;
If you like to win,
but don't think you can,
It's almost a cinch you won't.
If you think you'll lose, you're lost;
For out in this world you'll find
Success begins with a fellow's will;
It's all in a state of mind.

For many a game is lost
Before even a play is run,
And many a coward fail
Before even his work is begun.
Think big and your deeds will grow,
Think small and you'll fall behind;
Think that you can and you will;
It's all in a state of mind.
If you think you are out-classed, you are;
You've got to think high to rise;
You've got to be sure of yourself before
You can ever win a prize.
Life's battles don't always go
To the stronger or faster man,
But sooner or later, the man who wins,
Is the fellow who thinks he can.

B. R. Pruett
"Head" Headhunter

Sure enough, the next day another letter waited. This had one section I found especially relevant to my life. Coach wrote:

... Football, more than any other sport, is built upon desire. It's attitude that makes a football player, not size or strength or playing skills. As a sport, football is quite different from baseball or basketball. You need highly polished athletic skills to be able to hit a hard-thrown baseball three or four times out of ten, or to be able to hit a jump shot consistently at long range. But in football all you need is the desire and the determination to throw blocks and to "cream" a runner ....

Then, in reference to our loss to the Blue Devils earlier in the season, he wrote:

... Sometimes in life, God gives us a setback in order to bring out the fighting spirit. Everything that happens to you can happen for good, if you have this spirit. If you forget everything else I have ever said, or will ever say, I hope you will remember this:

LIFE DOES NOT DETERMINE A CHAMPION; A CHAMPION DETERMINES LIFE.

Those with fighting hearts don't let anything beat them. They struggle on. They overcome. They turn difficulty into greatness!

Although I hated to lose that first game, it may well be that we are a better team (and better men) for having had to suffer through that disappointment. But let's not do it again!

B. R. Pruett
"Head" Headhunter

By now I was as psyched up as a kid could be! Friday came and by this point I was sprinting home from school to see the latest letter from the coach. He didn't let us down. Friday's letter focused on pride:

... You demonstrate pride with your aggressiveness, all-out effort, never-halting hustle, team spirit, determination to win, and "never-let-up" attitude. That's what winners are made of. I challenge you to have enough pride to be all that you can be, and to settle for nothing less than that.

Let's take their heads off Sunday!

B. R. Pruett
"Head" Headhunter

On Saturday the final letter arrived. The coach was still pushing:

33

Dear Headhunter:

Football is a sport that demands a great deal of you!

Mentally, it requires that you be alert and sharp-thinking anytime you're on the practice or playing field. You have to use your head to avoid foolish mistakes. The team that makes the fewest mistakes usually wins.

Because it is a contact sport, football requires that you keep your body in good condition, that you avoid needless injuries and illnesses which will hurt you and your team, and that you like to "pop" the other guy harder than he pops you.

But football is more than a sport where a bunch of guys run around a field and knock each other down.

One way or another, you are going to become a man. How much you become depends on how you are allowed to grow up and the set of values you form. You can do a lot of growing on the football field!

Football can teach you many things. It can teach you the value of teamwork and pride. It can teach you to be unselfish, and it can teach you the true meaning of loyalty, courage, leadership, self-discipline, alertness, and the never-say-die spirit!

Yes, football does demand much of you. To measure up, you must have the desire to win! After all, this is the point of competing in any sport, to win. Now I don't mean that you should want to win at any cost and by any means--that's wrong. As a real athlete, you must have deep within you the burning desire to win and the willingness to give the best that is in you, no matter how many handicaps are placed in your way, no matter what the odds, no matter how discouraging the outlook. These qualities which you develop on the football field will prove invaluable throughout your life. There's an expression in football: "When the going gets tough, the tough get going."

Let's take their heads off Sunday, Headhunters.

B. R. Pruett

"Head" Headhunter

I could barely sleep Saturday night because of the anticipation of this big game. Church never seemed longer than it did that Sunday morning. Finally, it was Sunday afternoon! Coach Pruett had truly outdone himself with that series of letters. "The Epistles of Pruett" were incredibly effective. Not only were all our players geared up, but the notes had done a nice job of getting the parents into the act as well. Believe it or not, I don't remember all that much about the game, except for one important fact: By the slim margin of one touchdown-WE WON!

The Headhunters had taken off the heads of McCrary's Blue Devils! We were the Champions!

The following football season was all a ten-year-old kid could have asked for. I had finally earned enough respect for my playing ability that I was picked by Coach McCrary himself to be on his team. Many times the name of the team was determined by the local business that served as its financial sponsor. There was a gas station-or "filling station" as we called it back then-that sponsored Coach McCrary's team that year. The name of the station was "Studs," and that name was too good to pass by.

The Studs

What a fun season! Here I was-Billy Bates, number 12, linebacker and running back for Coach McCrary's Studs. My two best friends, Conrad and Brian McCrary, were on the team as well, so I was one happy boy. Incidentally, lest you think Conrad and Brian found positions on the league's best team because their dad was coach, nothing could be further from the truth. Both boys grew up to be fine young men both going off to major universities on full football scholarships. Conrad attended the University of Mississippi and played linebacker for their football team. Brian went off to Florida State University and played cornerback for the Seminoles.

Needless to say, the Studs won the league championship that year.

The year 1972 was my fourth year in Memphis ... and my fourth year in community football. I joined the Mason YMCA Youth Football League that

35

year and was put on a team called the Colts. I'd become very comfortable in my dual positions as linebacker and running back. This was to be the year I really started to blossom in terms of my athletic ability. I remember we had a good team and a good record, but my most exciting memory was of being awarded the Most Valuable Player award for the league that season. I had never received an MVP award before. It was fulfilling for me on a personal level, to be rewarded for all the hard work I had begun to put into my athletic pursuits. I was also named to the YMCA All-Star Team.

Later that same year the YMCA named me to their All- Star Baseball Squad. Things were starting to go my way athletically. It was a good feeling to be known and recognized by the coaches in the Memphis area. It took some of the pressure off of having to prove myself in every new season, with every new sport. I was sailing!

I guess that's why I felt a little less wind in my sails the day Dad came home and announced: "I've been transferred back to Knoxville .... we're moving."

"Dream and Shoot for the Stars!"

Life after Memphis went right on.

In 1973 we moved to west Knoxville, in Knox County. Being only twelve years old, I was able to make the adjustment pretty smoothly. I have always been a pretty optimistic person. I did well in school, made new friends, still got into my share of trouble, but found new venues for football.

We weren't in Knoxville very long before we discovered the Concord Farragut Optimist (CFO) football league. I quickly signed up and started all over to prove myself to a new cadre of coaches.

Every coach has his own individual style when it comes to coaching. I've been very fortunate to play under some of the most admired men in the coaching business. But there's often fun along the way. I distinctly remember one of the coaches I had in the CFO. His name was Hogan Harrison, and his most distinguishing characteristic was his chew of Red Man Chewing Tobacco that enlarged his cheeks at every practice. Not just a chew, but a huge chew.

One brisk autumn day he was particularly irate with the running backs. He felt their efforts were halfhearted, and he was a man who believed in all-out ... all the time. "I'll show you how to run with a football!" he exclaimed to the exasperated runners. He grabbed a ball and began to look around at the defense behind him. He was looking for someone he could run over, as an example to the team. For some unexplained reason, he spotted me and announced: "Bates, get over here! Let's see if you can tackle me!" He smirked and looked over at his running backs. "Watch this, boys-this is how to run with a football!"

Sooner or later it will become obvious that I rarely do anything in life at half-speed. This has been both an asset and a liability in my life. Nevertheless, I decided to accept this challenge from the coach and give it my all. I decided to not only tackle him, but to tackle him hard! Well, my resolve paid off.'

I did tackle him.

And I did tackle him hard.

I tackled him so hard that he landed on his backside and immediately swallowed his chew of tobacco.

Practice was over early that day.

I can still recall going over to our car, where my mother was waiting to drive me home. Mom was parked right next to our coach's car. Imagine how I must have felt as I got in our car and turned to discover our coach alongside his car, violently throwing up.

In sixth grade I entered Farragut Middle School. I was an average student who enjoyed school and especially enjoyed after-school sports. I still got into a fair amount of trouble, but in school I tried to play it pretty straight. I learned a lot about what not to do in school from one of my cousins, Jay Graham. Jay is a colorful guy who likes to have fun.

One day Jay and his friend were able to procure some sodium from the chemistry class. They went straight to the boy's room, put the sodium in one of the toilets, and caused an explosion! Apparently, someone had witnessed this bombing incident (I envision some little skinny kid hiding in a stall, shaking like a leaf). Anyway, someone reported them to the principal, and they almost got expelled. Thanks to Jay's example, that was the day I learned to behave myself in school.

Jay had influenced me earlier in life as well. He talked me into running away from his farm with him when we were little kids. I remember hiking down the road in the steamy summer heat. We were only gone for a few hours, but it really upset our parents. As a matter of fact, my most vivid memory of that entire incident is the hickory switch my dad used on me to help me fully understand the lack of wisdom in running away from home. Dad could be pretty intense when he wanted to be.

Fortunately for me, Jay and I went to different schools (although we were to meet up again, competing against each other in a very important high school football game). My entrance at Farragut signaled the start of my school-related sports career. I wanted to play everything-football, basketball, baseball, and track. I had a contagious energy about any and all athletic endeavors. I am so grateful to have met up with adults, especially coaches, who could channel that energy into something positive.

My first coach at Farragut was a wonderful man named Bobby Henry. He was a master motivator and a tough disciplinarian. He's the most sincere person I've ever met in my life. I often joked with him in later years that he was the only guy I knew who could give punishment while smiling!

Coach Henry had a major impact on my life. I was playing basketball as a sixth grader on Coach Henry's "B" squad. Because of our status-or lack of it-about the only time the court was available for practice for the sixth grade "B" team was at six o'clock in the morning! It's hard for me to believe the sacrifices my parents made for my love of athletics. Five days a week the alarm would explode at 5:00 A.M., taking them out of their warm bed into the freezing, predawn winter darkness. They would wake me, feed me, and drive me to practice.

Part of Bobby Henry's coaching style was to make up all sorts of signs and banners that he put on the walls surrounding the basketball court. Every morning a new quote or saying would be placed in a position in the gym where all of us could see it. Coach Henry would talk to us about the quote a little bit, and then we'd move right on into practice.

I'll never forget the day I walked in and read the saying that has stuck with me all my life. The coach unrolled a banner that stated:

Dream and shoot for the stars.
You never know ... you may reach your star!

Coach wanted us to be unafraid of lofty goals. He wanted us to believe we could do more than people gave us credit for. Don't let anybody tell you that you're too small or too slow ... think big!

"Dream, boys!" he would say to us. "Shoot for the stars! Who knows? You may even reach your star. But even if you don't, you'll land pretty high anyway."

I can't fully express how much of an impact that little saying has had on me. To this day I believe it with all of my heart. When I am asked to give speeches around the country, some- where in every speech I encourage the audience to "shoot for the stars." I did, and I have been richly rewarded as a result. The same can happen for you too. My best friend, Mike Baird, made certain that I had another special memory from that year in basketball. Since he was my best friend, I let him in on a secret known by no one else-I had a crush on a girl. Her name was Kim Pankey, and I was genuinely smitten, as any twelve-year-old boy could attest from his own personal experience.

One morning after practice-but before school-Mike had arranged for Kim to be in the gym just as we finished our workout. With Mike's encouragement, I went over to speak to Kim. I was pretty nervous-this was big-time stuff for a sixth-grader.

As I got closer to Kim, it suddenly became apparent why Mike had so "kindly" set up this meeting. Just as I was about to speak to Kim-standing no more than five feet from her- Mike came up from behind me and did the unthinkable with my elastic waist gym shorts. He pulled them down, right there in front of Kim!

39

I think that was the day I decided to work on my running speed.

School was an excellent environment for me. I was playing football in the fall, basketball in the winter, and running track in the spring. I was consciously attempting to shoot for the stars, especially in athletics. Throughout much of my life, I had heard that I was too small to excel in sports. No one could convince me that statement was true. Part of shooting for my star was showing people what I could do. Just give me a chance, I would think, and I'll show you what I can do.

Coach Henry not only coached me in basketball, but the next year he coached me in freshman football. I still played running back on offense, but I moved from linebacker to safety on defense. It was to be a perfect season. In all of the years of his illustrious career as a coach, it was to be Coach Henry's first undefeated season.

I loved playing for Coach Henry. He brought out in me an intensity that would characterize all of my future athletic pursuits. I had the pleasure of being on the platform with Coach Henry at a banquet years later. It was then that I dis- covered he felt I was the most intense player he had ever coached in more than twenty years of coaching. He went on to say that when I graduated from high school, he was still coaching freshman football, and he started a club in my honor. "It used to be called the Slobber-Knocker Club and you could only get in it for one reason-you had to hit some- one as hard as you could," he told me later.

"That's it, Bill," he said. "Just one good lick and you're in that club."

"So we've renamed it," he continued. "Now it's called the Bill Bates Slobber-Knocker Club. We give each player a T-shirt to commemorate the event. It's the most sought-after T-shirt on the squad every year."

Coach Henry helped me in numerous ways. Not only did he bring out my own intensity, but he also assisted me in learning how to read the intensity on the other side of the football.

How do you know if your opposition is full of intensity?

How do you know if they came ready to play, ready to hit someone hard? Coach Henry taught me a simple method: You can tell by looking in their eyes.

A player's eyes give it away every time. I've never seen a player I would describe as intense who didn't show it in his eyes. Thanks to Coach Henry, I learned how to look for it. In my mind.

Looking for a slobber-knocker in Super Bowl XXX – **Intense**

The only thing that went better than freshman football was freshman basketball. I had a good season and found myself thinking it might be time to start concentrating on one sport instead of playing them all. So it was, in that spirit of single-minded concentration, that I made an important decision: No more football. I'm concentrating on basketball.

In all honesty, there was really more to that decision than to focus on one sport. Looking back, I see now that a lot of what was going on at that time in my life had to do with my physical growth. I was going through a little growth spurt that resulted in my bones growing faster than the rest of me. My knees were really bothering me. My folks had a doctor examine me, and he concluded that I had Osgood Slaughter in both of my knees. He explained that there was no reason for alarm, stating the fact that many kids experience this condition at my age.

Typically, you just grow through it and everything ends up fine. All I knew was that my knees hurt. I didn't have to be a genius to realize that my knees hurt more during football season than at any other time. I could wear knee pads on my knees playing basketball. Therefore, it was easier for me to put aside football in favor of basketball and its lesser demands on my knees.

I felt comfortable with my decision. Looking back, it's amazing to me how God seems to bring people into our lives to point us in the right direction.

I truly believe there are no accidents in life. Everything is designed by God for a specific purpose.

Enter Coach Bill Clabo.

Coach Clabo was the varsity football coach. I didn't know him very well. The only time I had ever talked with him was during one of those awkward little moments freshmen get themselves into. I took his daughter, Jill, who was in eighth grade at the time, on a "date" to the Homecoming Dance at school. Being the suave, debonair, man of the world that I was, I had my sister Rosemary drive us to and from the dance. I don't know what triggered the reaction, but when we arrived back at her house, Jill bolted out of the car and quickly ran up to her front door and went inside. Coach told me later that she sprinted up the stairs and went straight to her bedroom. She never spoke of the night again. Despite that unflattering beginning, Coach Clabo had been observing me on the football field from a distance during my year on the freshman team. Apparently he liked what he saw, and the idea of me not playing football anymore didn't sit well with him.

One Sunday afternoon-a gorgeous Tennessee spring day-the phone rang at our home. It was eight days before spring practice was to begin. My mom knocked on my bedroom door and called me to the phone.

"Son, it's Coach Clabo."

"So I hear you're not coming out for spring football," he said to me.

"No, sir," I replied. "I've decided to concentrate on basketball."

"Why's that?"

"Well, sir," I stammered. "I think I need to focus my attention on just one sport ... and I think basketball is the right one for me."

"What's wrong with football?" he prodded.

"To tell you the truth, sir," I paused. "My knees hurt real bad. It seems that basketball is a lot easier on my knees than football, so I'm sure that plays into my decision as well."

"I see," Coach Clabo responded. He was silent for a moment and then added: "Well, I think you're pretty good at football, myself. And I think there's a future for you on the field."

"What are you saying, Coach?" I prodded.

"Listen to me, Bill. I'm not making any promises or predictions. But next year, even as a sophomore, I think you have a real chance to shine here on Farragut's football field."

"On the varsity team?"

"Maybe so, son. Maybe so."

I sat in a dumbstruck silence.

"Listen to me, son. I can work around your knees in practice you know what I mean? I'll see to it that you can avoid some of the drills that are especially painful. Do you understand what I'm saying?"

"Yes, sir."

"Just do me a favor, Bill, okay? Think about your decision carefully. You don't have to decide right now. I know you're not asking for my advice, but I'll give it to you anyway. I'll make it real clear for you--don't quit football. If you do, I think you'll be making a big mistake." He hung up.

That was an important conversation for me. Thanks to Coach Clabo, I didn't quit football. Actually, I decided later that Sunday evening that I would be there the next Monday at spring practice. I couldn't wait to get to school the next day to tell him of my decision. He was pleased and he let me know it.

And sure enough, I was honored to make the varsity squad as a sophomore. It was a good season for me. Coach Clabo moved me from safety to cornerback, so I was certainly getting a lot of experience in varied defensive positions.

It was great to play for a coach who believed in me. In some ways Coach Clabo was a little distant, in much the same way that people perceive Coach Tom Landry. But this man offered more encouragement about football than anyone I had ever met. I learned an awful lot about football from Coach Clabo that sophomore year, not to mention all that he taught me about life itself. He was helping me shoot for the stars ... and I was grateful.

So I didn't know what was going to happen when I heard the news in the winter of my sophomore year. . . . . Coach Clabo was retiring from coaching.

"Trust in the Lord"

When Ken Sparks arrived as the new coach of the Farragut High School football team, he didn't come alone.

He brought God with him.

Although it seemed to me that it would be difficult to replace Coach Clabo, I have to admit I took an immediate liking to this tall, thinnish, blond-haired young man. For one thing, I liked his style.

Coach Sparks was the kind of guy who could make things happen. For example, it was during his coaching tenure that Farragut built a new football stadium. I can still see him driving one of the tractors or one of the graders around the site or planting grass on the field itself. He was a man who led by example. The winter of my sophomore year was a cold one, but I was rarely outside to experience it. After school we'd go right into basketball practice. Once that concluded, Coach Sparks had arranged for something he called "Winter Workout Drills." My sole recollection of those drills is that they were so intense, we'd all wind up over at the side, throwing up.

Varsity Coaching Staff

KEN SPARKS
Head Coach

LENDON WELCH

BRUCE LUSSIER

PETE BILLINGSLEY

DENNIS PAYNE

EDDIE COURTNEY

Coach Sparks was also a magnificent motivator. "I want our team to be committed to excellence," he told us in one of our early sessions together. "When I think of excellence in professional football, I immediately think of the Dallas Cowboys and their head coach, Tom Landry. I admire him greatly and have deep respect for his team. Let's make the Farragut Admirals the same kind of team. That's a very important goal for us to achieve."

As if to underscore this significant comparison to the Cowboys, Coach held up a helmet and jersey for the team to see. "We'll be wearing new uniforms from this point on, and I want you to see what I've chosen." He proudly displayed a silver helmet with a blue star, along with a white jersey with blue numbers-exact replicas of Dallas Cowboy uniforms.

"So start working on what's inside, guys. What will you be putting these uniforms over? The most important thing is what's inside. What you think about is what you are."

Coach Sparks was a player's coach. It wasn't long before he and I became close friends. I would sit and watch him work and think to myself, Man, I really respect this guy. He has real integrity. He's a man of his word, a hard worker, and a man of conviction. It was soon after that I discovered where all of this came from.

"I've got an opportunity I'd like you to consider," Coach mentioned to me one day. "There's a sports camp up in North Carolina that has a great program. I'd like you to think about going up there for a week this summer, Bill. I think it would really make a difference. You see, I believe that if you're going to be everything you can be, it's got to come from the inside. You've gotta have the power that comes from inside. This camp will teach you where that power comes from."

I went home and talked it over with Dad and Mom. As usual, they were 100 percent supportive. So, with about ten of my teammates and Coach Sparks himself, I was off to Black Mountain Summer Camp in Asheville, North Carolina; This particular camp was sponsored by the Fellowship of Christian Athletes. I had heard a little about FCA, but didn't know much about it. I knew Coach Sparks was all for their program and had even talked about starting "Huddle Groups" this coming fall.

Once I arrived at the camp, I registered, received my room assignment, and went to unpack. After I got all settled in, I took a look at the daily schedule. As I read it through, I quickly became aware of the fact that this camp was for more than sports.

The first thing I noticed was that, as soon as you got up each morning, you were to take one hour for "Quiet Time." I soon discovered that meant an hour of reading the Bible and praying by yourself. After Quiet Time, you went to breakfast. After your meal, the rest of the day was given to sports. But it was the after-dinner schedule that intrigued me. "Speaker" was all it said on the program.

Those evening speakers became the focal point of my week. Each night a guy would get up and talk about what the Lord meant to him in his personal life. I was fascinated by the way they described their "relationship" with Jesus Christ. I was brought up in church-we faithfully attended every Sunday without fail. I knew about Jesus and considered myself to be a Christian.

But the speakers kept referring to a "personal relationship" with Christ, and this was a new wrinkle for me. I had not thought of a one-on-one type of relationship with God before that time.

By the end of the week I had received a steady dose of teaching that caused me to realize I needed to accept the Lord as my personal Savior. I wanted that personal relation- ship with Him. When the speaker gave us an opportunity to come forward to talk with someone about receiving Christ as Savior, I stood up and walked to the front of the room.

That was the most meaningful decision I've ever made.

There weren't any bells or harps or angels or singing. In my case, there were no tears or overpowering emotions. I simply wanted Jesus Christ in my life.

The man who met with me at the front of the room opened his Bible to a couple of verses in the Book of Proverbs:

Trust in the Lord with all thine heart; and lean not unto thine own understanding. In all thy ways acknowledge Him, and He shall direct thy paths.
-Proverbs 3:5-6

That passage really spoke to me ... as it still does to this day. From that point on, I've tried my best to look to the Lord for the strength, wisdom, and direction that I need in all of life's decisions. To me, it was a much different story-having Christ as the guiding force in my life as opposed to a God I thought about only in Sunday school.

When I finished talking with the man at the front of the room, I got up, shook his hand, and turned to leave. As I turned around, I saw a man with a smile spreading from ear to ear.

It was Coach Sparks.

Immediately I ran over to him, threw my arms around him, and gave him a big Ol' bear hug. "I did it, Coach! I did it!" was all I could say. But he knew exactly what I meant.

At that point I understood more fully what made this man the way he was. He was, first and foremost, a Christian. If he could have had his way, all of his players would have been Christians as well. Coach Sparks brought God to our high school. When we returned to school that fall, we began Fellowship of Christian Athlete Huddle Groups among our teams. We also added pregame chapel services to our schedule. Coach had observed firsthand how many college athletic programs were incorporating these types of Christian influences on their teams, and he followed their example. We even had a revival meeting going on at one point in the year!

Those high school years can be difficult years for any teenager. There are so many influences in a young person's life-both positive and negative. Looking back, I am so grateful to Coach Sparks for his positive influence in my life. Right when I could have gotten mixed up in drinking, drugs, and the like, he pointed me in the right direction. Instead of being so influenced by those around me, I started trying to influence them. Sometimes it's difficult to stand up to others, but I've never forgotten Coach Spark's most important maxim:

Trust in the Lord.

Because I seriously started trusting the Lord, I began to see little changes in my life. One of the most significant changes I recall is reaching a decision about how I would treat other people. I had never been purposely cruel to people, but I still had some of that "bully" from my playground days inside me. From reading my Bible, I learned that Jesus was not a bully- so I didn't need to be one either! I started treating people with more respect and, in doing so, found that people treated me better as well. It was very encouraging to see my Christianity at work in my everyday life.

The change in my life that was closest to home-and most difficult-was making a stand with my friends. There were three guys I had hung around with for a couple of years- forming something as close to a gang as you could get. We were inseparable. We lifted weights together, played golf together, swam in the lake together, fished together . . . we did it all together.

We also got into some trouble together. We experimented a little with drinking, and that got us into plenty of hot water with our parents.

When I got back from camp, I knew I didn't want to be a drunk or anything else that would be a poor reflection on the Lord. But how was I going to tell my buddies about the change in my life?

I opted to keep quiet instead and show them the change.

They would ask me if I wanted a drink and I would decline. At first they were shocked, and made fun of me. But I found out that after I said "no" a couple of times, they knew where I stood and they stopped asking me. The Lord was looking out for me. As I became less and less involved with these guys and more involved with Christian friends, I realized that later that year two of them were almost kicked off our football team because Coach Sparks found out they had been out drinking during the season.

I very well could have been with them, if I hadn't met the Lord. It was at this time that a new friend entered my life. His name was Stan Cotten. Stan was the quarterback on our team, and the talk around town was that this guy was headed for greatness. I took an immediate liking to him-not only because of our shared love of sports, but also because he was a strongly committed Christian.

I learned so much from Stan. In my junior year, he was injured and had to sit out the season. You see a person's character demonstrated in times like those, and Stan's character ran deep.

Another big change that occurred that year was written all over my chest. The number on my football jersey had varied through the years. During my sophomore year I was wearing number 42 and playing cornerback for Coach Clabo. When Coach Sparks came in with his new uniforms, I quickly went for my favorite number. Now that I was a junior, I had a little more clout on the team, so no one protested when I grabbed the jersey with number 40 on it. That number has been kind to me. At the writing of this book, I've been wearing number 40 for Thirty Seven years straight. My website is even www.BillBates40.com

I started to see some dramatic improvement in my football abilities during my junior season. Coach Sparks had moved me to strong safety on defense and I was also returning kick-offs and punts. We were winning games and I was steadily improving personally. Part of my personal growth came through learning from my mistakes.

Coach was big on giving us opportunities to replay our strengths and weaknesses from each game. Every week we would review game films from the contest the week before. If a receiver had bobbled a pass and dropped it, Coach would stop the film and say, "Baird, did you see that missed opportunity?"

"Yes, sir," Baird would reply.

"Okay, now forget it," Coach would continue. "What I want you to concentrate on is catching it."

At first we all nodded our heads and thought to ourselves, Well, that makes sense-think about catching the ball. But there was more to Coach's plan.

"Baird, I want you to visualize in your mind that you are running the same pattern as we just saw on the film. Run that pattern. Now Jeff is dropping back into the pocket. He plants his feet and he passes the ball. It's being thrown to you, Baird. See yourself catching that pass, Baird. Visualize it. Do you see it happening, Baird?"

"Yes sir. I see myself catching the ball."

"Good," Coach continued. "Now I want you to run that same play in your mind ten more times. If you can see yourself catching the ball that many times, you're on your way to actually making the catch tomorrow in practice."

Although it wasn't original to Coach Sparks, it was my introduction to positive mental reinforcement. By replaying the situation positively in your subconscious, you were establishing a mental pattern that would work in your favor on the playing field. I started using that positive patterning in many areas of my life. And it really helped. I would dream big dreams, shoot for the stars, and visualize it happening.

In my junior year my big dream-the dream I would carry within me for the next six years-began to crystalize. I began to zero in on exactly which star it was that I was shooting for. I began to press toward just one goal, and that goal began to dominate all other dreams.

What was my big dream ... my star? The dream of one day playing professional football for the Dallas Cowboys. From then on, I found myself shooting for just one star-the Dallas Cowboys STAR.

Wearing the Star for Farragut

The dream was actually an easy one for me to visualize, since every weekend I'd suit up in Cowboy blue and silver. Each time I put on the silver helmet with the blue star, I'd dream of the day it would happen in Texas Stadium instead of Farragut High.

Some people make fun of dreamers, but I don't. I think of all the people who have realized major accomplishments in their lives. All have dreams of achieving as their common denominator. When I speak to young people, I always encourage them to dream and DREAM BIG. Find a star- then go after it! That's what I encourage people to do.

My junior year continued to progress well. I made some plays that were starting to earn me some attention. I returned two kickoffs and one punt all the way back for touchdowns, and the team was steadily making its way to the playoffs. By the last week of the season we were nine and zero, playing our final game at home against Oak Ridge. We played well. We wanted Coach Sparks to have the distinction of an undefeated inaugural season. We wanted the playoffs. We wanted a championship. We wanted all these things.

But Oak Ridge wanted us more. We lost.

I thought back to one of the letters that Coach Pruett had sent me during my season as a Headhunter.... many champions are made champions by setbacks.

51

They are champions because they have been hurt. The experience moved them, and pulled out this fighting spirit, making them what they are. Sometimes in life, God gives us a setback in order to bring out the fighting spirit. Everything that happens to you can happen for good, if you have this spirit those with fighting hearts don't let anything beat them turn difficulty into greatness ....

That loss to Oak Ridge was a good lesson.

Next year will be different, I was soon telling myself. I could already visualize it.

To take a little of the sting out of the loss to Oak Ridge, we were invited to a bowl game that postseason. It was called the Nurseryman's Bowl and our Farragut Admirals played with great pride.

The highlight of the game for me was returning the opening kickoff of the second half for a touchdown! The crowd went wild! It was so loud, it was almost impossible to hear the official, who was in the process of calling the playback, due to a Farragut penalty. Unfortunately, penalties count even in noisy stadiums, so the return was in vain. But we did win, and I was awarded Most Valuable Player of the game. Coach Sparks confided in me years later that this was the game that caused all of the college scouts to stand up and take notice of this little scrapper called Bill Bates.

So entering my senior year, people were expecting big things from Farragut and big things from Bill Bates. As a defensive back, I had gained more yards than the leading offensive back in the entire Knox County area! Coach Sparks had people realizing that his commitment to excellence was a reality.

I don't think I can fully communicate how much of an impact this man had on my life. Here was a man in his mid-twenties who had so influenced me that I wanted to do any- thing I could to please him. Thankfully, he was a godly man, so his goals were pure. I wanted my senior year to be memorable. I wanted it personally, I wanted it in gratitude to my family, and I really wanted it for Coach Sparks. I began praying, asking God to help me do whatever I could to make my last year at Farragut a special one. Please Lord, let 1978 be our best year!

My partner in these prayers was my friend, Stan Cotten.

We felt some of the burden of leadership for the team, since we would be seniors. It felt good to have someone to share this with.

When training camp began that summer, there was a sense of excitement that I had not previously felt. Part of it had to do with Stan's return from his injury. Will Garland had played for Stan all during my junior year. Will did a good job, but Stan was an exceptional athlete.

Stan was the starter, with Jeff Joslin as his backup. We felt like we were a good team, with some real depth. That depth would be important sooner than we realized.

Very early in training camp, while running through a routine play, Stan was tackled to the ground by one of our defensive men. When he didn't immediately get up, we knew there was trouble. Stan was really hurt. He had blown out his knee. He was in agony.

It was a scene I'll never forget. Coach Sparks and I ran to Stan and carried him off the field. As the two of us joined hands to hold Stan, all three of us were crying. Here was a top prospect, cut down in his prime.

Stan wouldn't come back. Jeff Joslin came in and quarterbacked my senior year.

Now I had an even greater reason to make 1978 a great year.

"We Are Counting on Bill at Tennessee"

GOD was good to us. He heard our prayers.

My senior season opened August 25, 1978, at home against Crossville. With very little trouble, we won 48-0. We played five games that September and remained undefeated. October found us on the road, picking up a 27-6 win at Karns.

With our record 7-0, it was a great delight to match up with last season's nemesis: Oak Ridge. This year the game was played at their field. With the thoughts of our near-perfect season last year vividly running through our minds, we played hard and won ... but not by much. We eked it out 17-14. Only two more games to go for a perfect regular season.

By October's end our dream had been realized. Our final regular-season game was also on the road. Our opponent was Carter, and we took care of them 27-14. We were 10-0 and headed for the state play-offs!

Our first postseason competition was a school called South-Young. They had a running back that was the leading ground-gainer in the city that season. Coach Sparks had created a special defense built around this guy. The plan was simple: I was to follow the guy wherever he went. So, early in the first quarter, we were destined to meet. And we did. I ran up and hit the guy as hard as I could. Later Coach Sparks said it was the most horrible collision he had ever seen in all of his coaching. I rammed the guy so hard that we both hit the ground. We lay motionless for a brief moment that must have seemed like an eternity to our friends and family. South Young's trainer came out on the field and revived their fallen hero. They escorted him off the field, removed his jersey and shoulder pads, and sat him down. He remained on the bench for the remainder of the game.

I walked off the field on my own power, feeling a little shook, but basically okay. Coach Sparks called another player's name, instructing him to go in for me right away.

It was one of the few times I ever challenged a coach's decision.

"No, Coach!" I screamed. "I can play! I can play!" Coach looked at me doubtfully.

"Coach, 1 don't want them to think I'm hurt," I confessed.

"I'm fine. Please let me play!"

So Coach Sparks allowed me to return to my position, never missing a play. The first half was a struggle all the way, and we were behind 7-6 with only twenty-three seconds left. With a fourth down and nine facing us, Jeff Joslin, our quarterback, surprised everyone by handing the ball to our running back, Jim Compton. It was a simple draw play, but it so shocked South-Young, that Jim dashed straight down the field for a forty-three-yard touchdown. That play returned our confidence and gave us the momentum we needed to go on and defeat them 35-7.

That victory sent us one step further on the road to a state championship. Our next opponent was Newport, a school I knew a little about. My adrenaline was pumping for this game because I was playing against kin! My cousin, Jay Graham, was on Newport's team. Yes, the same person known for blowing up the boy's room toilet with sodium had turned his energies to football. And he was good.

But we were better. Farragut beat Newport 21-0 on their home field! Next up was the state semi-finals. We were pitted against Red Bank from Chattanooga. By now there was an increasing amount of pressure being put on us from the outside. We went into the Red Bank game ranked number one in the state. We were expected to win.

We took a 10-0 lead through the second quarter, but they scored on us just before half time, cutting our margin to 10-7 at the half. They scored on us early in the second half but missed the extra point. It was 13-10 for most of the second half. We just couldn't score on them. With only seconds on the clock and no time-outs, our kicker, Dwayne Burchfield, came in, kicked a twenty-seven-yard field goal, and put us into overtime.

The method of playing overtime at this level of high school ball was to put the ball on the ten-yard line and be given four plays to score. Then the other team was given the same opportunity. Pressure! Red Bank got the ball first and scored on a pass play. The extra point was good so it was 20-13. But we came right back. Our running back, Jim Compton, bowled over for a score and Burchfield once again added the extra point. It was 20-20 and now double overtime.

This time we got the ball first and scored on another run.

The extra point made it 27-20. Red Bank reciprocated with a run and score. With the scoreboard reading 27-26, the Red Bank coach decided to put it all on the line and go for the two-point conversion.

I can still recall Coach Sparks standing on the sidelines, his hands folded as if in prayer, his eyes riveted on the ball. The Red Bank quarterback called a pass play. He threw the pass perfectly. His receiver was there waiting, caught the ball, and pranced across the goal line. Our hopes for state championship were dashed by one point, 28-27 in double overtime. I was on the field when it ended. I fell to my knees, then sprawled flat on my face. I was crying like a baby. We had put so much into this season and it just ended too abruptly. Even in the midst of my tears, I found myself thinking, I'm never going to give up. Even though we lost, it was such a thrill to make it this far. This is such a great game! I'll never, ever quit.

Both my father and my mother had attended the University of Tennessee and both had graduated from the school. They were loyal alumni and avid supporters of the school's athletic program. As far back as I can remember, Mom and Dad had season tickets to Tennessee Volunteer football.

And, of course, when they attended those games, I was right at their side. I still get goose pimples on my neck when I think about the excitement that was generated in that stadium! Before the game the Tennessee band would form a huge orange "T" with their band members. As they played, the crowd would shout, "HERE COME THE VOLS!" and the football team would sprint onto the field.

The University of Tennessee has a huge stadium. While I was in high school, they added onto the existing 76,000 seats, increasing them to 97,000. It was the second-largest stadium in the United States, behind the University of Michigan. It looked like an orange sea.

I'm recounting all these facts for one simple reason: I always dreamed about playing football for the University of Tennessee. The head coach at the time was Johnny Majors. The man was greatly admired by so many Tennessee fans. He had played at Tennessee in his college days, as had two of his brothers. His brother, Bobby, was only six years older than me, so I can very distinctly remember watching him play. He was so enjoyable to watch. By your senior year in high school, your choice of college becomes a focal point in your thinking. And when you're a young athlete who has the opportunity to receive scholarships from major universities, it becomes a very exciting time.

My parents wanted me to make up my own mind ... but, of course, they were partial to Tennessee. Early in my senior year it was arranged for me to meet Coach Majors. He actually came to our house. We chatted amicably and he made it clear that he wanted me as a Volunteer. Naturally, I was thrilled, as were my parents. Even though I had always dreamed of playing at Tennessee, I just had to be certain there were no other places that were better for me. The fact that I wanted to look around a little may have made for a little more effort on Tennessee's part to sign me. But I had to be sure.

The week after Coach Majors' visit, my folks received this personal letter from him:

Dear Mr. and Mrs. Bates:

I am very appreciative for the opportunity to have visited in your home last week.

Bill is the type young man that we must sign at Tennessee to play the schedule that we have in the Southeastern Conference. I know Bill has a lot of pride in his heritage. He has a lot of University of Tennessee background from both his mother and dad.

We are going to make every effort to see that Bill is wearing the Orange of Tennessee in September 1979 in front of 85,000 people. We are counting on Bill at Tennessee.

Sincerely,
John Majors
Head Football Coach

Recruiting was an all-out blitz. To see if you were interested in their program, a university would send you a letter through your head coach. If you responded, they could invite you on campus for a visit. Sifting through the letters was a major task because Coach Sparks received hundreds of letters expressing interest in me. And Coach had a good team, so you can be sure he was getting plenty of mail for other players as well.

With Coach's counsel, I was able to narrow down all the requests to four or five schools. We made contact and started scheduling visits. This was tricky as well, since it all occurred in the winter, during basketball season ... and I was a starter on our varsity squad.

My first trip was to Auburn University. Coach Sparks was especially excited about this school because one of the assistant coaches, Dal Shealy, was a close friend of Coach Sparks. (By the way, Dal Shealy is now president of the Fellowship of Christian Athletes.) It was a great trip. The campus was gorgeous, the football program exciting, the students friendly. I tried my best to keep an open mind, but I was already leaning strongly toward Tennessee.

The next visit was to Ol' Miss. This visit did not go as well as the visit to Auburn. The arrangement was rather impressive: Ol' Miss would send their Lear jet to pick me up for the visit. I was getting the big-head just thinking about it-a Lear jet just for me!

Then reality came crashing in (perhaps a poor choice of words). The "Lear jet" turned out to be an antiquated, propeller-driven airplane. Far from impressive, it looked dangerous to me. So in that context, I really got rattled when the pilot deplaned from his craft. I was told later that he was a gentleman in his mid-fifties, but to me he looked to be a hundred! The entire flight found me locked in concern over this man. I never took my eyes off him, for fear he would die at the controls. Since I didn't know how to fly, I wondered if this would be my first chance to sky dive. The truth is we did arrive safely, without a scratch, but I already knew I didn't want to attend Ol' Miss before we touched the ground.

The University of Kentucky was my third visit. One of their coaches, Coach Catalovis, had actively pursued me for several years. He had come to several of my high school games and had expressed great interest in me.

Kentucky knew how to throw a visit. I saw some of the nicest dorms I had ever seen. I was taken to see the most beautiful thoroughbred race horses on earth . . . several of them Kentucky Derby winners. I attended a Kentucky basketball game at a time when Kentucky was in the top five in national rankings. It was a fabulous time. The visit to Kentucky made me realize how difficult this decision would be. I was still leaning toward Tennessee, but I was making friends at other schools, creating relationships which would make it hard to choose to go somewhere else.

Even though I had been on Tennessee's campus dozens of times, my fourth visit was to UT in order to "make it official." I had just about decided on Tennessee for certain. There was one last trip I had to make. Visiting Auburn, Mississippi, and Kentucky had seemed like a drive down the road. There was a part of me that was asking inside, What would it be like to go to school someplace far away from home? Did I want to break away from my southern heritage in my choice of college?

These were the types of questions I was asking, and it prompted me to visit one final university. My fifth college visit took me all the way to southern California to visit UCLA ... but not without a measure of confusion.

Tennessee people are loyal supporters of their state and their state's schools. It was no secret that I was planning a visit to UCLA, and this news did not set well with some ardent Volunteer fans. How could I slap

Tennessee in the face by leaving its hallowed ground, even if only for a visit?

UCLA informed me that on the day I was to leave for Los Angeles, I was to go to the Knoxville Airport, where my pre-paid ticket would be waiting for me at the airline ticket counter. My dad drove me to the airport and accompanied me to the ticket counter. It's a good thing he didn't just drop me off at the door.

"I'm here to pick up my ticket to Los Angeles," I said to the woman at the counter. "You should have it in your computer. My name is Bill Bates."

She did some typing and replied, "No, Mr. Bates, I'm sorry. There are no tickets here for you, and I have no record of any reservations being made under that name."

I tried to stay calm. "The ticket was paid for by UCLA. Do you have any record of it?"

"No, sir. Nothing there either."

"William Bates?"

"No, sir."

"Are you sure?"

"Positive."

My dad came to the rescue, just like he did so many times in my life.

"Are there any seats available on this flight?" he asked.

"Yes, there are still seats available," she replied.

"Fine. I'd like to buy my son a round-trip ticket to Los Angeles."

Dad whipped out his wallet and made sure his son would get his visit to California.

Much later we found out that UCLA had, in fact, purchased a ticket for me and that it was in the computer. Apparently some well-meaning Tennessee fans had access to the computer and erased my name, in an attempt to sabotage my trip and keep me a Volunteer! (UCLA later reimbursed my father for the ticket.)

The visit to Los Angeles was a great experience for me. I loved California! I was intrigued by so much of what UCLA had to offer. It quickly became apparent to me the choice was between UT or UCLA. Underneath it all, the decision was whether I should leave home or stay. Less than twelve hours after I landed back home in Knoxville, I signed scholarship papers with the University of Tennessee.

During my entire senior year I dated a wonderful girl named Cindy Reavis. She is-among many positives-a strong Christian. We went through a lot together, especially since we attended different high schools. She went to our archrival, Bearden, and I was at Farragut.

After the senior prom, our lives headed in different directions. My decision to play football at Tennessee was the choice that ended our relationship, but I've never forgotten the memories of our youth and the strong Christian influence she brought to our time together.

My senior year had so many highlights for me. Many of my friends on the football team were signing scholarship papers, and it was so much fun to be a part of it. Three of my friends from school signed with Tennessee, so Farragut would be well-represented on the freshman squad.

It was a great day for Farragut High School when the Vols signed me, Jeff York and Rusty Rennie

As I mentioned, I was part of the basketball team and we had a noteworthy season. We won our league championship and went to the state semi-finals (just like the football team)! That spring I ran track, as I had done throughout my high school career. My goal in track was to improve my speed for football. In doing so I qualified for the state finals in both the 100 meters and the long jump. All along I continued my vigorous weight-lifting regimen. I had a goal in weight-lifting, as well. I wanted to be able to bench press three hundred pounds before going off to college.

I did it ... one week before I left.

"Winners Never Quit and Quitters Never Win!"

When an athlete is highly sought after in high school, hey often refer to him or her as a blue-chip player or a blue chipper. I was very fortunate to be considered this type of football player during my senior year in high school. It was an exhilarating feeling to accept the awards that were coming my way. During high school, I was All-State two times, twice I was named to the All-East Tennessee League, and twice I was on the All-Knoxville Football League. One of our local newspapers, The Knoxville Journal, considered me number three on their list of top college prospects.

During my career at Farragut High School, I put together a good set of statistics. I was the first person to ever return kicks for more than 1,000 yards in the Knoxville Interscholastic League. I intercepted fourteen passes, made almost two hundred tackles, and had matured into a six-foot- one, 183-pounder who was ready to take on anything.

And being a person who was ready to take on anything was exactly what I needed to be when I first walked onto the practice field at the University of Tennessee.

It was hot and humid, a typical summer scorcher for the beginning of August in Tennessee. When the freshmen assembled, it was amazing to see the thirty guys who had been recruited and signed from all over the country. I remember thinking how impressive this freshman squad must be. I looked around and saw Willie Gault, who would go on to a major career with the NFL's Los Angeles Raiders. I saw Mike Cofer, who would do the same for the Detroit Lions. There was Anthony Hancock, who would play at Kansas City for the Chiefs, and Anthony Miller, who would play for the New York Giants. Thirty blue chippers. I was one proud boy.

And that's where the problem started. "Pride goes before destruction," it says in the Bible. It appeared that the main focus of freshman practice was to destroy you!

Thirty blue chippers had to prove themselves all over again. Since the coaches hadn't worked with us all that much, they would write our last names on a piece of white athletic tape and slap it on the front of our helmets. That way they could scream our names across the field, providing truly personal embarrassment.

"Gault, you ran the wrong pattern!"

"Rush him, Cofer! Let's see some speed! You call that fast, Cofer?"

"Come on, Bates! My granny can defend that play better than you did!"

I thought about a lot of things during summer freshman practice. I thought back on how I had really prayed about where to attend college. I felt God's peace about Tennessee. It's a good thing too, the way I was being humbled out there each day. But, then, everyone was being humbled out there ... it wasn't like I was being singled out. I also began to realize the lessons to be learned through humility. I knew I wanted to be the best football player I could be and if this sort of proving myself accomplished that goal, then I was all for it. There's a big difference between humility and humiliation. I didn't always see the contrast on the field, but I truly believed these coaches cared about me and used these methods to bring out my personal best.

Before long the upperclassmen arrived, and we were practicing together as a full unit. I'll never forget my first scrimmage with the whole team. I lined up to defend Kyle Aguilar, a six-foot-eight tight end, whose assignment was to catch the ball right over the middle. I knew this was coming, so I positioned myself to be in the best spot for the hit. Sure enough, he pulled down the pass over the middle and turned, heading right toward me. I don't know what it was, exactly. It could have been the old offensive-defensive hatred ... or it could have been the senior-freshman contrast ... or the seasoned veteran-nervous rookie thing. For whatever reason, I ran toward Kyle with all the speed I could muster and, without pulling back an iota (which is probably not a smart thing to do against one of your own teammates), I nailed him to the ground.

Frankly, I wouldn't have thought that much of it, except that when I got up after tackling him, the whole team was silent. As I looked around, everyone was looking at me- players, trainers, reporters, and coaches. It's the first time I remember Coach Majors focusing right in on me.

I swallowed hard and thought, Well, I guess I got myself some attention! I just wished I knew whether that was good or bad. I've pretty much concluded that when you get attention for doing something right ... that's a good thing. I was working hard at these summer practices. I'd sweat so profusely, I'd be convinced there was no liquid left in my entire body. I pushed and pushed, hoping and praying it would pay off.

Back when I was being recruited, I looked very carefully at each of the schools I considered. Part of that analysis was to determine which school would provide me an opportunity to play early in my college career. I didn't want to wait until my junior or senior year to play.

For example, while I was visiting UCLA, I observed a sophomore in the safety position who was a great player. His name was Kenny Easley. I quickly ascertained that if I went to UCLA, I'd be sitting on the bench behind him for another two years.

Proud to be a Volunteer!

Autumn arrived and with it, the start of our regular season. Our first game was on the road in Boston, against Boston College. The day the roster was to be posted was as nervous a day as I had had in a long time. I don't recall eating, sleeping, or paying much attention in class. I sprinted to the locker room at the hour of truth and skimmed the lineup quickly. Please, Lord, please! I prayed silently and fervently. God was to provide an answer of five little letters. There at the bottom of the list was the word "BATES." I silently thanked God and then let out a scream that echoed through- out the entire locker room! Here I was a freshman and I was part of the traveling squad. I was going to play special teams, and I was pumped.

Besides my special teams' responsibilities, I was playing backup to our starting strong safety, Greg Gaynes. I had great respect for Greg. He went on to a pro career with the Seattle Seahawks and now coaches for the Los

Angeles Rams. I expected him to have a banner season at that position. I had no expectation of taking his place.

And then Greg hurt his ankle.

So without a moment's notice, Bill Bates, freshman, took over the position of strong safety as the Tennessee Volunteers went on to defeat Boston College!

The next week provided an even greater thrill. Greg was going to be sidelined for a while, so I was now a starter! It was the ultimate thrill of my short life ... a freshman starting for the University of Tennessee for their first home game of the season.

The game was against Utah State. It was an important game for me, because I had the chance to show what I could do. I had a great game. I made ten or eleven solo tackles in an all-out effort. We won, and you'd have thought I had just claimed the Super Bowl It was a magic moment for me.

As the weeks went on, Greg healed from his ankle injury, putting Coach Majors in a tough spot-Do I play Gaynes, my proven commodity, or do I use Bates, the freshman boy-wonder? He ended up using us both for a time, but he wanted one of us to take hold of the position. Who would it be, Greg or me?

Football was my love, but there was also the realization that I had classes to attend. I quickly discovered there were many places on campus where I could not park my vehicle. Campus parking tickets were coming my way at the rate of two or three a day. It seemed like there were more campus police than there were students!

I was also introduced to Tennessee's great Gibbs Hall This athletic dormitory was state of the art for its time, but it was not home sweet home. The bed I was assigned did not have the comfort of my bed at home at "Momma Peggy's" (my mom's). But even though the bed was not great, it became my true love. Any free time I had found me on that mattress.

My roommate was Jeff York, one of my high school buddies who also signed with UT. The 7:50 A.M. classes were not our favorites but occasionally we managed to make a few! Now I understand how playing backgammon until 2:00 A.M. didn't help matters.

I remember beginning to visualize myself playing in front of the great Tennessee fans. During the summer months the UT Stadium was locked up pretty secure, but they couldn't keep me out. Late at night I'd jump the fence and make my way to the middle of the field. I'd lie down right in the center of the big "T" on the fifty-yard line. Hours would go by as I visualized the plays I would make. In my mind I'd hear the "Voice of the Vols," John

Ward, exclaiming, "Bates makes a bone-crushing tackle and is joined by a host of Volunteer defenders!"

It may be hard to believe, but my life at UT consisted of school, practice, the mess hall, and the sheets. Being a student athlete gave me little time for anything else.

Johnny Majors was considered a national treasure in the state of Tennessee. He had returned to the university as head coach-fresh from a national championship season at the University of Pittsburgh-with their sensational running back, Tony Dorsett. My freshman year at Tennessee was his fourth year there as head coach.

Coach Majors is a hard-worker and a quality football coach. He knows his "X's" and "O's" as well as anyone I've ever played for. He understands the technique of how to play football. He knows how to push players to get from them what he wants. As a player, he was at the safety position {like me} and he was the runner-up for the Heisman Trophy his senior year. As a coach, he was very involved in practice. Because of his special expertise in the defensive backfield, he had greater interest in that part of the lineup than anywhere else.

One time after a game, I received a note that simply said:

Bill Bates:
Please come see me in my office.
Coach Majors

I went into the meeting with a positive feeling. As far as I was concerned, I was doing a good job. Being a freshman starter was a responsibility I took very seriously. When I arrived at Coach's office, I found out I had not been invited there for praise.

Coach got right to the point. "You're missing tackles out there, Bates. I need you to work harder, especially on your tackling. We can't afford to have missed tackles on this team. Do you understand what I'm saying?"

"Yes, sir," I managed to get out in a weak tone.

"I don't want to see you missing tackles out there anymore, Bates. Now, get outta here and get to work!"

And with that, our "conversation" ended.

I walked across campus, filling up inside, nearing an explosion. I was angry, discouraged, disillusioned, and disheartened. Finally I arrived at my dorm room. I opened the door, fell on the bed, and cried like a baby. I don't think Coach Majors knew how much this meeting would affect me ... or did he? He always seemed to know which buttons to push to get what he needed from his players.

I soon discovered that criticism pushes me. I'll try so hard, I'll pass out. I threw everything I had into those practice sessions. I began to put tremendous pressure on myself to improve. It was to be one of life's ironies. I did improve, but not without cost.

I was trying so hard to please Coach Majors that my friendships suffered, my love for the University of Tennessee suffered, and my overall excitement for football-especially practice-was greatly diminished. I was improving but I wasn't very happy.

Criticism affects different players different ways. Coach Majors seemed to achieve his goal by criticizing me. I worked even harder.

Not long after my meeting with Coach, another "meeting" took place. Coach invited Greg Gaynes into his office with an agenda similar to the one he had with me earlier. Greg didn't respond the same way I did. He felt the coaches were putting unfair pressure on him and he let Coach Majors know he didn't like his criticism. Apparently, it was quite a verbal tussle between these two guys and, unfortunately, no one wins in an argument of this nature. But the result was clear. At the end of their conversation, Greg made a decision. He quit the team.

After the shock of his announcement sank in, I realized this would only add increased pressure on me. And it did. Starting as a freshman is highly unusual, so my every move was continually scrutinized.

My freshman year wasn't all gloom and misery. There were some wonderful moments as well. One such moment had to be the biggest game of the season for any Volunteer fan ... Tennessee versus Alabama.

The Alabama Crimson Tide was in its prime in 1979. Bear Bryant was consistently producing champions, and he was a man I greatly admired. Their Wishbone Offense was an effective tool, to say the least. By the time we met them, late in the season, they were undefeated and we wanted nothing more than to upset them. This wouldn't be an easy task. The game was in Birmingham, which cannot be overestimated.

On top of it all, it was an unseasonably hot afternoon. The fans in the stands were stripped down to T-shirts and shorts, so you can imagine how much more miserable it was down on the field in full uniform!

We played inspired football in the first half. Alabama was utterly shocked by our intensity, and we went into the locker room at halftime leading 17-0. We felt good ... maybe too good.

The Crimson Tide began to roll in the second half. Part of the difficulty in defending their Wishbone Offense is the number of options it provides their quarterback. He had so many possibilities, and we knew we should be covering all of them on defense. My responsibility was to cover the "pitch" man. This would be a running back who would come out of the back-field, moving toward the sideline on each play. Since the pitch man was the quarterback's final option, there was no holding back for me. I ran all-out each time toward the sideline, whether or not he had the ball.

If this hadn't been a football game, it would have appeared that all I did on a horrendously hot day was run wind sprints-one right after another. Their offense hammered away at us. The Wishbone allowed them to make consistent gains on us. The gains were small but, if done consistently, produced first downs.

Major Ogilvie was the running back who came out of the Wishbone the most that afternoon. He'd gain four yards, then six, then four more, then eight, then four, then four again, then six. This resulted in first down after first down. Plus, they were wearing us down. Ogilvie had 109 yards rushing that day, but I stopped him as often as I could. He'd go back to his huddle after each play, and I would return to the defensive side of the field. While their quarterback called plays, I'd be in the defensive secondary dry-heaving.

We played our best but we lost. I was among a field full of orange-jerseyed guys who thought we should have beat them. We were a better team that day, but somehow they squeaked it out.

After the game I went over to the Alabama sideline. I wanted to congratulate Coach Bryant, and most of all, I just wanted to shake his hand. What a wonderful surprise to have him turn toward me as I approached him. He held out his hand and said, "Bill, you played a great game! Y'all deserved to win." I shook his hand, honored to be recognized by him and so pleased to discover what a class guy he was. Also, I was honored that day by being named Defensive Player of the Game.

While we're talking about Bear Bryant, I should mention that we lost to Alabama two more years, before beating them my senior year. That made eleven straight years of losing to Alabama! After our victory my senior year, I went over to the sideline once again to shake hands with Coach Bryant. Guess what he said to me this time? "Bill, you played a great game and y'all deserved to win!" Ever gracious, even in defeat-no wonder the man was a legend.

We stuffed Alabama at the Goal line....Mike Casteel and Reggie White

We had a good season that year-good enough to be invited to Houston for the Bluebonnet Bowl. What a thrill for a nineteen-year-old kid to be playing in the Houston Astrodome against the Purdue Boilermakers! Along with the thrill came the reality that Purdue had a tough team that year. We got beat, which was only compounded by the fact that I got hurt. I took a hit to my right knee, bursting my bursa sack. The excess fluid caused my knee to begin swelling almost immediately. It hurt horribly, but I was determined to play right through the pain. I did just that, but by the end of the game my knee was swollen beyond belief.

After the game I sat in the locker room, not knowing whether I'd play football again or not. I vividly remember my dad coming down to the locker room. He took one look at my knee and his eyes began welling up with tears. Sometimes I think it's harder on family and loved ones to see an injury than it is on the player himself. Fortunately, the injury healed and I was back to full strength quickly.

At the end of the 1979 season, I was honored by being named to the Freshman All-America Team and I was the number one punt returner on our squad. The message around the locker room was coming through loud and clear: Because I had such a good freshman season, big things were expected of me next season ... big things.

We began the 1980 season at Tennessee believing we were the team to beat. This wasn't simply a subjective idea on our parts. We were given the number one national ranking in several preseason polls. Coach Majors had his hands full trying to get us to see that polls are worthless if you don't get out there and win every weekend.

To make things more exciting, our opening game was to be against Vince Dooley's University of Georgia Bulldogs, who were also highly ranked. A true test was on tap for the first match-up of the season. But I had no idea how big this game would be for me. September 6, 1980 was to produce a situation that would follow me around for years and years. It was "The Play."

On that particular Friday evening there were more people in Tennessee's stadium than had ever been assembled to watch a football game in the history of the whole state. Now, that's a sea of orange. I was pleased that so many people were there-especially the way the game started off. We were leading 9-0 when the sound of the gun ended the first half. We came back, scored a touchdown, tried for a two-point conversion, missed, but still had a comfortable 15-0 lead.

It was about midway through the third quarter when my nightmare began. Georgia, once again unable to move the ball, elected to punt on fourth down. They had gained some pretty good yardage on the drive, so as I took my position as punt returner, I was lined up pretty close to the goal line. The Bulldog punter let loose with a fabulous punt.

I stood ready to receive it, just like I had done a thousand times before. But this punt was different. For some reason, I couldn't bring it into my grasp. No excuses ... I fumbled the ball.

Georgia capitalized on my mistake. My fumbled attempt at the punt return resulted in a safety for the Bulldogs. Now it was 15-2. But, more significantly, we felt the momentum swing Georgia's way.

It was on the Bulldog's next possession that the world was introduced to the effectiveness of Coach Dooley's newest offensive weapon. We had seen glimpses of this freshman running sensation. At 220 pounds, he was strong and fast. But this was to be the drive that would present Herschel Walker to the world.

Herschel had run pretty well so far, but I had been hitting him hard throughout the game. We decided to send a blitz in the direction he was running, with me as the last line of defense. Sure enough, first down and ten, with the ball on our sixteen-yard line, quarterback Buck Belue handed off the ball to number 34.

I saw the flow going to my right and immediately I sprinted over to that side. I didn't expect Herschel to break through the line, but somehow he found a gaping hole over their left tackle, and suddenly there I was ... with him coming straight at me.

I was at the five-yard line, dead in front of him, set up for the tackle. I expected him to make a move one way or the other, and I'd gotten there soon enough to be ready to go whichever way he went. He had been running around people all night, so I was mentally prepared for the pattern of running he had developed.

To my surprise, Herschel didn't go left or right. I looked into his eyes, deeply set in his helmet, and quickly ascertained that he was going to go straight ... straight over me! I felt a helmet on my chest ... then footprints on my chest. My mistake had been that I reacted too quickly. I got there and set up to make the tackle so fast that I completely stopped. Herschel, on the other hand, was going full speed. So he ran right over me and scampered into the end zone for his first touchdown as a collegian.

I remember looking back and watching him go through the end zone. It hurt ... real bad. I wasn't injured or anything like that-truthfully, Herschel didn't hit me that hard. He had hit me harder several times earlier in the game. It wasn't the fierce intensity of the hit-it was just the way it looked. It was destined to become "The Play."

We were up 15-9 after Georgia's extra point. We got the ball and began an effective drive. However, Jeff Olszewski, our able quarterback, uncharacteristically fumbled the ball and the Bulldogs recovered.

With the momentum clearly in Georgia's direction, they once again handed the ball to Herschel Walker, fresh off his first collegiate score. Quickly Herschel doubled his effort. He scored on us again, making it 15-15. Dooley elected to kick the extra point. It was good. Georgia led 16-15 in the fourth quarter.

They ate up the clock very effectively on us that night.

Our last and best effort to score on them occurred with four minutes left in the game. We moved the ball all the way down to their five-yard line.

Olszewski handed off the ball to Glenn Ford, one of our running backs. Ford fumbled. Georgia recovered and held onto the ball. We lost 16-15.

The University of Georgia would take the momentum from that opening game and carry it through their entire season. Catapulted by Herschel Walker's seventeen touchdowns that season, Coach Dooley's Bulldogs would go on to an undefeated season and a national championship.

When the game was over I was so disappointed that we had lost. I knew I had made some key mistakes in the contest, but I didn't single out Herschel running over me as being any different than the fumbled punt or the fumbles by Ford or Olszewski. I was embarrassed by the defeat.

I went back to my dorm room and slept away most of Saturday. On Sunday, I got up and went to church as I always did. As I was walking down the aisle to be seated in church, I could hear people whispering, "There's Bates ... did you see him get hit Friday night by that Herschel Walked" It was the strangest sensation! I tried to put it behind me and just pay attention to the service. I hustled out of church, back to my dorm, where I settled in to watch Sunday's offering of NFL games.

This will get my mind off that stuff, I told myself. And it almost worked. At halftime, CBS turned its attention away from pro ball to let the whole world see the newest running sensation in the collegiate ranks. My jaw dropped as I watched Herschel Walker running over me on national television. "This kid is really something!" gushed Brent Musberger. That little clip of film was to travel all over the country, not to mention the exposure it got in the Georgia Bulldogs' highlight films.

I walked away from the TV with an overwhelming feeling of defeat. I don't need to deal with this kind of stuff, I complained to myself. It's not worth it ... I'm gonna quit football.

The more I thought about quitting, the better it sounded.

I just needed it confirmed by one person. I called my dad.

"Dad, I've made a decision, and I wanted you to be the first to know about it," I told him over the telephone.

"What's that, son?"

"I'm quitting football. I don't need the kind of junk that's going on from the reporters and the TV sportscasters."

"I see," my dad responded quietly. I felt awkward with the silence so I asked his advice.

"What do you think I should do, Dad?"

He paused a little longer, then finally spoke. "Bill, it's just a game. I know this is hard on you. Remember, though, Georgia won on the scoreboard, but you won on the field."

"So what are you saying, Dad?"

"I guess what I'm saying, son, is this: Winners never quit and quitters never win."

When I hung up the phone, I knew it was vitally important for me to see this through. So I did.

When I went to practice the next day, I had this horrible feeling that I had let all my teammates down. It was a haunting feeling. Nobody really said anything, but I had that sense that everyone was watching me. I wondered what was going on behind my back.

The hardest thing I've ever done was to put "The Play" in its proper perspective and get on with my life. It was even harder than making the Cowboys-it was the hardest.

Bill Bates
Defensive Back

Today I look back on that situation and see the positive.

Herschel Walker went on to establish himself as a premiere running back in college and pro ball. I have great admiration and respect for him. But look how he got his start! He received national attention because he ran over one of the hardest hitting guys in college ball at the time! I'm no longer embarrassed. I've learned to turn it around. I'm honored. If it hadn't been for that incident, I wouldn't have learned to tackle the way I did throughout my NFL Career.

Another part of this story that helped me tremendously was putting into practice a simple truth: "The Play" turned out exactly the way God wanted it to. You can't change your past, so the best thing to do is accept it, learn from it, and move on.

Do I have any animosity toward Herschel? Absolutely not! He is one of the greatest guys you'll ever meet. He is a wonderful Christian man, a true humanitarian. We were teammates on the Cowboys for two seasons and we got along wonderfully. He and his wife have had dinner with Denise and me on many occasions.

Actually, Herschel and I have never discussed "The Play."

I think it's probably better that way.

The week after the loss to Georgia really tested my ability to focus. The University of Southern California was our next opponent. They, too, had a running back of major status:

Marcus Allen.

To the utter shock of all of us, USC beat us. It wasn't a trouncing-it was just the opposite. They beat us 20-17, thanks to a forty-seven-yard field goal by Eric Hipp, with only six seconds left on the clock. He had nailed a forty-five- yarder in the first half as well. The Trojans had a great day, while we at Tennessee were all in disbelief. Two weeks earlier we had been ranked number one in so many preseason polls ... and now we were 0-2. This didn't set well with any of us. We knew we'd be looking at practices that would be likened to cruel torture. There was a lot of bad press that week about the Volunteers. Radio call-in shows were butchering us with cutting ridicule. There was no question that losing our first two games at a major university was leaving a bad taste in our mouths. But it was particularly distasteful to an important person in my life ....

Johnny Majors.

"What More Do You Want from Me?"

My special teams coach on the Cowboys has become a wonderful friend of mine. His name is Joe Avezzano. I'll have a lot more to say about Joe as we go on, but one of the things that's amazing about him is that during his college coaching days, he coached under Johnny Majors for eleven years.

That's a real testimony to Coach Avezzano's staying power. He was with Coach Majors four years at Iowa State University, moved with him for four more years at the University of Pittsburgh (which produced a national championship behind that sensational running back, Tony Dorsett), and then three years at the University of Tennessee, which is where I first met him.

I asked Coach Avezzano to describe the coaching philosophy of Johnny Majors to me one afternoon after a run at the Cowboys training facility at Valley Ranch. He sat next to the track, dripping sweat, still breathing heavily, but very willing to talk about a man for whom he has great respect. "Johnny Majors is a very demanding coach," he began. "He's that way on his coaching staff and his players. Bill, you have to remember the circumstances surrounding his arrival at Tennessee. To begin with, he was an alumnus of the school. Along with that, he was a former football player on their team-and not just another player, but a highly decorated player. He moved to the head coaching position at Tennessee right after winning the national championship at the University of Pittsburgh-so he's a highly decorated coach as well. The expectation level was phenomenal. I imagine that added to his already demanding style."

"Anyway, Coach Majors is basically looking for three things in his players. One thing he demands is a technically sound performance. He'll accept no substitutes or excuses on that count. Second, he looks for players with a high level of intensity because he feels that will further enhance their performance on the field. Thirdly, he likes to find a player with strong character. If he can find a guy with all three of those attributes, in his mind, he's found the perfect player for one of his teams."

"That makes for a pretty tough coach," I responded.

"Yeah, but that also explains why you did so well at Tennessee," added Coach Avezzano. "Majors loved your character, your work ethic, and your intense desire to succeed."

I just wish I had known all that when I was back in college. It would have alleviated so much stress.

After the humiliating 0-2 beginning of my sophomore season, we were put through some real character building. Coach Majors was determined to get this team back up to the performance standard he knew we could realize. So we worked.

And it paid off. We defeated Washington State 35-23 the following week in Knoxville and then won our next two games on the road. We beat an always-tough Auburn 42-0, and the next week we took Georgia Tech 23-10 in Atlanta. Were we on our way back?

At 3-2 we regained our confidence. We began preparing for our rivalry with Alabama. We were back at the level of play that gave us hope that we could knock off the Crimson Tide on our home turf.

When I woke up that Saturday morning, I looked out my window to see an ominous sight-it was raining. Not just raining, but pouring-buckets and buckets. A perfect day for a running game.

And that's exactly what Bear Bryant brought with him.

The Wishbone Offense totally dominated us. They racked up 301 yards on the ground, while we could only muster up a dis- mal twenty-two. We didn't even make a first down until halfway through the third quarter! When it was all over we were wet and disheartened.

We lost 27-0.

The downhill skid started all over again. We ended up losing the next three games. Practice was excruciating. Coach Majors wouldn't tolerate a team with a record of 3-6. I thought it was a good sign that we went on to win our final two games of the season. The year ended with our record at 5-6. I could only hope that Coach Majors would look to next season with optimism. If he decided to continue the punishing practices from last season, I was afraid he was going to kill me. He was changing the way I felt about football.

Not too long after the regular season ended, the next season began. Coach Majors was a real believer in year-round training. While it was the freezing cold of winter outside, he'd have us inside for his own version of winter workouts.

Winter workouts were designed to test you physically and mentally. The workouts took place in the afternoons . . . unless you had missed the previous workout. If you had missed an afternoon workout, you were expected to be in the gymnasium at 6:00 A.M. the next day so, believe me, the players made every effort to be there in the afternoons. A common regimen at these workouts was circuit training. The players would divide into four groups, each going to a different corner of the gym to participate in sprints or crab walks or up-downs or the like. You'd work fifteen minutes in each corner, then rotate to another until you completed the circuit in an hour.

Those drills after my sophomore season were especially difficult for me. Maybe the workouts were no harder, but I was struggling ... mostly on the inside. Try as I might, I just couldn't shake "The Play." The Georgia game, Herschel Walker, and the fumble kept speeding around in my mind.

Thus, it was particularly distressing to have Coach Majors right in my face in those workouts. He'd wander over to the sprint portion of the circuit while I was running as fast as I could. He'd watch me for a couple of seconds and then he'd scream at me: "Push yourself, Bates! You gotta run harder! Push yourself!" Looking back, I don't know whether Coach was singling me out or not, but it felt that way. Deep down inside, I was so burdened by the previous season, I was discouraged. Winter workouts ended only a couple of weeks before spring practice began. Mentally, I tried to shake the nightmare of the past, but it was still there looming in my mind.

Everything came to a head during one spring practice.

The regimen started up as usual. We did some stretching, and then the defensive backs moved together for defensive back drills. All of that went without a hitch.

After those drills we began tackling drills. Open-field tackling is vital to any football player. There is a skill to mastering it. Typically, one of the coaches would give a player a ball and send him running down the field. Fifteen yards away, a defender would be waiting for his chance at an open-field tackle. That's an open-field tackling drill.

In those days we had an excess of kickers. A bunch of guys would show up at practice as walk-ons for the kicking position. So, besides kicking, they'd also serve as the ball carriers for the open-field tackling drills. On this particular day, one of those walk-on kickers was given the ball and sent running ... with me lined up fifteen yards away. I almost always made the tackle, but for some reason, on that day I missed the tackle. It was always embarrassing, but it was especially so on this practice because the drill was being conducted by the head coach.

Before I had time to catch my breath, I heard a voice growling loud enough to be heard in Wyoming. "BATES, DO IT AGAIN!" It was Coach Majors and he was steamed.

As I turned around to do the drill over again, the horn blew on the practice field, indicating it was time to move on to the next drill. Coach Majors wasn't through with me, however.

"All right. Everyone move on to the next drill," he barked. But then he looked right at me and added, "Bates, you stay right where you are and get that tackling right!" I hung my head in embarrassed disbelief. By the time I looked up again, there were ten or fifteen new walk-on kickers, ready to attempt to get by me. In anticipation, I quickly got set.

I think Johnny Majors knew how to push my buttons. He had observed me for two years now and made careful note of my style. Basically, when you get me angry enough, I'll move into hyper-warp speed. That's how I've always been and that day was no exception. After eight or ten tackles at this out-of-control pace, I was completely exhausted. It got so bad that I had to stop the drill myself-something I never do. I was over on the sideline hyperventilating when the trainers came over to me. They sat me down and gave me water. I was as close to passing out as possible. My head was spinning.

I rested no longer than twenty minutes, and I was back out on the practice field. By this time practice was almost over. The team was participating in a full-speed scrimmage when I rejoined them. I pushed myself as hard as I could and some- how survived.

The final aspect of my practice was kicking practice. I was to go over to another part of the field to practice returning punts. I ran with the little energy I had remaining. It must have been adrenaline alone that got me through that horrible afternoon. As fate would have it, on the final punt of the practice, I got tackled and twisted my ankle in the process.

With practice concluded, I slowly picked myself up off the ground and began the painful limp back to our locker room. I had only taken a few painful steps when my mind started screaming inside of me. What am I doing? Why am I putting myself through this? I'm the only one out of ninety guys being put through anything like this!

About that time Dom Capers, our defensive back coach (now a coach in the NFL), came over to check on me. Before he could even open his mouth, I exploded:

"Why am I doing this? Why do I have to go through all this? What do you want from me?"

Poor Coach Capers. None of this was his doing, but he was the most convenient coach to absorb my wrath. In a cool, calm manner, Coach quietly responded, "I think you need to speak with Coach Majors."

Normally I wouldn't have considered something so radical, but I was furious. I quickly surveyed the field and spotted Coach Majors by the far goalpost. I must have been quite a sight. I was limping on the outside and burning on the inside. I got over to him just as he finished with another player, so I swallowed hard and spoke right up.

"Listen, Coach," I began. "This has been the most traumatic day of my life. I cannot have many more days like this and continue to play football for Tennessee. What more do you want from me? I just don't know!"

I had an immediate feeling of venting a lot of frustration and exasperation. But you just don't talk to Johnny Majors that way. He responded forcefully, coming right back at me in a confrontational manner. No fatherly advice here-just hard words.

"Let me show you what I want from you," he snapped. And with that, he proceeded to demonstrate to me how to make an open-field tackle ... as if I had never seen one before.

"Do you understand now?" he asked after his demonstration.

"Yes," I replied weakly.

"Fine," he snapped. He turned his back and walked off the field. I limped off alone.

I showered, dressed, and hobbled back to my dorm. I laid on my bunk, face down, my mind reeling with the latest incident, the Georgia game, "The Play," and any other failure I could conjure up. Over and over I found myself saying, Is this really worth it?

At this point God graciously brought to mind a brother and helper who could give me some much-needed perspective. I went to the phone late that night and called Coach Sparks. The next day Coach Sparks was on the practice field at the Tennessee campus. Interestingly enough, he seemed to sense that I needed serious encouragement, so he brought along another friend ... Stan Cotten.

The two of them watched me go through an uneventful practice. But it was clear to them that my heart was not in it. This wasn't the Bill Bates they were used to seeing.

After practice I showered, changed, and met them in the parking lot. Coach Sparks immediately came up to me and put his arm around me. That's when the healing began.

As we talked that evening, Coach reminded me of some fundamental truths that I had let slip by in my life. "Remember who you are, Bill," Coach encouraged. "You are a child of God. Think about all you have in Christ."

I had to admit I hadn't been doing much thinking that way lately.

"It goes back to a simple premise," Coach went on to say.

"Trust the Lord. Remember, Bill, you don't have to fight this battle. This battle, like all others, belongs to the Lord."

I remember we ended the evening by having Coach Sparks pray for me. It was the best I had felt in quite a while.

I'd like to say that everything turned around the very next day, but that wasn't the case. I had become so discouraged that it took a few weeks for me to regain my healthy perspective. Actually, Coach Sparks and I met a second time, shortly after our first visit. He sensed that I was losing heart. As a result he gave me one of the most serious talks he had ever given me.

"Listen Bill," he said to me in his loving manner. "You and I both know that God has a plan for Bill Bates. His plan may include football at the University of Tennessee-but then again, maybe not."

Those words shocked me. What was God's plan for me in this mess? I asked myself.

Coach Sparks continued, "The important thing to remember is that you don't have to perform for God to love you and take care of you. Trust Him, Bill. He'll always be there for you, no matter what you do or how you play."

That night we prayed together. I remember how simple my prayer was. I was hurting so badly that I could only think of one thing to say.

"Dear God," I prayed. "Please help tomorrow to be better than today. Thank You. Amen."

I didn't know it at the time, but as that prayer ended, one of the biggest turning points in my football career began. Without my realizing its full effect, that prayer was the start of me putting the heavy burdens of my mind behind me. I put Johnny Majors behind me.

I put Herschel Walker behind me. I put the past behind me.

Each day was a fresh, new opportunity to trust the Lord ... to allow Him to direct my path.

I started thinking to myself, "Maybe since I had that little conversation with Coach Majors, he won't be in such a hurry to get all over me." There was, of course, no basis for that thinking, but that's how I filled my mind.

The strangest thing occurred. My thinking-built on no basis-was 100 percent correct. Coach Majors started picking on other people. He left me alone. It was as if we both silently understood what had transpired that late spring afternoon, and there was nothing else to add.

During this whole episode in my life, another situation occurred that brought further perspective. One of my good friends, Kenny Colquit, was enjoying an outing at a swimming pool with his buddies. Diving across the pool for a football, he hit his head on a pool step. The blow paralyzed him from the neck down. The accident has kept him down physically ever since. But his ability to overcome his limitations has inspired me on numerous occasions. Whenever I experience any type of pain, I realize it is nothing compared to what some people have to overcome, especially Kenny.

The entire Johnny Majors incident caused me to mature.

I started taking my role as an upperclassman seriously, providing leadership to the players around me. And then, on top of it all, Coach Majors began to say nice things about me ... even publicly ... in the newspapers!

Part of what was so amazing about this pivotal incident in my life is that it all happened so quickly. I didn't miss a beat on the outside. To the casual observer--completely oblivious to the wrenching going on inside-it would have looked like business-as-usual.

My junior year as a Volunteer began very much like the previous one. Once again, our season opener was against Georgia, and once again they defeated us.

Herschel Walker had another memorable day, gaining 161yards. I should point out that, it was an exciting contest between him and me. There was no hint of revenge or anything personal. Both of us are consummate competitors, so we each gave it our all. Tennessee came back from Athens a 44-0 loser.

The next week we were in sunny southern California for a rematch with the University of Southern California. Marcus Allen was unstoppable, running for 210 yards and scoring four touchdowns. We lost 43-7. So it was two weeks into the season and once again, we were 0-2.

But then, just like last year, we won the next three games, so we were 3-2 entering the Alabama game.

When we lost to Alabama, this time with a score of 38-19, it was the eleventh straight time they had beaten us. But, unlike the last season, we won four of the last five games to end up with a 7-4 season.

To commemorate a winning season, we were invited to East Rutherford, New Jersey, to compete against the University of Wisconsin in the Garden State Bowl. The Badgers scored first but we were energized by our kick returner, Willie Gault, who returned their first kickoff eighty-seven yards for a touchdown. We went on to win 28-21.

As that bowl game reached its conclusion, I realized I had only one more season of college football. I was hopeful it would be a good one. After all, I had made peace with Herschel ... and with Johnny ... and most importantly, with myself.

The future was bright.

We opened our 1982 season at home against the Duke Blue Devils. On the one hand, we were expected to beat Duke. On the other hand, we had lost five of our last six openers. Unfortunately, the other hand prevailed and we lost a one- point heartbreaker, 25-24.

The next week we defeated Iowa State, so we were able to go into the third week 1-1. We traveled to Auburn for a con- test with the Tigers. On the plane trip to Auburn, something occurred that had never happened to me before-1 became violently ill on the airplane. I had the works-high fever, chills, vomiting, all for unknown reasons. When the plane landed, I was taken immediately to the hotel, given some medication, and put to bed.

It turned out that a blister on my right heel had become infected and the infection had spread throughout my entire body, poisoning me and causing the violent reaction.

But when I woke up the next morning I felt great. I hadn't felt that rested in a long. time. The autumn afternoon in Auburn was perfect for football. I anticipated a good game.

Everyone was talking about Auburn's freshman running back. My first tackle against this guy convinced me he was worth talking about. When he shot out of the backfield, I hit him low-right on his thigh, to be exact. He went down, but the impact of my head on his thigh caused me to see stars! That was my introduction to Bo Jackson.

Auburn beat us 24-14. We won the next week against Washington State and then tied LSU in Baton Rouge. This brought our record to 2-2-1, before facing Alabama for the last time in my collegiate career.

The game was home for us. Because they had defeated national powerhouse Penn State the week before, Alabama was ranked number two in the nation. That, we knew. What we didn't know was this was to be Coach Bryant's last season before retiring. This was the stuff dreams were made of for a Tennessee fan. More people were in Neyland Stadium than ever before. As we sat in the locker room, waiting to go out on the field, the noise generated by 95,342 people was deafening to our ears, even down below.

Coach Majors knew that we all understood the importance

of this game. A long, flowery pregame talk was unnecessary. I'll never forget his words. Gathering his team around him, he merely said: "They've beaten us eleven years in a row." He paused and added, "It will not strike twelve."

We got on the scoreboard first with a field goal by our kicker, Fuad Reveiz. The Crimson Tide came right back with a touchdown, and the first quarter ended with us behind 7-3.

Halftime found us behind 21-13, but we felt that the momentum was moving our direction. Midway in the second quarter our wide receiver, Willie Gault, caught a pass from our quarterback, Alan Cockrell, and ran it fifty-two yards for a touchdown.

We scored two touchdowns in the third quarter to lead 27-21. In the fourth quarter we scored another touchdown and successfully went for the two-point conversion. Leading 35-21 in the fourth quarter, we felt good.

But Alabama came right back and scored a touchdown.

With the score 35-28, could we hold on?

YES!

After eleven years of frustration, it finally happened. My senior year would now possess the absolute highlight of my entire collegiate career!

The fans went berserk. They mobbed the field, grabbing any orange jersey they could find and hoisting him on their shoulders. We were exhilarated, but we somehow fought our way through the crowd to get into the safety of our locker room.

While we were in the locker room, the fans took down the goal posts. They kept screaming for us to come back up. After a few moments alone as a team, we went back up. Once again the fans mounted us on their shoulders and marched us all around the field, as if we had just won World War II. I guess from a Tennessee perspective, we had.

It was heady stuff. Coach Majors was named National Coach of the Week by United Press International. The press was treating us with a respect that can only come from knocking off a titan like the Tide.

I remember I couldn't even sleep that night. My buddy, John Cook, and I were so stoked, we were like two little kids. Part of our return to childhood included a little fishing. But not the kind with a pole, a hook, and some bait. That's not childish enough.

No, John and I came into the possession of two goldfish, and in our kid-like glee-we ate them! It was hard to explain to the owner of Herbie and Moe-the two fish-how they escaped from the tank!

Everyone celebrates his own way.

"Denise Can't See You Right Now!"

After the victory over the Crimson Tide we were unbeatable ... *or so we thought.*

The next game was an away game in Atlanta against Georgia Tech. We were fairly confident in practice that week, still basking in the glow of our great defeat of Alabama. We moved up to number fourteen in the national rankings, and were told that Saturday's game at Tech was to be televised nationally.

Coach Majors was still pushing us hard, but in a demonstration of uncharacteristic kindness, he made an announcement after practice early that week. "Since the game is in Atlanta this week, it's close enough from Knoxville to take buses. So as is our custom, we'll all drive down together on the team bus."

We all looked at each other and winced-those bus rides could be long and uncomfortable.

"However," Coach continued, "after the game on Saturday, if you'd like to, you can find your own ride home."

The team lit up. Saturday night in Atlanta! This had some promising possibilities. It became the only issue we discussed for the whole week. Some of the guys weren't certain if they were going to stay after the game or not, but for us seniors there was no discussion. We had a simple schedule:

Go to Atlanta.

Beat Georgia Tech.

Stay and party!

You would think that with such simple plan, we could have carried it out with little or no effort. Unfortunately, that was not the case. Looking back over the schedule, we accomplished number one with no problem. The bus ride was filled with exciting stories of how each of us was going to fulfill number three in our plan. By the time we arrived in Atlanta, we were so pumped up for number three that we forgot about number two.

Because we put victory parties ahead of victory, we were prime candidates for upset ... and that's exactly what happened. Once again we suffered the embarrassment of defeat on national television, as Tech did to us what we had done to Alabama the week before.

At the game's end, many of the guys who had made post- game plans just discarded them and rode the bus home in silent sadness. This would have been my normal procedure as well, but for some reason I decided to stay.

I met up with David Keith, one of my buddies. David is an actor and at that time was relishing the prominence of his role in An Officer and A Gentleman. He's a Tennessee alumnus and a staunch supporter of our football team. We met that night at a party he had told me about at a club in downtown Atlanta.

When I arrived David was sitting at a table with his date and another couple. I recognized David's date as one of the Tennessee cheerleaders. Apparently she brought along another Tennessee cheerleader who was accompanied by this other guy I did not know. I recognized the other cheer-leader as Denise Conrad. I had seen her cheering on the sidelines during our games, but I had never had the chance to actually look at her or spend any time with her before this evening.

No wonder I fell so hard for Denise!

So I sat down at the table as the proverbial "fifth wheel" two guys and their dates ... and me. I felt a little uncomfortable, but noticed that there was another feeling overtaking the awkwardness of the situation. I found that I couldn't take my eyes off Denise. She was beautiful. Her blonde hair and blue eyes were complemented by the most wonderful smile .... I was in the process of being smitten!

Denise and I started up a casual conversation. Before we knew it, we were totally absorbed in each other's words. Somewhere along the line Denise's date must have seen what was happening, because he apparently got up and went away.

I asked Denise if she would like to dance with me and she consented. Out on the dance floor I felt so comfortable with her. I knew from the start that she was different than anyone else I had ever dated. I had never really thought much about love at first sight, but suddenly and without warning, I was in it. And it felt absolutely fabulous!

We went back to the table and continued our conversation. She was so easy to talk to. We had a lot of things in common, not the least of which was an avid love for sports. She was a real fan, just like me. I also discovered that she was one year older than me. Because she had changed her major, it had taken her an extra semester to graduate, which explained why she was still in school the fall of my senior year.

God's timing is so perfect. I had seen Denise on and off for my four years at Tennessee, but He waited until this moment in Atlanta to put us together. It seemed so perfect to me ... it was almost corny. Here was the captain of the football team and the homecoming queen. It almost drips sugar to think about it, but I was totally taken by her charm and her beauty.

When our evening in Atlanta came to a close, I gave her a good-night kiss. As far as I was concerned, the kiss sealed it. I was smitten ... infatuated ... head-over-heels in love. And suddenly, that was all that mattered in my life.

"I'd love to see you back in Knoxville," I told her. "I'll call you," I promised.

"Great!" she responded.

I was on top of the world.

I had to plan my next move very carefully. How was I going to see Denise again? If I called immediately upon my return to Knoxville, I might look a little overanxious. But if I waited too long, I might appear disinterested.

I had no idea how Denise felt toward me. I sensed that she enjoyed me as much as I enjoyed her, but there was no way to be sure. Unbeknownst to me, Denise was having her own timing crisis.

Denise had a boyfriend. This fact certainly complicated things from her perspective. She liked the guy, but as I found out later, the Atlanta encounter had made the same impact on her that it had made on me .... she was equally smitten with me.

To further complicate the matter, we were seen by a lot of people that night in Atlanta. Included in the group that evening were ten fraternity brothers of Denise's boyfriend. They quickly reported the information to their brother, who had no intention of giving up Denise. Thus, everyone in Knoxville knew about Denise and me before either one of us got back from Atlanta.

While Denise was attempting to figure out how to break off with her boyfriend, I was patiently waiting for the appropriate time to call her for another date. To hear Denise retell this story nowadays, I waited far too long to call. She was in agony trying to figure out why I wouldn't call her. All this top of the end of the semester class demands made for a particularly stressful time in both our lives.

By the middle of the week after our magic Saturday night, I could no longer wait. I really wanted to call Denise, but decided it would be safer to call one of her friends. That way, if I was too anxious, her friend would advise me of that and I'd wait a little longer.

"Hi, Tracy, this is Bill Bates," I said over the phone. "I met your friend, Denise, last Saturday in Atlanta, and I really want to go out with her. But I'm worried that our date was a bigger deal to me than it was to her, so I don't know what to do. Plus I think she has a boyfriend. Can you help me out?"

I really wasn't prepared for Tracy's response.

"Listen to me, Bill Bates! Denise is very agitated with you for not calling her. She thinks you don't want anything to do with her! So, if I were you, I'd hang up on me and turn right around and call her immediately!"

Taking her advice, I hung up on her. I redialed the phone and got Denise on the line.

"Hi Denise ... this is Bill." I started to back-pedal, "Sorry it's taken so long for me to get back to you, but I'd really like to see you again."

"Well, that's nice," Denise responded politely.

"So can I take you out?"

"Sure."

"Great! How about tomorrow night?"

"Tomorrow night sounds just fine."

"Dinner and a movie?"

"Wonderful."

"Okay, I'll pick you up at seven."

I hung up and started doing somersaults all around my apartment!

The next day as soon as class was over, I was out washing my car so it would look as impressive as possible for this new queen in my life.

I showered, shaved, put on my brand-new black leather sports jacket my dad had just given me, and drove over to Denise's apartment. I parked the car, checked myself out one last time in my rearview mirror and, with a spring in my step, walked up to the front door. I knocked on the door and waited for my angel to appear.

Unfortunately, my angel's roommate answered instead.

Tammy Brogan came to the door and opened it just the slightest little bit.

"Hi!" I announced. "I'm Bill Bates. I'm here to pick up Denise for a date."

From the crack in the doorway came the most shattering of replies: "Denise can't see you right now!"

With that, Tammy quickly closed the door, leaving me alone on the front step feeling about as foolish as I had ever felt in my life. I gained enough composure to spin around on my heels, find my car, and speed back to my apartment.

I walked into the front room, which was in total darkness ... and I chose to leave it that way. Sitting in that room, alone and in the dark, my mind was racing.

Why did this happen? I asked myself. Is she trying to pay me back for waiting so long to call her? What does this mean? I wonder what she's doing right now?

What Denise was doing at that moment was going through a scenario right out of a romantic comedy of the 1940s. Without me realizing it at the time, Denise was in a jam. That particular day she was finishing up some extra work she was doing for one of her classes. Her plan was to get home in time to get ready for our date. What was not in her plan was for her boyfriend (soon to be ex-boyfriend, I hoped) to decide to come over that day as well.

Denise had only been home a short time when the door-bell rang. Busily getting ready for our date, she didn't even stop to answer the door, so Tammy got it.

"Denise!" Tammy whispered, her face pale with shock.

"Steve's out there in the living room. He wants to see you."

"This couldn't be a worse time!" Denise lamented. "I'll have to get rid of him somehow."

"Hi, Denise!" Steve said, as he wandered down the hall to see her. "What are you getting all dressed up for?" Stammering around, desperately looking for an answer, Denise decided to tell Steve a story. That way, she could tell him the truth later, when everything had calmed down. "Well, I'm heading over to work on the homecoming decorations," she said.

"Well, I know you're under a lot of stress and pressure right now, so I had my mom cook up a whole basket of fried chicken. Take a few minutes and eat this with me. You'll feel better, I'm sure."

What could she do? She was stuck! So it was while they were in the apartment together that I knocked on the front door. Poor Denise didn't even know I had come and gone. Tammy had taken care of the whole thing.

It took Denise almost an hour to get rid of Steve. When he finally left, she came out to the living room and said to Tammy, "I'm sure glad Bill is running late. I'd hate to think what would have happened if he had been here on time."

Tammy swallowed hard and said, "Sit down, Denise.

There's something I need to tell you."

When Tammy told Denise about my visit, Denise immediately went to the phone and called me. But, as I said, it had been an hour since I had been there, so I was fuming.

I had decided to occupy the evening with the next most important thing in my life-football. I had opened my play-book and was going over plays when my phone rang.

"Hi, Bill. It's Denise." She was trying to sound as cheerful as possible, but I was in no mood for it.

"Hello," I said, with the coolness of a glacier.

"I'm sorry about the way Tammy treated you at the door." remained silent.

"I'd still love to go out with you." More silence.

"Is it too late for our date?"

"Yeah." I was still ice-cold.

Now Denise paused for a moment. "How about if I drive over and meet you at your place? Would that be okay?"

"Fine," I snapped. I was certain she wouldn't come, so what difference did it make what I said?

"Great. I'll be right over."

As I hung up the phone, I could tell I was already weakening. My brain told me she wasn't coming ... my heart was hoping she would. I returned to studying my playbook-my one true friend in this world of unfaithfulness. Occasionally I'd glance up at the clock on the wall. Twenty minutes went by ... no Denise. Thirty minutes ... She's not coming, I continued to tell myself. Forty-five minutes ... It's all over, I concluded.

And then my doorbell rang.

Denise looked radiant. I tried my best to stay mad, detached, and glued to my playbook, but it wasn't working.

"I'm sorry about the incident at my apartment," Denise said. "I stopped by the store on the way over and bought a bottle of wine. How about if we start tonight all over again? Okay?"

She was so sweet, I was overpowered. As we sat and talked, I once again realized how special this young lady was. Before long we were off in my car to see that movie we originally intended to see.

It was a wonderful evening.

I fell in love with Denise Conrad that November evening in Atlanta, and that love has continued to grow ever since. I remember how I floated around campus during that time in my life. My greatest love up to that point had been football, but suddenly the game had no meaning to me at all. Football had nothing to do with my life-my life was Denise. Of course, there was a reputation to uphold, so very few people knew how totally taken I was by her.

But I knew.

That December Denise graduated from the University of Tennessee. I remember attending her commencement exercises ... seeing her in her cap and gown. I was filled with a mixture of pride and love. I knew she was "the one." As our story would unfold, it took me several years to finally make her my wife. But it wasn't because I was uncertain. Denise Conrad was destined to become Denise Bates-that was for sure.

Why else would a grunt like me send a girl two dozen red roses just for graduating college?

"You'd Be the 13th Pick of the Dallas Cowboys!"

After the loss to Georgia Tech our record was 3-3-1. This meant we had to get serious again, if we had any expectations for an invitation to a bowl game. With this being my senior year, I wanted that to happen more than ever. So we buckled down as a team and went for it.

We went on a scoring spree. We beat Memphis State 29-3, then traveled to Jackson, Mississippi, to defeat the Rebels of 01' Miss 30-17. That final game at home against Kentucky was truly an experience everyone should have. Running through that "T" set up by the band on every occasion was great, but this would be the last time for us seniors. My insides were bursting as the public address announcer proclaimed, "Announcing Senior Captain Bill Bates!"

We went on to overpower the Wildcats 28-0. Now, this was the sort of senior year I desired-three wins in three weeks. With our record at 6-3-1, we were invited to Atlanta to play in the Peach Bowl December 31,1982. Our opponent was to be Iowa.

Once again we were feeling fine! A 6-3-1 record, a bowl invitation, and the defeat of Alabama ... all was well with the world.

Our team drove to nearby Nashville for our final game of the regular season. It was against our interstate rival, Vanderbilt University. We didn't take the Commodores very seriously, despite the fact that they were headed to a bowl game themselves, because everything was going our way. Right? Does this sound familiar?

One of the unusual qualities of the Tennessee-Vanderbilt game was the impact it had on one of our coaches. George Cafego was an assistant coach in charge of the kicking game. He was legendary in Volunteer circles. Born in 1915, he was an All-American at Tennessee in the 1930s (back before they wore helmets, as we used to kid him). He had been coaching at UT since 1955.

Normally Coach Cafego was silent before games. But once a year, like clockwork, he would ask to say a few words to the team about a real concern in his life: He hated Vanderbilt! In his own crude way, he'd give us a speech laced with profanities that would get us all pumped up ... if for no other reason than to go out there and win it for him personally. Thus, the out- come of this game was disappointing for a number of reasons.

Saturday, November 27 was a dreary day for more reasons than one. It was a cold and bleak afternoon in Nashville. The rain was pelting the field mercilessly, causing the playing conditions to be sloppy, to say the least. We played to a 14-14 score at halftime.

Our offense bogged down in the second half. We just couldn't get it going. The Commodores scored in the third quarter, making it 21-14. We finally got on the scoreboard in the fourth quarter, tying it at 21. But with less than three minutes left in the game, Vanderbilt produced an amazing drive-including a sixty-Five-yard pass play-that set up one final touchdown.

When the gun signaled the game's end, we were defeated 28-21, in another game we thought we would win. Losing to Vanderbilt was the worst form of torture any of us could think of. We shook it off as best we could. We could deal with losing our last game by turning our attention to the Iowa Hawkeyes and the Peach Bowl. This game turned out to be one of those ironies in a sporting event. Personally, I played a great game. But as a team, we didn't look good at all.

To be frank, by halftime it had all the makings of an Iowa routing. We were down 21-7 by the end of the second quarter. Fortunately for our team, we came back strong in the final half. We scored 12 in the third quarter and 3 in the fourth, giving us 22 points. Unfortunately, Iowa scored another touchdown in the second half, so the game ended in a 28--22 Iowa victory.

The only bright lights on our defense that day were my teammate Joe Cofer and myself. Together we made twenty- and four tackles-twelve each. But nothing can take the place of a win.

I consoled myself by thinking, I had a great game! Surely this will solidify my position to be one of the top picks in the upcoming NFL draft! My dream of playing for the Dallas Cowboys is coming close to reality. If I just keep shooting for the star, it's gonna happen!

It was difficult for me to fully comprehend that my college football days were over.

When Denise graduated in December, she moved from Knoxville to Nashville. This was the beginning of a long- distance relationship for us that would wind its way all over the United States in the next two years.

Fortunately for me, the two of us had grown very close ... very quickly. We had only dated for two-and-a-half months while living in the same city. I helped her move her stuff to Nashville. Driving back alone on that cold night in early January, I realized how difficult it would be to have a relationship that was defined by long-distance phone calls and weekend visits. But I was in love with Denise and I knew that if it were up to me, somehow we'd make it work.

My love continues to grow for this beautiful woman

Then, just a few weeks later, a big career opportunity came Denise's way. Her major at Tennessee had been in interior design, but all along the way she had taken jobs in the world of modeling. A modeling agency from Atlanta called in February to offer her a full-time job as a fashion model. Since modeling was much more lucrative at the time-coupled with the fact that she enjoyed it more than interior design, she accepted the position.

Denise and her roommate decided they could move her by themselves with no trouble. They rented a U-Haul trailer to pull behind them and headed off to Atlanta, with Tammy driving the car with the trailer and Denise following behind in the second car.

Everything went fine until they ran into a murderous snowstorm just outside of Dalton, Georgia. The roads were treacherous. Even with traffic crawling along, it was still quite dangerous.

Suddenly, as the traffic ground to a halt, Tammy applied the brakes a little too gingerly and the trailer jackknifed around on her. When it was over, three cars had piled into each other, and Tammy and the trailer were off the side of the road in a ditch.

Denise called for a tow truck. The local Dalton towing service was quite busy that evening, so they decided to charge accordingly. They charged Denise $50 to tow the car and then another $50 to tow the trailer. She reluctantly agreed to pay, feeling stuck.

Tammy and Denise found lodging at a local motel. When morning came, the two girls went to the service station where the car and trailer had been towed, only to find out they were no longer there.

"No, ma'am," the attendant replied. "Your car and trailer were only left here because we were closest to the highway. You'll find your vehicles over at the station down the road, where you actually called for the tow truck."

When Denise and Tammy arrived at the gas station, sure enough, the car and trailer were there, all ready to go. But their friend, the tow truck driver, presented them with a bill for another $100 for towing the vehicles from one station to the other! Two hundred dollars for a tow in 1983-true highway robbery! At that point Denise called to tell me all that had occurred. I raced to Dalton like Superman to the rescue.

The move to Atlanta did end up to be a positive one for Denise in terms of her modeling career. She signed on with agencies in Atlanta and Charlotte, North Carolina, finding her new job both exciting and fulfilling. We tried our best to see as much of each other as we could, but living so far away presented its constant challenges.

As my college years were coming to a close, I began looking back at the things that had made college such a positive experience. One of the

100

good things in my college life was my association with the Sigma Chi fraternity. A number of my high school friends joined this fraternity, and it came to be considered the "jock frat." I learned a lot from this group, especially about dealing with people in a proper manner.

Being a scholarship athlete gave me a lot of opportunities.

One of the trainers at Tennessee, Mike Rollo, had assembled a campus intramural recreational league. I was chosen by Mike to be on the UT Lakers basketball team, which was a true honor.

We took these things seriously. Mike was the head coach of the Lakers, but we also had a board of directors and an advisory committee that oversaw all the Lakers' transactions like trading or acquiring players.

Our team dominated this league, which included teams from fraternities as well. This brought its own difficulties, since Sigma Chi had their own team. Having to divide my loyalties was not something I was used to. I ended up "lettering" four years with the Lakers.

My time away from the books and football always seemed to center around sports. I always felt that the better all- around athlete I could become, the more it would enhance my ability to play football. I now see how it has given me the ability to play so many positions. At the post-season football awards presentations, I was honored to be the recipient of the Bill Majors Award. The award is presented every year to the player who best exemplifies the dedication toward football displayed by Bill Majors, a Tennessee player and coach who died in 1965.

101

As my four years at Tennessee came to a close, their sports information department released this final career summary:

NUMBER 40 BILL BATES-21 YEARS OLD, 6' 1 ", 186, 4 LETTERS SENIOR DEFENSIVE BACK FROM KNOXVILLE

Four-year starter who became the leader of the Volunteer secondary during junior and senior campaigns. As a senior, was an intangible leader not only among Vol defenders, but also in the eyes of the entire Tennessee squad. One of the most dedicated players in recent UT gridiron history, and also a laborious off-season weightlifter. Has been a starter since second game of freshman year and made his first collegiate interception in that contest. Led defense with four thefts in 1981 and was second last year with three. His strength, however, lies in his ability either to break up passes at last possible instant or jar the ball loose with savage tackling. He was regarded as team's surest and fiercest tackler in '82, and was given "Hardest Hit" incentive award for crunching tackles twice against Auburn and Kentucky. He contributed eleven solo hits against UK and also intercepted a pass, earning Defensive Player of the Game award in the process.

He was also bestowed that honor for two other games in 1982, against LSU and Memphis State. He made eight solo tackles and four assists in the 24-24 standoff at Baton Rouge. He ended season with eighty-six hits to rank number two on Tennessee tackle tally. A Nolan Cromwell-type at either safety position, Bates' dependable play will be noticeably absent from future Tennessee secondaries.

In some ways, I felt like I was reading an obituary. But with credentials like those, it was gratifying to know that scouts from the NFL and USFL had been coming around asking about me. For any life in football after college, the only alternative is playing professionally. Like hundreds of other college players, I hoped for a pro career. Of course, this normally meant the National Football League, but in 1982 there was another option. The United States Football League (USFL) had come into operation, providing another field of play for those who would not play in the NFL. However, the NFL was still everyone's first choice due to its history, and, more importantly, its money.

The USFL had an unusual drafting arrangement. The league would assign the entire senior squad of a university to a particular USFL team. In our case, the right to draft Tennessee players was owned by the New Jersey Generals. It seemed pretty safe to guess that they would draft me. But my heart was with the NFL, especially if there was a chance with the Dallas Cowboys.

It was no secret that there were NFL scouts on the Tennessee campus on many occasions. Walt Yowarsky, the scout for the Cowboys, had been to Knoxville to check me out. It was a thrill for a college kid to be working out, knowing he was being observed by someone from the Green Bay Packers, Miami Dolphins, or the Seattle Seahawks.

I had hoped I would be picked to play in a postseason contest like the Blue-Gray Game or the East-West Game. That was an NFL scout's heaven. They would be able to see the best of the senior class in game conditions. But I was not invited to participate in any of those games. I didn't get discouraged though. Because I had a good college career, I knew that scouts were looking at me, among others on our senior squad at Tennessee. I had heard from a few teams off and on during my senior year. I started getting correspondence from the New Jersey Generals of the USFL. And from the NFL, there was interest from the Pittsburgh Steelers and the Seattle Seahawks. But most of my focus was on the interest from the Cowboys. My hopes ran high every time I saw an envelope with my name on it, along with a return address from Dallas, Texas, that included a silver helmet with a blue star on it. I expected to be drafted early, and I hoped the Cowboys would jump in front of everyone else to claim me as their prize.

The USFL ran their draft that March and, as expected, the New Jersey Generals picked me up. My initial hesitancies were realized as I met with them and they offered me a contract for only $20,000 a year. The rumors of little money in the USFL were true.

By the spring of 1983 the letters from Dallas were beginning to look more promising. In March I received this note from Gil Brandt, vice president for personnel development for the Cowboys.

Dear Bill:

Ever hear the expression, "It's a whole new world?" Well, this is the best way of describing what will be happening to you in the next few months. As one of the very best players to come out of college, the situation is more confusing than ever this year. In the past collegians had to be concerned with one thing-showing enough ability to make the team that selected them. After that, everything else fell into place.

Today, making the squad is still essential If you don't, you suddenly become an ordinary citizen and the majority of those "new friends" interested in your financial welfare vanish into thin air.

But now, the choice of which team you join might be yours, and that responsibility is a heavy burden.

If dedication is yours, you had better take a long, hard look at the various teams because a mistake on your part at the outset could affect the next ten, twenty, even thirty years of your life!

Enclosed is a booklet about the Dallas Cowboys. It answers some important questions that you should have about coaching and management stability, past record of success, career potential outside of football, national exposure, city lifestyle, etc.

We are sending the booklet to you because these are things you need to know about the Dallas Cowboys. In turn, please fill out and return the enclosed questionnaire to finalize our top prospect file on you.

But what really sets this informative booklet aside from any other is the very thing that should be the number one priority in your mind at present.

All Dallas Cowboys have been and will continue to be given a fair chance to make the squad and play. Why? Because the Dallas Cowboys have a commitment to the future, and the future is you.

Sincerely,
Gil Brandt
Vice President
Dallas Cowboys Football Club

I was like a wide-eyed kid, filled with wonder as I looked through the booklet that accompanied the letter. It was only fourteen pages long, but each page had facts, figures, quotes, and pictures that caught my attention. Page one was given entirely to seven simple facts:

A Team with a Winning Tradition ... Dallas Cowboys.

-seventeen consecutive winning seasons, 1966-82

-sixteen trips to the playoffs, 1966-73, 1975-82

-twelve division championships

-five NFC championships for a record five Super Bowl appearances

-two World Championships, 1971 and 1977

-thirty-four playoff game appearances, most in NFL history

- Winningest team in the NFL since 1966

The more I read the booklet, the more excited I became.

With Tom Landry as their head coach, the Cowboys were already legendary. Could I play for this great man? The Cowboys were sure proud of their leader on and off the field ... and justifiably so. I read on:

As a young quarterback, I felt that Coach Landry helped me understand the game a lot quicker than any other coach could possibly do. He's so well-disciplined and well-organized himself that he was able to instill that discipline and organization in me more quickly than anyone else could have.
  -Roger Staubach former quarterback

I became discouraged at times, but Coach Landry always made me believe that I had a place on the team. That helped me through the tough periods and I think it made me a better player when I moved in as a full-time starter. No matter what happens, he's always in control. You don't know how much that means to us. You're just glad he's on your side.
  -Charlie Waters former safety

I have nothing but respect for Tom Landry as a coach and a man. You always count on him to put an excellent, well- coached team on the field. They play clean, hard, aggressive football.
-Don Shula Miami Dolphins

Tom Landry is the best coach in the NFL.
-Frank Gifford

If I was going to play, I wanted to play for the best! I wanted to play for the Cowboys.

"The Dallas Cowboys will never make you a promise that cannot be kept," the brochure explained. "If we offer you an opportunity to become part of our organization as a professional athlete, we believe sincerely that you have the qualities necessary to succeed."

Two weeks later another letter arrived from Dallas. It was from Coach Landry.

Dear Bill:
Traditions are important factors which contribute to the stability of any athletic program, be it on the collegiate or professional level. Whether it is

105

your traditional college homecoming bonfire or our long-standing tradition of wearing white jerseys at home, these traditions integrate themselves into our programs and become positive influences on the road to success. The Dallas Cowboys organization has been associated with a number of traditions over the years which have proven to be positive and motivating factors for our club. One tradition which has been most successful for us has been our ability to sign our draft picks and free agents, then if need be, many of these quality performers are brought back to our active roster during the regular season.

We like to think of our organization as a stable one which promotes from within. As a rule, we do not look outside our organization for additions to our active roster. We feel that the veterans, draftees, and free agents who initially signed with Dallas are the players we want. When we want to fill a spot on our active roster, be it due to injury or some other need, we look to our own people, the draftees and free agents who have been through our drills and are familiar with our system. Of the forty-nine players who were on our active roster at the end of the 1982 season there are those who had been released by us during their career and brought back for one reason or another.

We are proud of that fact, as well as the fact that a great number of players signed as free agents by the Dallas Cowboys are now members of active rosters throughout the National Football League.

Another longstanding Cowboys tradition is that of winning, and our ability to utilize our draftees and free agents when needs arise during the regular season has been a big plus to our success. We attempt to sign players who we feel have the ability and work habits to play in the National Football League. As the 1983 NFL draft draws nearer, and with it the need for you to make important decisions as to your future, I hope you will consider the stability of the Dallas Cowboys organization and the importance to us of our traditions.

If we can be of any help during the days ahead, please do not hesitate to call on us.

Sincerely,
Tom Landry
Head Coach
Dallas Cowboys Football Club

Another two weeks went by ... and another letter, once again from Gil Brandt. This one informed me of a Dallas Cowboys Draft Hotline that would be in operation during the NFL draft scheduled for April 26, 1983-

less than two weeks away! He gave me the toll-free number and closed the letter with the words, "Good luck in the draft!"

I just knew I would be drafted early, especially after receiving such encouraging letters like these from the greatest team around. I just hoped the Cowboys would pull the trigger first. It's also important to remember that back in 1983 there were twelve rounds of picks, unlike today's shortened version. Nothing was guaranteed, but I truly felt I had what it took to be a draft pick. My hope was riding on the Cowboys, and the only real question in my mind was what round I'd go in.

I was ready. I had even hired an agent who would help negotiate my contract. I am not mentioning his name for reasons- that will be apparent later in the book. I hired him during the USFL draft, and he was very helpful in sorting through all the "fine print" of the legal documents that accompany a union of this nature.

The day of the draft arrived. I stayed in my apartment all day to be close to the phone. My roommate, Chris Wampler, was hoping to be drafted as well, so he and I invited some friends over to help us pass the time. Brad White, who had been drafted by Tampa Bay the previous year, Barry Bauguss, and John Cook (my goldfish buddy) came over to our "Draft Day Party."

My friendship with Brad meant a lot to me. He was two years older than me and he took me under his wing in many ways. He showed me how to work hard. He helped me through my difficult days with Coach Majors, and showed me the ropes at Tennessee. Even when he went off to join the Buccaneers, he kept in touch with me.

Barry and I went all the way back to Farragut High School. He was one of those guys who was always there for me, and I truly appreciated the long-standing friendship we had developed. John Cook and I go back to high school days as well rather than being good friends back then, we were bitter enemies. He attended the archrival high school, Bearden. He used to chase after me on kickoffs. On one occasion, I ran a kick all the way back for a touchdown. Showboating a little bit, I raised my hands in triumph and did a little dancing in the end zone. As I turned around, I didn't realize that the shot putt circle was in the back portion of the end zone. While I was doing my victory dance, I ended up sliding across the circle-the steel on my spikes creating sparks on the circle.

I quickly jumped up, only to hear the laughter from the Bearden players. And, of course, the loudest laughter came from John Cook.

I didn't realize then that I was listening to the laughter of the guy who would become one of my best friends. He became the player I took under my wing, much like Brad had done for me.

So it was a special group-Brad, John, Barry, Chris, and me. The draft wasn't televised back then (before ESPN). We watched brief updates on television, but basically it all came down to waiting for the phone to ring. I was as nervous as a cat in a room full of rocking chairs. I was fidgeting all around-sitting down, getting up, taking a walk, coming back, sitting down, getting up-continuously waiting for the phone to ring with the good news on the other end. By the end of the draft, the unthinkable had happened.

The phone didn't ring. It didn't ring for Chris. It didn't ring for me.

I was in a daze. I couldn't understand what had transpired.

Why all the interest from the NFL scouts? What about all these letters from teams ... especially the Cowboys?

I went to bed that night thoroughly disheartened. What am I going to do? I asked myself. Should I reconsider the USFL?

You'd Be the 13th Pick of the Dallas Cowboys!

No, I just don't feel right playing in that league. Should I just focus on graduating and getting into business somewhere?

My thoughts shifted to prayers. Help me, Lord. I need Your wisdom and direction. I don't know what to do.

The next day was a day to sit back and watch God work. At 7:00 A.M. the following day, I was awakened from a fitful sleep by pounding on my apartment door. I stumbled to the door, still groggy with sleep. I opened it and was greeted by an excited man who introduced himself to me. To this day I still can't remember the guy's name, but his position was clear. He was a scout for the Seattle Seahawks.

"Hi, Bill," he said cheerily. "I'm here to ask you an important question. Will you sign as a free agent with the Seattle Seahawks?"

I was stunned. I didn't know if this was real or if I was dreaming. "I don't know if I'll sign or not," I confessed. "I'm not totally awake. Why don't we talk later this morning, like after breakfast." I was stalling him. I needed some time to think.

His response threw me.

"Great! I'd love to stay for breakfast." He came right in and made himself at home. It quickly became apparent to me that this guy was not leaving until he had an answer from me. I fixed him breakfast, and we sat and talked over eggs and bacon. I was getting real confused. On one hand, the Seahawks weren't the Cowboys, but on the other hand the Cowboys didn't appear to be interested ... and this was an NFL team. I needed some time alone.

The apartment where I lived had a swimming pool. That year I had the responsibility of getting the pool ready for use in the spring. "I need to go out and clean the pool," I told the scout.

"Fine. I'll just wait here until you come back."

Out at the pool, I tried to think calmly, rationally, and objectively. But it was all so overwhelming-I needed help.

When I returned to my apartment I told the scout I needed to make a phone call. I grabbed the phone and walked down the hall as far as the cord would reach so the scout couldn't hear what I was saying.

I called my dad. I told him about this most recent development with Seattle. As you can tell by now, when I needed good advice, I called my best friend and he always gave me the best advice.

"What should I do, Dad?" I asked.

"Well, first of all," my dad responded, "you need to call your agent. He deals with this stuff all the time. He's in a much better position to give advice than I am. So call him."

I hung up with Dad and called my agent. I explained the situation to him, and he responded quickly. "Tell the scout you want to wait a little bit. You never know, Bill. Some other team might call you."

I went back out to the living room and told the scout I needed some more time. He understood, but he had obviously been sent to get an answer. "If you don't mind, I'll just wait here until you decide."

By now it was 11:00 A.M. The guy had been with me for four hours already. I didn't know how long it was going to take me to decide. Suddenly my life was about to be changed.

A few minutes after 11 o'clock, the telephone rang.

"Hi, my name is Bob Ford and I'm with the Dallas Cowboys. I'm here in Knoxville and I'd like to know if I could come over to your place to talk with you. I have something very important to discuss with you. I think you'll find that it's worth your time to do so. Will an hour from now be okay? I really want to sit down and talk with you."

"Uhhhh," I stammered, walking down the hall with the phone to get out of earshot of the Seattle scout. "I really want to meet with you, Bob, but it's probably not a good idea to come to my place."

"No problem," he replied. "I'm here at the Holiday Inn.

Can you be here in an hour?"

"Sure," I said.

"Then I'll see you in an hour."

We hung up, and I went sheepishly back out to the living room. "I need to run a few errands," I told the guy.

"Okay," he answered. "Mind if I wait here?"

"No, that's fine," I responded. I thought to myself, I may have some interesting news for you when I get back.

An hour later I was at the Holiday Inn. Bob and I reintroduced ourselves and small-talked for a few minutes, but the conversation quickly turned to business. He made a statement that made my heart race:

"Bill, I've gotta tell you the truth. I'm Sure you're disappointed in the way the draft turned out, but listen to me ... If there were thirteen rounds in the draft instead of twelve, you'd be the thirteenth pick of the Dallas Cowboys!"

I sat in silence, barely able to breathe.

"So, Bill, I'd like you to sign this contract as a Cowboys free agent. That will allow you to come to our training camp this summer in Thousand Oaks, California. We'll be able to get a real good look at you during camp. If you perform like I think you will, I imagine there's a place for you on the Cowboys roster. It's a great opportunity!"

Once again I was silent ... and close to flying out of the chair with excitement.

"How 'bout it, Bill," he pressed. "Do we have a deal?"

I was ready to sign anything at that point. Fortunately, I had the presence of mind to make a couple of phone calls first. I called my dad, who was genuinely excited for me. And, as he had done earlier that morning, he advised me to call my agent.

I called him. He, too, was excited for me. He asked me to give the phone to the representative from the Cowboys. The two of them hammered out some negotiations on the contract. The phone conversation ended. All that was left was one thing.

I signed the contract and with that signature, I became a free agent with the Dallas Cowboys.

Bob and I shook hands and I left the meeting with those words still floating around in my head:

"If there were thirteen rounds, you'd be the thirteenth pick of the Dallas Cowboys." It was music to my soul.

My mind flashed back to the maxim hanging on the wall of Farragut's gym the winter of Coach Henry's "B" basketball squad:

Dream and shoot for the stars.

You never know you may reach your star!

It was happening my dream of playing football for the Dallas Cowboys was coming true! I was the happiest guy walking on the planet! The Lord had heard my prayers and answered them. My Star-Jesus-had given me my heart's desire-to play professional football for the Dallas Cowboys!

Driving back to my apartment, I was almost home before I remembered I still had company. I decided the truth was the best way to handle this delicate situation. I went into the apartment, sat down, and told the Seattle scout all that had transpired since I had left on my "errand."

To his credit, the guy was genuinely happy for me. Of course, he was disappointed for Seattle, but he had real class. He congratulated me, got up, and left. He had his answer he had waited for all day.

A week later the following letter arrived:

Dear Bill:

Let me take this opportunity to extend our sincere congratulations from everyone within the organization upon your decision to join the Dallas Cowboys Football Club. We are happy to have you.

Ours is a proud history-the culmination of sacrifices, dedication, and hard work by many people. The fact that you were afforded our extended hand of invitation is indicative of our belief that you are the type person willing to pay the price to maintain such a heritage.

With the pressures associated with your signing now having subsided, I urge you to direct your concentration toward one endeavor only-that of preparing physically and mentally for the demands you will face beginning July 9 in Thousand Oaks. There is nothing easy about training camp. However, your desire to succeed will determine your ultimate destination, not something you might express verbally.

Do not sell yourself or your chances of making the Cowboys short because you are a rookie. Too many before have discarded that label and contributed vitally toward our aspirations of reaching the Super Bowl. You can do the same.

Believe me. It is good to have you with us.

Sincerely,

Gil Brandt

Vice President

Dallas Cowboys Football Club

I did exactly what the letter suggested. All of my focus was turned toward Thousand Oaks on July 9. My desire was to be as ready as I could be. I wanted to beat the odds by being a free agent who actually made the team. It would be the greatest challenge of my life to that point.

I called Denise to tell her the good news. She was excited and happy for me. But she also knew the uphill battle that lay ahead for me. Even during my years at Tennessee, people often thought of me as "too small" or "too slow." I may have gotten away with that in college, but it would be quite another story in the National Football League. We both prayed fervently during this time.

The loftiest goal of my life was sitting right out there in front of me. I wanted to wear the star on the side of my helmet.

I wanted to be a Cowboy.

"It's Thursday, Before the Last Saturday Preseason Game!"

Arriving at Cal Lutheran College in Thousand Oaks, California was an experience I'll always remember, mostly because it was filled with surprises.

I flew from Knoxville to southern California, where the Cowboys promised to have a bus waiting for my ground transportation from the airport to Thousand Oaks. All the way out on the plane I kept reassuring myself. If there had been thirteen rounds, I would have been the thirteenth pick. That truth seemed to equalize things in my mind. I knew that being the thirteenth-round draft pick meant it would be tough to get some playing time, but I beamed with childlike glee at the thought of dressing in that Cowboy uniform for the 1983 season.

When the plane landed, sure enough, a representative from the Cowboys was there to meet me. We went downstairs to baggage claim and after retrieving my bags, we walked out to the curb. The air was warm, but it wasn't nearly as humid as Tennessee. For that, I was grateful.

As the Cowboy representative pointed me toward the bus, I got my first clue that I was in for a surprise. I was directed onto a bus for the ride to Thousand Oaks. As I boarded, I immediately noticed that the other people on the bus looked like football players ... they were BIG! Silently I began counting. There were about twenty guys on this bus. Why so many big guys? I asked myself, but I quickly shook it off.

The plot thickened. I poked my head out the window of the bus and to my surprise, I saw more buses. And each of them was filling up with big guys ... football players.

So I started thinking, Relax, Bill, you're in California, the home of the Raiders and the Rams and the Chargers and the 49ers. That's what it is. Those buses are full of the draft picks from all those teams! It'll be great to be close enough to all these teams-maybe we can all practice together. More competition will only make me better!

But the further the buses rolled down the road, the sicker the feeling in my gut. It certainly appeared that all the buses were headed for the same destination . . . Thousand Oaks, California. What could this mean? When I arrived, I was in for the shock of my life. It turned out that all the guys in my bus-plus all the guys in the other buses-were all here for the identical reason: We were all Dallas Cowboy free agents. The truth was that even though I had signed a contract, it didn't mean I was on the team. But the thirteenth pick surely meant that I was a shoe-in, I erroneously concluded. How naive I must have been to think that!

As Coach Landry would explain to me years later, the Cowboys have a network of people all over the United States, poised and ready to sign free agents the moment the NFL draft concludes. To my utter amazement, I was one of more than 100 guys! It may have been closer to 150. But, suffice it to say, I was far from alone.

At that point I had this horrible thought speeding through my mind: What this means is that all over the United States, well over a hundred guys were signing free agent contracts because the guy on the other side of the desk was saying the same thing in each location-"If there had been thirteen rounds in the draft, you'd be the thirteenth pick of the Dallas Cowboys!"

"This is great, just great," I mumbled. "One hundred thirteenth picks!"

I had come prepared to prove myself, but the proving ground was multiplied by 100 before my very eyes! I remember walking around the campus like a dumbstruck country kid making his first visit to the big city. I was in the process of watching a dream come true ... my dream! But now I knew it was going to be much more difficult than I ever anticipated.

After we were shown around the campus and given time to settle in, we were instructed to report to the locker room to get our equipment. When I walked over to my cubicle in the locker room, my uniform was all laid out for me.

My emotions were running high, which was to be expected during such a big day in my life. But for reasons intimately personal to me, when I saw my uniform in the cubicle, I broke down and wept.

I knew why I was crying. It was the sight of the silver helmet with the blue star, and the jersey with the number 40. It was as if this uniform had been waiting for me since I last wore it four years earlier at Farragut High School. I had visualized this scene in my mind ten thousand times over the last few years. To actually have it transpiring was overwhelming to me. My mind was in overdrive with thoughts of the past.

I thought back to Coach Sparks. I imagined he would be real proud of me right about now. One of his boys made good. I was glad ... glad for him.

I also remembered how he always counseled me. "Remember, Bill," he would say in his deep southern drawl, "Trust in the Lord with all your heart and lean not unto your own understanding." Trusting the Lord had been a successful plan for me. Look where it got me!

I sat in front of my locker, wiping away the tears, and silently asking God to continue to guide me in my life. And if it's Your will, Lord, I prayed somewhat selfishly, please help me to make the team. I knew the way to do it was to do some- thing to impress somebody.

My defensive coach was another legendary figure-Gene Stallings. He was so good to me in our years together. I'll always be grateful for our relationship. He started out camp by assigning me the position of strong safety. I was eager to prove myself at any position, so I approached it with my usual flair for the overstated.

Ripped groin muscles couldn't keep me down

Later in the camp the coaches actually made a position especially suited for me. They put me in as a middle linebacker on third-down pass plays. This was to be called the Nickel Defense and the Cowboys were the pro team to pioneer that scheme.

I was thrilled with the position because it gave me more time to be on the field, proving myself. As I recall, I was looking pretty good until

115

another surprise cropped up. I had never even thought about the possibility of getting injured. It was just unimaginable. But, in a very normal play during that first week of training camp, I pulled my groin muscle. It turned out that I had multiple tears in both groin muscles. It was a serious injury.

I did my best to give the outward appearance that nothing happened, but everyone-including Coach Stallings-was aware of the injury. It didn't help matters that by the next day, blood had risen to the skin level on my upper, inner thighs. "It's a deep muscle bruise," I was told by the trainer. "And, based on how it looks, I imagine it hurts like crazy." Why, Lord? I was screaming inside myself. How can 1 make the team if I'm not 100 percent? As I prayed, I began to realize the answer to the very question I posed to the Lord. I've got to play with the pain, I concluded. That way, the coaches will see how tough I am.

So, with that strategy as my guide, I went out to prove that Bates felt no pain. We had a scrimmage against the Rams that week and I performed as well as a guy could with torn groin muscles. I was so taped up, I looked more like a mummy than a football player.

When the preseason games began, we played the Miami Dolphins in Dallas and beat them 20-17. But it was in that second game-in Anaheim-against the Los Angeles Rams when things started happening.

I had demonstrated to the coaches that I could play, even with an injury like a groin pull, so I was getting some playing time. That game against the Rams was like a dream come true for me in more ways than one. The most obvious way was that I had an exceptional game. I made some key tackles and in the end, we won the game 30-7.

But it was the day after the game when another dream came true.

Like most coaches, Coach Landry liked to use the day after the game to look at film of the game with his players and coaches. It was a real time of instruction for everyone involved. He felt it was an absolute necessity to make improvements as a team. To be totally honest, it was a difficult and awkward experience to sit there and watch the film because Coach Landry rarely pointed out the good things. But once he found a mistake-be it a missed block, missed tackle, blown coverage, incorrect pattern, or just plain fatigue or laziness- Coach would run that piece of film over and over, backward and forward, stressing how terrible it was to make that mistake.

The obvious feeling was that you had let your teammates down. So, in front of the rest of the team, you'd make a note, to improve on whatever it was you had blown.

The day after our preseason victory over the Rams, we were watching the game films with Coach Landry in his usual position as "pointer-outer" of mistakes.

After looking at a few plays, a play was run where I made a bone-crunching tackle of a Rams kick returner. In totally uncharacteristic fashion, Coach Landry stopped the film at that point and said, "Bates, that was a great hit on that play. Nice job." He turned to the rest of the team and added, "See guys, that's how you make a positive impression on the coaches." Then he went on with the film.

I don't think I heard anything else during that entire session. I was pumped a mile high by receiving a compliment from Coach Landry. But it went even deeper than that praise.

As I mentioned previously, back in my high school years, I was introduced to positive mental imaging. I had developed the discipline of seeing in my mind the right way to run a play. I imagined myself running downfield on a kickoff and making a tackle, time after time after time, so it would be as much of a natural reaction as possible to make that play.

When Coach Landry stopped the film that day to compliment me on the hit, I found myself thinking, I've seen this play before! This is the exact play I have visualized in my mind for a long time now.

Exciting things were happening. I was trying my best to "trust the Lord" and play hard. Perhaps it was going to turn out exactly like I was hoping it would ... and I would make the team!

The most important thing in camp was to make an impression on your coaches ... hopefully a positive one. As practices continued, I at least knew I was making an impression on some of the other players.

Two veterans took it upon themselves to taunt me at every occasion. Tony Dorsett and Ron Springs were the type of players who would run around joking with guys a great deal of the time. So it was obvious that their tune would change when they came by the defensive backs.

They would point their fingers in my direction and chant, "Master, Master, Master," in a condescending manner. Just as I was about to let it bother me, Coach Stallings called me over. "Don't pay them any attention, Bill," he counseled. "You just keep eating their lunch out there on the field in your man-to-man drills. You've definitely got them worried about you out there."

I thanked Coach for his encouragement. It was at that point that I knew I was making an impression on the entire team. It was just that I still couldn't figure out if it was positive or negative.

Another aspect of training camp that would leave a permanent impact on my entire career involved our rooming situation. As is always the case, the players were given roommates. Whether at training camp or in hotel rooms on road games, one never roomed alone.

That first summer I was given John Warren, another rookie, for a roommate. John and I got along great, so it looked like a positive experience for both of us. That is, until the fateful night.

I have an unusual quirk-I walk in my sleep and do a variety of things of which I have no knowledge at the time. Early in the rookie training camp, I scared John to death with my sleepwalking.

The dorm rooms at Cal Lutheran had two beds, a bureau, and some portable closets that could be used to divide the room. I began a bizarre sleepwalking incident one night by getting up and forearming one of the portable closets toward John's bed.

Fortunately, the noise of the forearming woke John up, and he was able to bolt out of bed just as the closet tumbled onto his mattress!

He was really shaken by this experience, but he calmly got me back in my bed. He set up the closet this time over by the wall-and then went to sleep. Not long after that, I was up again. This time I stood up on my bed, assumed a three-point stance, and attempted to run after John in order to tackle him! Because I was standing on my bed when I took off after John, I only took a step or two before I was at the edge of the bed. I went right on, falling off the side of the bed-completely off balance. I ended up on John's bed, looking into the eyes of a man who was full of fear.

I point out this incident because it helps explain why I receive such unusual treatment in the NFL: For the last the twelve years I've always roomed alone.

As the preseason went on, the inevitable started to occur. The coaches began to make their cuts. After the Rams game, we played Pittsburgh in Dallas and lost 24-7. It was the week before our last preseason game and the pressure was really intense. We were going to end the preseason at home against the Houston Oilers. I was working as hard as I could because I knew the final cuts would be made after that game. Those who survived that cut would be on the roster for the opening day of regular season.

We were on the field, running through plays at half-speed - a normal activity two days before the game. I was on defense, as usual, when Coach Stallings motioned to me to come over to the sideline. I hustled right over to hear what he wanted to say. He looked at me with his steely eyes and said, "On this play I want you to cover Tony Dorsett man-for-man."

I nodded in agreement, turned, and sprinted back to my position. In 1983 Tony Dorsett was the franchise in Dallas. He was always to be treated with great care. The last thing anyone wanted to do was put Tony in a situation where he possibly could sustain an injury.

The ball was hiked to our quarterback, Danny White. At half-speed he faded back and passed the ball to Tony. With the ball tucked in tight, Tony set off at a medium jog heading right toward me. I had been in this situation hundreds of times before. Sadly, it is so difficult for me to do anything at half- speed. I felt the adrenaline coursing through my body and, in the rush of the moment, forgot all about half-speed.

I sped over to Tony, put my head down, and rammed my helmet into his gut as hard as I could.

I decked him.

He was rolling around on the ground, desperately trying to catch his breath. It was obvious I had knocked the wind out of him. The question everyone within a mile was thinking was, Is that all that happened or is he injured? I was in a daze. Why did I wait 'til the Thursday before the last Saturday preseason game to totally screw up my chances of making the team? I thought, in utter disgust.

It was one of those moments that seemed frozen in time.

Before too long, Tony regained his ability to breathe. He celebrated that return by bellowing some choice words to this wet-behind-the ears rookie. "You #$&!" he screamed.

"What the @#$ did you do that for?"

Actually, I wasn't really sure myself. I mumbled an apology and added, "Sometimes it's necessary to knock another person's light out to let your light shine!"

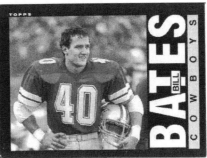

Topps honored me with a Rookie Card

Tony walked off the field grumbling. He didn't buy that for one minute. I can't say I blamed him either. The Lord had a reason for everything that was happening to me, including my full-speed hit during a half-speed drill. I was certain they were going to release me after that incident. But, ironically, it was that incident and incidents like it that caught the coaches' attention in a positive way-particularly the attention of Coach Landry.

Years later after he retired, I asked Coach Landry what he remembered of my rookie training camp.

His answer? *"You were a tremendously aggressive player. In that way, you were a good guy to follow. You were determined and possessed a confidence. To put it in its simplest terms,"* he added, *"you caught my eye in every practice."*

So, as training camp came to a close, I didn't know if I had made the team or not?

No one had come knocking on my door. No one had called me to the office. Was no news good news?

I soon discovered that the way you know you've made the team is when they don't call you to inform you that you've been cut. You just keep going to the team meetings with your trusty playbook.

In that sense, making the team is somewhat anti-climactic.

There are no bells and whistles announcing your addition to the roster. It's more of a business-as-usual type of situation.

Since I received no call after the final cut, I went off to the day's meetings, hoping there wouldn't be any more cuts. As time went on that morning, I realized my dream had come true! With all the excitement and energy of a high school kid, I bounded off to that first meeting.

The first meeting I attended after making the final cut was a tense one. It was a meeting of all the defensive backs. When I walked in, I immediately noticed that all the other players were wearing black armbands.

"What's going on?" I asked innocently.

"We're protesting the cutting of Benny Barnes," one of the veterans fired back at me. It didn't take Einstein to figure out what was happening- Benny had been cut to open up a space on the roster for me.

I felt horrible, which was exactly the way they wanted me to feel. I was nervous. The guys most offended were the black players. Was this a "race thing?" Benny, a black player being cut for a white one? I didn't know. All I knew was there was tension in the room that could have been cut with a knife. I swallowed hard and just went about my business.

What a group!

That first season was like a ride at an amusement park for me. Sure, it was a lot of work, but I was so grateful to be playing in the NFL. I was loving every minute of it. And for the new kid on the block, I couldn't have had a more exciting beginning.

The regular season began Sunday, September 4,1983. We opened our season the next day-a stellar season premiere for Monday Night Football. The Cowboys versus the Washington Redskins at RFK Stadium in Washington, D.C. Since this match-up was historically a fierce one, everyone expected a good contest. But no one could have predicted how good.

To this day ABC television surveys indicate that September 5, 1983, wins first place for the most exciting Monday Night Football game ever. It certainly gets my vote.

The reason why it gets the nod as the most exciting game is because we got in trouble quickly. The Redskins simply overpowered us, putting us in the hole. The score was 10-0 at the end of the first quarter, and we went into the locker room down 23-3 at the half. We had to pull a rabbit out of our hat to grab this game as a victory. Coach Landry, as captain of our ship, charted a masterful plan to get us back on course. The most exciting game is aptly named because it includes what many feel is the greatest comeback in NFL history.

Danny White threw a seventy-five-yard touchdown pass to Tony Hill to start the second half. On our very next possession, White once again connected to Hill for a fifty-one- yard touchdown.

We were now back in the game, 23-17. One more touchdown, a thirty-three-yard interception by Ron Fellows, and another score put us up 31-23. Late in the game the Redskins scored one last time, but it wasn't enough. A bleak first half was completely turned around.

We came back to win the game 31-30. It was a delirious locker room at the game's conclusion. I remember feeling that if all the games were going to be at this level of excitement, I might die from cardiac arrest from the postgame jubilation! I was awarded the first Specialty Team Award from Haggar for combining on three stops of kickoff returners. It was a wonderful way to start a professional career.

That first season was a great experience for me. The Cowboys won seven straight games before dropping a game to the Los Angeles Raiders. By season's end we were 12-4 and heading to the playoffs. We were to host the Los Angeles Rams in the NFC Wild Card game.

The game was scheduled for the day after Christmas. That week I received a most unexpected Christmas present.

I had been a backup safety for Dextor Clinksdale the entire season. He had an okay season, but I was really pushing for his position. I had somewhat resigned myself to the fact that, as a rookie, I couldn't really expect to start. But it didn't stop me from pushing myself as much as I could.

The day before Christmas, the coaches announced they would be starting me instead of Dextor! I was flabbergasted, but definitely ready for the challenge. I'd show them they were right in starting me.

When game day arrived I had a fire in my belly to go out there and do my best. It's a good thing there was fire because it was absolutely freezing that day in Dallas. It was a whopping zero degrees with snow and ice everywhere. People now affectionately refer to that game as "The Ice Bowl," and most people watched it from the cozy warmth of their living rooms or dens. There weren't many people in Texas Stadium that day. I guess I can't blame them.

Thanks mostly to an outstanding running game from the Rams' ace back, Eric Dickerson, the Rams prevailed over us, winning 24-17. I felt badly about our defeat but did feel like I had played a good game. It was the next morning when I was packing up my stuff to go back to Tennessee for a visit that the phone rang.

"Hey Bill, it's Coach Stallings," said the voice on the other end of the line.

"Hi, Coach, what's up?"

"Have you seen this morning's paper?" "No, sir, I haven't."

"Well, good. I'm glad I got ahold of you first. I just want to tell you--don't worry about what Dextor said, okay? Just don't let it bother you, because it's not true."

I thanked Coach, hung up and, naturally went right for the newspaper. My eyes bugged out as I read Dextor's review of our game. He blamed the loss on the "poor performance of the defense." And he blamed the poor performance of the defense on the fact that I was starting and not him. Welcome to the NFL, Mr. Bates!

On the positive, I received this letter after the season concluded:

Dear Bill:

Congratulations! The greatest players in the history of football have selected you to receive their 1983 SPECIAL TEAMS PLAYER OF THE YEAR AWARD. Along with the eleven top NFL players of the 1983 season, the NFL Alumni will be honoring President Ronald Reagan with our Old Hero Award at the Second Annual NFL Alumni Player of the Year Awards Dinner in Tampa, January 21, 1984. Bob Hope will also be on the program, as will coaches Tom Landry and Don Shula.

Bill, we believe the "Pro's Pro" Awards are the most meaningful in all of football arid we again congratulate you for this great honor.

Sincerely,

Jim Campbell

Director of Communications

NFL Alumni

It was quite an honor for a rookie to be named the Special Teams Player of the Year. I also knew how much I learned that season. For one thing, we played twice as many games as we did in college and it felt like it. That particular year we played four preseason games, sixteen regular season games, and one postseason game-twenty-one games as opposed to eleven. I was ready to settle in for a much needed rest.

I felt I deserved it.

But the off-season would be somewhat tainted in my mind because of Dextor's words.

That first year was a real test for Denise and me. Trying to keep a relationship together by long distance was a draining experience. It turned out that we only saw each other every six or eight weeks. Denise would fly out from Atlanta for a visit for a few days every couple of months. To an outsider it must have looked like we were rolling in money-Denise being a model and me playing pro football-but that was simply nowhere near the truth. The real story is that our money was so tight back then that we swapped off buying her plane ticket to Dallas-I'd buy one ticket and she'd buy the next one six weeks later. It was far from the glamorous life, believe me.

On top of that-I have to admit-during football season I was so focused on football, little else mattered. Looking back, I'm sure this tended to drag out our relationship. I have to admire Denise's patience. She hung in there with me the whole time. Not only was I not very sensitive to Denise during the season, but it was also difficult for a new person to "break into" the little clique known as the Dallas Cowboy wives. Obviously, since Denise wasn't my wife, that gave her sort of a second-class status among the players' wives. Couple that with the fact that she was only in town once every six weeks, and it was a difficult time of adjustment. One wife bluntly told Denise, "Let us know when you get married and then we'll start inviting you to things!"

Word got back to Denise in Atlanta that I was experiencing a modest degree of popularity as a rookie. I'd agreed to go on a radio talk show where we took phone calls from fans with questions. Denise recalls those shows as "every other caller being a girl wanting to know if Bill Bates was married and if not, how could she get ahold of his phone number."

Denise came out for the Thanksgiving holiday that first season. I remember it well. As always, the team played on Thanksgiving. And, as always, the team stayed in a hotel the night before the game. Consequently, Denise stayed in my apartment that Wednesday ... all by herself. Most of her evening was occupied with phone calls. Believe me, after the game on Thanksgiving, I heard all about the phone messages Denise took on my behalf. All the callers were in the same basic category: Girls who somehow had gotten my home phone number and called to say, "I just feel badly that Bill will be all alone on Thanksgiving. Is there anything I can do to help?"

It was a real struggle for Denise. I so appreciate her love and understanding.

Incidents like those Thanksgiving phone calls point out her complete trust in me. She was a real trooper. Not every woman would have hung in there with me.

She also has a great sense of humor, and I believe it helped her get through some of those stressful situations. For instance, on the weekends that Denise was unable to be in Dallas, she'd stay home on Saturday nights there in Atlanta with her roommate, Cheryl Rosenbaum. Every Saturday night was a power-packed evening of non-stop excitement. They would sit in front of the television, watch "The Love Boat," and eat ice cream. Scintillating stuff. They even had a name for their Saturday night gathering ... The Big Fat Ugly Girls on Saturday Night Club. By invitation only.

"He's What Defense Is All About...Mean and Ornery!"

It was 1984-my sophomore year in the NFL. With the triumphs of my rookie season behind me, I turned my attention toward achieving some goals that would end up following me around for my entire professional career-making the final cut by being placed on the forty-seven man roster and making my teammates respect me ... especially Dextor.

There were a lot of people in my comer that second year.

Even the press was kind to me. One article that appeared locally in Dallas capsulized the feeling at that time:

Over in one dusty comer of the practice field at California Lutheran College is a blue tackling dummy. It is attached to a spring-like contraption that allows it to slide along a rail.

The harder a player hits the dummy, the faster it slides across the rail. It eventually reaches the end of the rail and when it does makes a loud clanging sound. Thus, the more intense the hit, the louder the clang.

It is a warm afternoon and defensive backs are lined up ready to throw themselves at the dummy. Assistant coach Gene Stallings urges them on. One by one the players lunge toward the dummy, creating various amounts of noise as the machine absorbs their efforts.

Finally a player wearing Number 40 on his blue jersey assaults the tackling dummy. There can be no question that he demonstrates more ferocity than any of those who have gone before. The clang from the machine echoes across the practice field. Bill Bates has struck again.

In the year that has passed since Bill Bates first appeared in Thousand Oaks, California, his name has become synonymous with hitting. He became an instant cult hero in Dallas with his play on special teams, gained the attention of network telecasters, and soon found himself the subject of hero-worship type mail from all across the country. It is almost too much for a young man from Tennessee to comprehend.

"It has all happened so fast," Bates said. "That's the thing about it. It's been so quick." And although his remarks may look a little corny in cold

type, they are spoken with fervor usually unheard from a professional athlete.

"It is a great honor to play for this team," Bates said. "A lot of people dream about playing for the Dallas Cowboys. I dreamed it too. But I never anticipated it would happen! And while I am here you are always going to see me giving it everything I have. I would hate it for the rest of my life if I didn't make the most of it while I had this chance. I don't want to look back and say I wished I had worked harder.

"Bill Bates is going to work as hard as he can while he is playing."

It was a heady time for me. Coach Landry had even been quoted as saying, *"Bill Bates is what defense is all about ... mean and ornery!"*

Gil Brandt told the press: *"They're going to rule him illegal pretty soon. He has captured the whole city of Dallas and the whole state of Texas with his enthusiasm. People are comparing him to Cliff Harris, who was a great defensive back for us."*

Coach Stallings told the Dallas Morning News:
"He's aggressive, he's excitable, he likes what he's doing. The fans can associate with that. He's a blue-collar worker who is happy to be here."

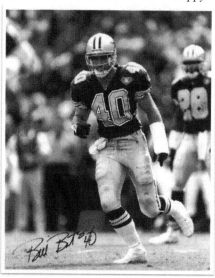

Our special teams coach at the time was Alan Lowry. He decided to put Jim Jeffcoat and me on either side of Rafiel Septien, our kicker. Based on what he had observed last season, this placement was by design.

"We put our biggest hitters on either side of the kicker so they'll be in the middle of the field," Lowry told the press. "The guys closest to the middle have a greater chance of making the play on either side of the field, regardless of which way the return goes."

"As a result," he continued, "the guys in the middle should make more tackles than anyone else on kickoff teams. That's what happened last year. Bates and Jeffcoat got most of their tackles off the kickoff team."

Training camp was Coach Landry's way of getting the team in top shape and focusing our complete attention away from any distractions in the Dallas area. We always had nighttime curfews, where one of the coaches would come by our rooms at the appointed hour checking to be sure we were there. One particular night after bed-check, a few guys decided they wanted to sneak out. But Coach Jim Myers-better known as "Night Cat"-was on the prowl, ready to catch the escapees!

My favorite memory of this story was when Coach Myers caught Ed "Too Tall" Jones. Hoping not to get caught, Ed stood in the shadows of the night with his arms outstretched, perfectly still, in an effort to convince Coach Myers that it wasn't him, but rather, a tree! Coach Myers wasn't fooled.

As camp progressed, I felt I was making my contribution.

The coaches were noticing me in a positive way, and I was beginning to feel confident in my position. Our preseason schedule opened in Dallas against the Green Bay Packers. I felt I played a strong game, especially on special teams, and we ended up winning the game 31-17.

But that Green Bay game stood out for me in a way that was far from pleasant. I fractured my hip in that game. I landed on my knee in a funny way. I was going underneath a guard to take away an end run on a play near the goal line, when two guys landed on top of me. The way the doctors explained it to me, it was like being in a car wreck without buckling my seat belt. The crash would jam my knees up against the dashboard of the car, and in doing so, it would fracture the part of the leg that holds the leg bone in place the hip.

I'm not diminishing the intense pain in my legs, but the real blow was in not being able to play football. Coach Landry decided to keep me around, placing me on the injured-reserve list for the first four regular season games. I kept going to the team meetings and jumped full-tilt into the prescribed rehabilitation program for my injury. My workout was pretty restricted. I was limited to upper body work with weights and swimming. The laps in the pool allowed me to do some work on my legs without putting a great deal of weight on them.

Finally, about the third week of the preseason, I was permitted to start running again. I wanted to get back. I didn't want to miss the whole season. But I never thought I would. I kept in constant touch with the doctors, making certain I was doing the right things, getting x-rays all the time. I was so pushy, I'd often tell the doctors how to run their business.

"I'm ready to go!" I'd announce to the doctors.

"No, you're not," they would reply. "Take a look at this x-ray, if you're so sure of yourself."

Once I looked, I knew they were right. I felt like I was a wild horse who had been roped in and put in reins. Each week they'd let me run a little looser, but they were always in control. On one hand, I hated it, but on the other, I had to respect the doctors for telling me what I needed to do to get back . . . and that if I didn't do it I would not get back. I wanted to run free.

It was the type of injury that could be overcome. But if I tried to come back too soon, I could reinjure it and be out all year ... or worse, for good. I had to keep reminding myself that I had to be patient. I didn't want to jeopardize my career over something like this.

Sitting out all of August and September really tested my patience. By the time I was activated, our team was 3-1, beating the Rams, the Eagles, the Packers, and only losing to the Giants. On September 30, 1984, I was brought back to play against the Chicago Bears in Soldier Field. It was a perfect day for football. The sun was shining its autumn rays onto a field that had the crisp feel of Chicago's famed breeze. It felt so good to be back!

No more street clothes on the sideline. I was in full pads, ready to hit someone ... anyone.

My first chance came less than three minutes into the game. On our first possession we were unable to move the ball, so the punt team was brought in, which included me. Danny White, our punter, lofted a beauty for about forty-six yards. The Bears' receiver, Jeff Fisher, who was later to become the Head Coach of the Tennessee Titans, was right under the ball, waiting with open arms to receive it.

When he caught it, I was right there. I hit him, hard, like it had been weeks-even months, since I had been allowed to really haul off and let it go. I hit him so hard, he couldn't hold onto the ball. As he fumbled, Cowboy rookie Norm Granger was there to scoop it up at the Bears' twenty-two-yard line. Although we were only able to turn it into three points, it was an important play as the day wore on. We ended the first quarter leading 10-7 and held onto that lead through the remaining three quarters.

We beat the Bears by a score of 23-14. After the game I was presented a game ball for my work on special teams. The next day the press described the Jeff Fisher fumble as the "Bill Bates is Back" play. This proved to be a big moment for me by giving me the respect I so desperately wanted from my teammates ... and especially Dextor Clinksdale.

As October unfolded I was back in full stride. Before the season started, Coach Landry had announced that he would personally select the team captains for this year. First he explained there would be a different set of captains for each of the initial six games. Then a decision would be reached for the remainder of the season.

After carefully observing all the possibilities, Coach announced his choices right before our game against the Redskins. He chose Tony Dorsett as the offensive captain, Randy White as the defensive captain, and from special teams he decided on me.

I was flattered beyond belief. This was incredible in itself, but--on top of that-to only be a second-year man was amazing. The press asked for a statement. This is what I gave them: *It's really a great honor, especially when the coach selects you. The special teams were playing well before I came back this year. I've been able to contribute a little, but the important thing is for the special teams to continue to play well and I contribute as much as possible. I know the special teams were a big concern of Coach*

Landry's this year. It's good that we're playing well. As for me, a lot of surprising things have happened to me in the past two years I've been here. I hadn't expected any of them, but I try not to get too caught up in them and just keep doing what I've always been doing. I've always believed you have to work hard in practice to be any good. Some guys are at the level where they don't have to do that, but I'm not at that level.

A team captain should be there to encourage people to do their own jobs without relying on someone else. A leader should be there to set an example. Among the best things that can make a good football player is giving 100 percent all the time, being committed to doing your job, and having fun doing your job.

I know a lot of people generate press releases containing what they think people want to hear, but I always try to speak the truth. I meant every word I said about being chosen captain, whether it sounded corny or not. Just playing for the Cowboys was a dream come true, and honors like being chosen captain were never taken lightly.

People often ask me what was the hardest hit I've ever experienced. It would have to be the one in the Redskin game at RFK. Early in the fourth quarter we were down pretty big. I was still coming back from the hip injury, so the coaches thought this would be a good opportunity to get me some playing time at the safety position.

Under head coach Joe Gibbs, the Redskins were famous for the counter trey (two big linemen pulling around the corner and wiping out the opposition). John Riggins had been running this play to perfection, gaining eight to ten yards a run. It was obvious to me the play was coming again. Instead of handling my responsibility-which was to contain-I headed for the five-yard hole. I hit Riggins head-on. We both fell sideways onto the ground. My bell had been rung, but I got up slowly and headed for the huddle. As I was trying to get the next defensive play, I suddenly realized I was surrounded by a circle of growling Redskins ... I was in their huddle, not ours!

So as not to look totally ridiculous, I acted as if I was picking a fight with them. As I headed back to the Cowboys' side, I noticed that John Riggins was just starting to get up. He didn't return to his huddle but, rather, staggered over to the sideline. When I saw this, there was no way I was going to the sideline!

We went on to a 9-7 record that year. It wasn't good enough for the playoffs, but it was decent. The big news that would come out the end of the season was more personal in nature.

For any player in the National Football League, the ultimate honor is being on a team that wins the Super Bowl. That Super Bowl ring is an award without peer. The next level of honor is to be chosen to play in the Pro Bowl in Honolulu, Hawaii. It is the jewel in any player's personal crown. But since its inception, the Pro Bowl overlooked any recognition for special teams players. Being a special teams specialist, I always thought this was a grave oversight.

To the delight of special teams players and fans, earlier that year the NFL announced that it was time to recognize the special teams' contribution ... and starting that year, a special teams representative would take part in the Pro Bowl set for January 27, a week after the Super Bowl.

Naturally, I coveted the honor of being chosen, but had to look at things realistically. Since I had missed the first four games of the season, I concluded that some of the other players had a better chance than I did. I'll be happy for whoever wins it, I decided. Maybe I'll get it some other year, was about the most positive thought I could muster.

So I was more astonished than anyone when I was named as the first recipient of the Pro Bowl's special teams position.

Again it was a heady time for me. The media were saying the position in the Pro Bowl was "created specifically for Bill Bates." It was flattering, indeed. I was feeling like a kid at Christmas.

Part of the attention I was receiving in the media was in no small way attributed to John Madden. The former head coach of the Oakland Raiders was now a sportscaster with CBS, and he was unreservedly excited about the way I played football. With his own excited style of commentary, Madden made each of my hits sound like bombs exploding on a battlefield. I will always be grateful to people like John Madden, who seemed to go out of their way to give a break to a guy like me. People have always kidded me that I have Coach Madden on my payroll. But now, with his new contract with the Fox network, I don't believe he needs to be on anybody's payroll!

As a matter of fact, after the Super Bowl ring and the Pro Bowl selection, the next level of honor would be selected to the "All-Madden Team." I've been fortunate enough to be selected by Coach Madden for his team nine of the last ten years (the exception being 1992, when I was injured). I was even further honored by being placed on the "Ten-Year All-Madden Team." Awards humble me and honor me ... and make me want to work even harder the next year!

Between season's end and the Pro Bowl I went back to Tennessee to see my family in Knoxville ... and more importantly, to visit Denise.

By Christmas of '84 we had been dating for two-and-a-half years. And with the exception of a two-and-a-half-month period, the whole relationship had been long distance. I had no doubt that I was completely in love with Denise. She was so selfless and giving in our relationship.

The previous summer I had moved out of my little apartment in Dallas to a condominium I had purchased. This gave me the opportunity to move all my stuff from Knoxville, since I finally owned a place of my own. Denise was right there to assist me in moving my stuff from Tennessee to Texas. There was even a strange sense of deja-vu during the trip.

Much like when I helped Denise move from Tennessee to Atlanta, all the earthly possessions I owned could be put in a U-Haul trailer that hooked onto the back of my car. Denise and I loaded up everything and headed off. Because there was no hurry, we decided to go by her place in Atlanta on our way to Dallas. (I know it's way out of the way, but you're only young and in love once, right") So as we were driving to Atlanta, we had an amazing experience. To this day I tell people this story and they can't believe it's true.

To put it simply, while we were driving, the U-Haul broke loose from the car. I know that sounds strange enough, but there's more. Because of the angle of the trailer at the time it broke loose, it didn't just roll off the highway and come to a stop. The trailer actually came up alongside of us and passed us on the highway! As hard as it may be to believe, it's the truth! It's not everyday that you see your U-Haul coming around you in the passing lane!

It sounds bizarre and funny looking back on it, but while it was happening, Denise and I were in a panic. I mention this because it was a deja-vu situation. This U-Haul incident occurred within one mile of the location where Denise had lost her U-Haul when she moved that winter two years earlier. For that reason, we're still not big fans of Dalton, Georgia.

It was incidents like these that helped cement a wonderful relationship between us. Denise and I knew how to have fun together, how to be serious together ... even how to survive U-Haul trailer mishaps together.

So two days after Christmas I was in Nashville to visit Denise. I decided it was going to be a special evening, so I invited her out to a four-star French restaurant in Nashville named Julian's.

135

Like me, Denise was tiring of this long-distance relation- ship. We agreed that something had to happen. There were things that needed to change ... and soon.

I decided we should make this the topic of conversation at dinner. I was a rat-I began to purposely lead her astray. Before long she was convinced that I had taken her out to dinner in order to break up with her.

"Denise, just how long have we been dating?" I asked over our appetizer, as gruffly as I could.

"Two-and-a-half years," Denise responded, somewhat forlornly. She waited for my response.

"Yeah. That's what I thought," 1 added, sounding like the answer was bothering me.

1 allowed enough time for an awkward silence to develop, and then I pierced the silence with an assault.

"Denise?" 1 asked, scratching my chin. "Do you think we really know each other well?"

"Well," she stammered, "Yes, I do."

"Hmmm," 1 mused. I could see her nervously fidgeting with her lovely blonde hair.

"I don't know," I threw out. "Do you think we really know how to communicate?"

1 could see her swallow hard. In a barely audible tone, she whispered, "Yes, I think we communicate just fine."

"Hrumpf," I moaned in a loud exhale.

I could see I was getting to her. She was trying to look into my eyes, but I avoided eye contact at all points of the conversation. Don't let her see your eyes, I told myself.

"I'll be right back," I announced suddenly.

"Are you all right?" she asked.

"Yeah, sure," I snapped. "I just gotta go to the men's room."

As I walked off to the restroom, I snickered to myself.

Sure, I was a rat, but it was lots of fun!

I wasn't gone very long in terms of minutes and seconds.

But I'm sure to Denise it seemed like years. When I finally returned, I slid back into my seat, cleared my throat, and with all the theatrics and drama I could muster, I asked her one last question: "Do you think we could get along together for a lifetime?"

I don't know what it was that gave it away, but all the stress and nervousness in Denise's face disappeared, replaced by the biggest grin I had ever seen.

I pushed my hand into my jacket pocket and took out a small felt box. I opened it to show her the engagement ring I had just purchased. I pulled it out of the box and placed it on her finger as daintily as a guy could-that is, a guy whose fingers pointed north when his hand pointed south. We hugged, kissed, cheered, and ordered a dinner befitting such an occasion. I was feeling like a million dollars! I had asked my girlfriend to marry me . . . and she said yes!

I guess she was willing to forgive me for putting her through such a horrible ordeal leading up to my proposal. But that's the way she is. More importantly, she was willing to accept me with all of my shortcomings and to love me in spite of them. It's that kind of unconditional acceptance that is so crucial to a healthy relationship.

With Denise I had nothing to prove. I hope she feels that I give her the same freedom.

When dinner and dessert concluded, Denise wanted to get right home to share the good news with her mom and step- dad. She ran into the house, screamed out the good news, and we broke out the champagne. I think we toasted everyone and everything imaginable, until about 3:00 A.M. I can still recall Denise and her mom crying over what had happened. There was plenty of emotion that night in Nashville.

Denise called her roommate, Cheri Lee, to tell her the good news. They screamed and cheered and cried like a couple of teenagers. After they hung up, Cheri called my good buddy, Mark Rosenbaum, to tell him the news. Mark and Cheri had been dating for quite awhile.

Mark called me to extend his congratulations sincerely, yet somewhat awkwardly. Certainly he was happy for me-he told me how excited he was that I had put that rock on Denise's finger. He said he was glad that I had pulled the trigger first. But I think it really got him to thinking about his relationship with Cheri. And sure enough, it wasn't long after that phone call that Mark asked Cheri for her hand in marriage.

"He Reminds Me of Me"

On June 8, 1985, Denise and I were married. The ceremony took place at the Vine Street Christian Church, which was right down the street from Denise's house in Nashville. We had been referred to David Beavers for some typical premarital counseling sessions. We ended up liking David so much that since he was a family counselor and a minister, we asked him to officiate in our wedding ceremony. He did a great job.

In our premarital sessions, David put us onto an aspect of our relationship that would prove to be a vital piece of counsel: "You two are very different from each other," he stated in stark simplicity. "Therefore, you'd better prepare for the appropriate adjustments that will need to be made." He turned to me and added, "Bill, you come off as a very confident person who is fairly self-assured. On top of that, you can be on your own-you even like to be alone."

"Denise, on the other hand," he contrasted, "is more of a personality who needs people in her life. She likes reassurance and approval from people. She'll especially want your approval and reassurance, Bill. You'll have to make a point of communicating these things to her on a regular basis."

David had read us like a book. He was right on. And so it was that he stood before us in church that Saturday evening in June. With 400 people witnessing our vows, Denise had eight attendants (all in dresses of Cowboy blue) and I had nine guys in tuxedos standing up with me. We also had Denise's two little nieces as flower girls and my little nephew, Benjamin, as ring bearer.

Benjamin did the best job he could, but this whole "wedding thing" was a big bore to a little boy. His father saw that it was going to be a problem so while Benjamin stood at the front of the sanctuary, he and his dad had an imaginary game of "catch." It was quite a sight to watch this kid in a tux catch pretend baseballs in church. But we all figured it could be a lot worse, so we accepted it as appropriate behavior.

After the wedding, we picked up an extra 250 people, because there were 650 people at our wedding reception, which was held down the road at the Richland Country Club. It was a classy affair, complete with a five-piece string ensemble from the local symphony. We spent the night in Nashville and headed off the next morning for our honeymoon.

We flew to the island of St. Martin in the Caribbean for a week of fun in the sun. We had arranged for our own private villa right on the sandy white beach. It was divine. However, the first day was pretty much given over to travel. We changed planes three or four times to get to our final destination. We arrived late enough that first night that we just collapsed into bed. The next morning was absolutely perfect, so we set out for a walk along the beach. We wandered so far away from our villa that, unbeknownst to us, we left the Netherland Antilles and crossed over to the portion of island belonging to the French. We spread out our blanket on a beach that was completely deserted. Still exhausted from all the events of the past few days, both Denise and I promptly fell asleep on our blanket. It was the sounds of other people who had discovered our beach that first awakened us. But as soon as we opened our eyes we were utterly awake ... and amazed. This beach on the French side of the island was not private, but public-very public. Denise and I were lying in the middle of a nude beach!

Rather than joining right in, we decided to hike back to our villa. The rest of our honeymoon was spent touring the island, snorkeling, eating breakfast feasts on the balcony of our villa, and just having a great time.

When the week was over we flew back to Nashville, where I stayed for one night before flying back to Dallas to prepare for training camp. Denise moved all of her stuff to Dallas, with the help of her brother. It was one more journey with a U-Haul trailer, but fortunately this trip didn't go through Dalton!

I had rented out my condo and made arrangements for Denise and me to move into an apartment I had rented. This way, Denise wouldn't move into a "bachelor pad" that she'd have to make her own. We both started in this new place at the same time.

Another reason for the move was that the Cowboys had just opened their new training facility in a section of Dallas called Valley Ranch. The apartment was close to Valley Ranch, so it was not only a new start, but it was also much more convenient.

Less than a month after our arrival in Dallas, we were invited to attend a Fourth of July party at the home of Doug and Sherry Cosbie. Just like our minister told us, Denise and I are different. Denise was absolutely thrilled to be invited and insisted that we go. "What's the big deal, anyway?" I mumbled back. "I don't want to go. What I really want to do is play golf."

This did not set well with my new bride. She was so incensed that I would be this insensitive that she had to show me in a vivid demonstration. Screaming all the time, Denise went to her shoe closet and began throwing shoes at me- and she has a lot of shoes! Needless to say, I didn't play golf that Fourth of July.

We went to the Cosbies' party and we had a great time.

Denise was immediately attracted to Sherry, who had a bunch of kids, just like Denise wanted. Sherry also introduced Denise to John and Carol Webber, who led team Bible studies for the players and their wives. Sherry, Carol, and Denise would continue to bond into close friends.

When training camp opened in 1985, I added a new credit to my pro football resume. I enjoyed a brief stint as the Cowboys punt returner.

It all started in practice. Since my style is so full-on all the time, I started volunteering to catch punts during practice. It was an area of vulnerability for us, since we really didn't have any other players interested in that position. So, just so I could prove that I could do it, I began punt returns. I felt like the more versatile I was, the better chance I had at making the team. Apparently Coach Landry liked what he saw because he began using me.

It was during our first preseason game that I returned a punt. We were in Dallas playing the Green Bay Packers.

After catching the punt, I took off up the field. I was met by a Packer defender who hit me as hard as I've ever been hit on a play. I was hit so hard, it knocked me unconscious.

The trainers came out onto the field. I was out cold, so nothing mattered to me. But to family and friends, it was a frightening experience. Denise told me later that I was unconscious for more than six minutes! As I laid motionless, an ambulance was summoned and they brought out a stretcher with the headboard to stabilize my neck. As I was being rolled off the field, I came to, lifted my hand, and waved to the crowd, who sighed a collective sigh of relief.

While the ambulance was taking me to Baylor Medical Center, I started to give the doctors a clue about my condition. I had a concussion. What gave it away was a telling statement I made to one of the doctors: "Hey, man, find my girlfriend and tell her I'm all right, okay?" I didn't even remember that I was married!

They kept me in Baylor overnight for additional observation. Although it was a fairly severe concussion, I remember Coach Stallings calling me the next day to see if I was all right.

I felt bad for Denise. This was quite an introduction to the world of an NFL wife. To make it even worse for her, as soon as I was released from the hospital, I boarded a jet to return to Thousand Oaks for training camp.

That was the last punt I returned for a while. Coach Landry didn't use me in that position again until the regular season was almost completed. We were playing good ball that season. Midway through the year our record was 6-2. We went on to win four more and lose four more, ending our season at 10-6, which was good enough to go to the playoffs.

That season Cincinnati had beaten us by scoring fifty points, the most I had ever experienced as a pro player. I recall it was bitter cold in Cincinnati, late in the second half, and we were desperately trying to get possession of the ball so we could score more than the twenty-four points we had. We called for a blitz. In this particular blitz, we lined up an extra man on the line of scrimmage. The scheme on this play called for me to line up as a noseguard!

It was comical, to be sure. Here I was-all two hundred pounds of me-sitting in a four-point stance, ready to go right over the center. The Bengals were ready for it and they picked it apart. I was told afterward, however, that John Madden went absolutely nuts about me playing noseguard! He couldn't stop talking about Bill Bates-"Now, that's my kind of player!"

I was honored to be chosen for the All-Madden Team. John sent me this incredible drawing that hangs on the wall in my great room.

The All-Madden Team print

We went to the playoffs by playing the Los Angeles Rams in Anaheim on January 4, 1986. The Cowboys had a bad day, while Eric Dickerson had a great one. Rushing for more than two hundred yards, he single-handedly beat us 20-0 in front of an adoring group of Rams fans.

The day was frustrating for us in several ways. Besides the obvious defeat, we were all kinda shaken when, midway through the second quarter, Coach Landry was escorted off the field by the police. There had been a death threat made on Coach, and the authorities decided it was not to be taken lightly. Jim Myers, one of the assistant coaches, took over on the sideline, while Coach Landry was forced to watch the game from the locker room.

Later in the game Randy White got into a brutal fight on the field. I'm sure he was as frustrated as the rest of us were that day, and he couldn't hold it in. Randy was a master at martial arts, practicing it religiously in the off-season. I guess it's a good thing he didn't kill someone that day. He, too, was personally escorted off the field and taken to the locker room.

It was a frustrating day for me as well. During the week I had been erroneously quoted as saying Eric Dickerson wasn't a good running back. As a result of that misquote and since Dickerson was awesome the press was all over me after the game.

There was a feeling of sadness and disappointment after the game was over. We didn't know it at the time, but it would be Coach Landry's last visit to the playoffs. I felt badly for him. He was always so complimentary of me, especially in public. He was even quoted as saying one of the reasons he was so fond of me was because "he reminds me of me. We're both overachievers. I wasn't very fast when I played, so you also, by renting the house, you could recoup your monthly payments. It sounded like a good deal. On top of that, before the law changed in 1986, an individual could buy as many rental houses as he wanted, using them all for this tax advantage.

The counsel I received from him was simple-buy as many houses as you can afford and avoid tax trouble. He went on to explain that houses in foreclosure were real steals in that market. I was so excited about this financial possibility that I told him I wanted to buy ten houses. That was a little too ambitious, but I did end up with six. I put the package together just like it had been explained to me. I found good people to rent the houses and even had a management group taking care of all of them for me.

I was breaking even and saving money on my taxes. I had no reason to suspect that anything was wrong.

About that time I was introduced to another agent/attorney. This gentleman had been helping Coach Stallings with some real estate deals of his own. A large group of athletes were pooling their resources to purchase an office complex in Dallas and this man was coordinating their efforts. So here was a guy familiar with a situation such as mine.

As he and I talked, I explained to him my situation with the six rental homes. He was impressed with my business acumen, but offered to check over the legal papers that spelled out the deal. I figured there would be no harm in letting him look over what I'd done, so I saw to it that he got the papers to peruse at his convenience.

When he read my papers an unfortunate circumstance came to light. I thought I was buying these houses directly out of foreclosure. I wasn't. I was, in fact, buying these houses from companies or corporations that were owned by my agent. In the process, my agent was having the houses appraised in order to finance a mortgage typically 80 percent of the appraised value. The appraised value of the house was always higher than the price he paid for them (since he bought them in foreclosure). He would "cut me a deal" and give me the houses for less than the appraised price, but more than the foreclosure price ... and he would pocket the difference.

I was horrified. I had trusted this man. Not knowing what else to do, I confronted him. He denied it all, saying this other agent was conspiring to drive him out of business.

I had no other recourse but to take him to court. Before it ever came to trial, he was willing to settle outside of court. He agreed to buy back four of the six houses at the price I had paid for them. I felt it was the best I could do, so I accepted.

Once legal expenses were added in, I took a bath over this deal. But one thing was certain ... I no longer had an agent. I actually negotiated my own contracts with the Cowboys for 1986, 1987, 1988, and 1989. Joe Bailey was the negotiator for the Cowboys in those days and he was a guy I felt I could talk with. So I was able to strike two, two-year deals with him for that time period.

My situation was not unique to me. Three other players also filed suits against my former agent. When the press got wind of the information about our financial crisis, it became public knowledge. By the end of the off-season, I was yearning to get back to something more familiar-like hitting people.

"The Greatest Hitter I Ever Saw"

The advent of the 1986 season was to be the beginning of difficult years for the Dallas Cowboys and their fans. The preseason unfolded in dramatic fashion, as we played the Chicago Bears in London. They beat us 17-6, which would be the first of our defeats in a winless preseason. With 0-5 as our preseason backdrop, we opened the season on September 8. It was an Indian summer-like day as we played at home against the New York Giants.

Midway into the game I was on the field in my linebacker slot for the Nickel Defense. Because of the offense that the Giants brought to the line of scrimmage, my responsibility was to go after their quarterback, Phil Simms. I pursued him with all the speed I could muster, determined not to allow him to get his pass off for a completion.

Thinking I had a good chance at the deflection, I waved my hands in the air as I got closer and closer to him. I threw my right arm at him just as he released the ball. So instead of hitting his passing arm for the deflection, my right hand ended up in his face ... or to be more precise, in his facemask. In a freak set of circumstances, my right ring finger became stuck in Simms' face mask. I tried to pull it back out, but I wasn't fast enough. My ring finger snapped as Phil tumbled to the ground. It hurt like heck, but I figured it was only dislocated. I nervously tried to snap it back into joint, but each time I did, the finger would fall back limply to its injured position.

I ran off the field for some assistance. The trainers jumped right to it and attended to my finger. They rushed me into the locker room to x-ray my finger. "It's broken," they concluded.

"Tape me up," I replied. "And hurry. I don't want to miss a play!"

Shaking their heads the whole time, the trainers taped me up and I was back on the sideline in time to go back in for the next set of downs. I got my wish. I didn't miss a play.

We beat the Giants 31-28, but I was headed for surgery after the game. It turned out to be a pretty serious injury. Between the hand and the first knuckle, the bone was shattered in fourteen places! They localized my finger and in a four-hour operation, they inserted four pins in the lower section of my ring finger right where a ring would go.

Usually when pins are inserted, the surgeons prefer to leave a portion of the pin exposed, so it is easy to remove once the area has healed. But they knew I was planning on playing with the pins in my finger, so they cut the pins as close to skin level as they could.

The following Sunday we were in Detroit, playing against the Lions. In order to play with this injury, my hand had to be taped and I had to wear a glove. The glove was so thick and bulky that it looked like a boxing glove. It was awkward and uncomfortable, but at least I could play.

As luck would have it, I had not one but two passes thrown my direction for simple interceptions. But because of the stupid glove I was wearing, I missed them both. Without much help from me, we beat the Lions and went to 2-0. Things looked good.

As the season progressed, I was allowed to wear a smaller, thinner glove each week. Before long it was time to remove the pins. This was a simple procedure in most cases, but I had a problem. Because the pins were cut so close to the skin, my skin had actually grown over the tops of the pins in a couple of places.

Miraculously, the doctors pulled three of the four pins out without too much trouble, but that last pin was a stinker. The doctor explained to me the difficulty. "Removing that fourth pin is like trying to pull a nail out of a piece of wood. It's complicated because the nail is bent and no longer has a head."

Their only recourse was to localize my entire right arm and yank. Blood was spurting all over the doctor's shirt. Denise got woozy, and came very close to fainting. After making sure she was all right, the doctor returned to my finger and eventually got the pin.

To this day my right ring finger is a testament to my injury-filled career. The knuckle on that finger is three or four times the size of a normal person's knuckle. People tend to notice it more than usual, since it is on this finger that I wear my Super Bowl ring. The beauty of that ring and the ugliness of that knuckle form a striking contrast.

The first Sunday in October we traveled to Denver. It was a rough day. Not only did we lose the game 29-14, but I twisted my right ankle. There's not much you can do for an injury of this nature except keep it iced. So that's what I did.

When we boarded the plane to fly back to Dallas, the trainers unwrapped the Ace bandage, put some fresh ice on the ankle, and rewrapped me.

148

I flew home tired and sore. Once home, I went right to bed. The next morning I went to the training facility to let the trainers look at my ankle. When they removed the bandage we all got a shock. I had a horrible burn all the way up my right shin. The ice pack they had wrapped inside the bandage contained dry ice. The dry ice stuck to the ice bag, which resulted in a nitrogen burn to my leg.

By the next Sunday my ankle was in good enough shape for me to play in our contest against the Redskins. But unfortunately the burns on my leg didn't heal in time, so I couldn't play. I was not used to being on the bench. In a last-ditch effort, I had the doctor give me a shot of Novocain to see if that would relieve the pain in my leg. It didn't.

We went on to a dismal 7-9 record that year.

Our last game of the season was a loss to the Bears at Texas Stadium. I recall running into an amazing guy. His name was Walter Payton, but his nickname was Sweetness. Why was he named this? Because he was so smooth and quick as he ran with the ball. He made many tacklers look silly and clumsy in their efforts to bring him down ... he was incredibly tough.

That day I was making a sure tackle on him. As I was grabbing him, he hit me with a hard forearm and spun away for another twenty yards. Later in the game I did tackle him. As we were getting up, I felt the hardest pinch on my butt. I wheeled around and discovered it had come from Walter himself.

He said to me, "Good tackle." Then, of course, he smiled, with that great sweetness.

It was a sad feeling not to make the playoffs, but you don't go into the postseason with a record below .500. For me personally, 1986 would be the "injury season" because of my finger, ankle, and the burns. The "injury season" was to be followed by the "strike season."

In 1987, besides my normal duties with the Cowboys on the field, I was chosen by the team to be their player representative, along with my buddy, Doug Cosbie. This involved speaking on behalf of the players in any discussions that occurred with the owners or the league officials. In many respects, this was more demanding than actually suiting up and playing the game, since it demanded an entirely different set of skills. There were many occasions when I wished I could simply line up against the owners and tackle them for a huge loss. How sweet!

The season began as normal. We lost our opener in St. Louis to the Cardinals. But we went to the Meadowlands the next week and beat the always-tough Giants 16-14. The Giants game was a personal triumph for me. I had two interceptions in that game and felt it was one of the best games I had ever played. It was such a bittersweet feeling to be mobbed by the reporters in the locker room after the game. I was basking in the warmth of the great game I played, yet deep down inside was a chill coming from the fact that I knew a player strike was going to happen right away.

And, as expected, after only two weeks of regular season play, we went on strike.

This was a traumatic time for all of us in the NFL. The players were stressed for two very important reasons. First, they weren't playing, so there was all this bottled up energy waiting to explode. Secondly and more significantly, since we weren't playing, we weren't getting paid!

To add to my personal stress level, I felt responsible for the strike since I was the player rep for our team. This, of course, wasn't true. But it was, nevertheless, how I felt. It was an awful time.

The owners decided they couldn't afford to let the season pass them by, so one owner suggested hiring replacement players to continue the schedule. After canceling just one week of play, the owners put together their own group of replacement teams, with players we affectionately referred to as "scabs."

The stress started to eat at me. It didn't help matters that the one owner who suggested the replacement players was the general manager of the Dallas Cowboys! Tex Schramm had come up with an idea that brought hatred his way from every player in the league.

I wasn't sleeping well. My old pattern of sleepwalking was beginning to intensify. One night I got up in the middle of the night and attempted to throw a dresser on Denise! When I headed for the window she knew I needed help. To this day I don't know if I was going to jump out of the window or what.

Shortly after that sleepwalking episode I made an appointment to see the team psychiatrist. He examined me and talked with me. "Your Rapid Eye Movement (REM) is carried over longer than most people," he explained to me.

"Therefore you tend to act out what you are thinking by sleepwalking." He quickly added that these thoughts were just like dreams. "They don't always mean what they look like on the surface. They often symbolize deeper feelings going on in your subconscious."

He prescribed the drug Halcion to help me sleep. I didn't like the way I felt the mornings after I took it, so I discontinued using it very soon after it was prescribed.

After several weeks that seemed like centuries, we were finally able to negotiate an agreement satisfactory to all parties involved, so the strike was over! The players reported to practice that Wednesday to receive one final slap in the face by the owners.

"We've decided to go ahead and finish out this week with the replacement players. They'll play this Sunday's game for us. So you guys can go back home ... and we'll see you bright and early Monday morning."

Thus, the season that looked so promising to the Cowboys ended up at a dismal 7-8 record. It was the sort of season to put behind you as quickly as possible.

Because of my stressful situation, I made an off-season appointment to visit a hypnotherapist. Pete Segal from Los Angeles had been suggested to me as a person who could help me get a better handle on what was at the root of my patterns of restlessness.

During the off-season I trained for a couple of weeks in Vail, Colorado. The high altitude aided me in my training ... plus Vail is a beautiful location! Pete flew to Vail that year to be with me. I gained a great deal from my time with him. I feel as if I learned all I could from him. He underscored in me the notion that you can control your mind from the subconscious level. I had felt this was true for years, since it went along perfectly with the positive mental imaging I had practiced since high school. It's a case of seeing yourself doing positive things.

Early in our sessions, Pete wanted to see what was in my past that affected me in positive ways and negative ways. So he hypnotized me. He didn't swing a pocket watch on a chain or put me to sleep. Rather, with the sounds of a tape recorder playing the crashing of ocean waves on the beach, he talked to me quietly, encouraging me to breathe deeply. This relaxed me to the point that I was almost asleep, but not quite.

When you're hypnotized, you know what's going on. You can even get up and walk around if you want to.

Once I was under, he took me back into my past as far as I wanted to go. It was amazing what came out of this session. With Pete guiding me, I went back to the incident that I considered most significant in my life. It was this incident that had shaped my behavior for years. Never in my conscious mind would I have thought this event was so important to me. But it was. What was the incident?

The fight on the playground with Brian McCrary.

I relived the entire experience for Pete. I was left on the ground, crying, thoroughly whipped by Brian . . . with his brother, Conrad, looking over at me and laughing derisively. Through my black eye and tears I vowed, "I'll never let this happen to me again!" That circumstance stamped something deep into my soul.

151

Once I was out of my hypnosis, Pete and I discussed the situation rationally. "The positive of this experience is that it made you more competitive," Pete explained. "You used this incident to insure that you were never laughed at ever again."

"But on the other side of this issue," Pete continued, "in order for it to never happen again, you became a person intent on satisfying those around you however you can."

"What are you saying, Pete?" I asked.

"What I'm saying, Bill, is that whether you realize it or not, you are a people pleaser." Pete helped me realize that the real damage to my insides was not created by Brian's punches, but by Conrad's mocking laughter. This session helped me understand that it was time for me to be happy in myself and not through trying to please other people.

The session with Pete was a pivotal point in my life. Before our sessions, I was fighting something inside and didn't even know what it was. And for that awareness, I am truly grateful.

When the regular season opened in September of 1988, no one could have predicted how crazy a season it would be. Our first five games were won or lost by six points or less. By October 3 we were 2-2 and heading for New Orleans. We lost by three points, but more significantly, it was the first of ten losses in a row.

It was really crazy. We lost ten in a row, then came right back to beat an awesome Washington Redskins 24-17 in Washington! What a season for Cowboy fans.

Our fans are loyal, but only up to a point. The press began to report the grumblings swirling around the Dallas Metroplex area. As is usually the case, the brunt of the criticism fell on the shoulders of Coach Landry. But it wasn't his fault. It was ours.

He put all the right plays in ... we just didn't have the players to execute those plays. As the season ended, the good news was that I led the team in tackles as the strong safety. The bad news was how poor the defense must be if the leading tackler was a safety!

With a record of 3-13, you didn't need a crystal ball to predict that there would be some changes in the season ahead. But none of us would have predicted that the change would involve Coach Landry.

I owe so much to that man. He taught me so much, and more importantly, he believed in me. Years later a writer asked Coach to describe Bill Bates. Coach replied: "Bill Bates and Cliff Harris are the greatest hitters I ever saw. "

"Turn Off That Machine!"

Football wasn't the only tension I was living with at that time in my life. There was stress at home for an entirely different reason. Denise and I wanted to be parents. It wasn't happening.

We had been trying to have children for a long time with no success. Only a couple who has gone through this experience can fully appreciate the emotional trauma it creates. The irony of situations like ours is that the stress created by wanting kids is often the factor that keeps you from conceiving. That's why the doctor is always saying, "Go home and relax! It'll happen, don't worry."

Yeah, right.

About midway through the '88 season, Denise and her mom went to New York City to see our game against the Giants. The two of them had a good time prowling around the Big Apple, although two blonde, attractive southern belles certainly stood out in contrast to most of what they saw on Times Square.

When Denise returned from the trip, she said she wasn't feeling well, so she made an appointment with her doctor. Since it was the middle of the season and the Cowboys were 2-8, I was totally focused on football. I didn't really give Denise much attention at that point. I'm sure I felt she was sick because the team was doing so badly! What else could it be?

I was in for a real surprise when I returned home from practice one night the following week.

"I went to the doctor today, sweetie," Denise began very casually over the dinner table.

"Good," I mumbled, still thinking about football rather than focusing in on her conversation.

"He came up with an interesting prognosis," she further taunted.

"Oh, yeah, what did he say?" I asked with halfhearted interest.

"I'M PREGNANT!" she screamed, with delirious delight. We danced around the table, hugging, kissing, and weeping tears of joy. For so long we had tried to have a baby. We had prayed about it fervently. It appeared that God was finally going to answer our prayers in the affirmative.

After we had settled down somewhat, Denise told me a little more about the visit. "One of the tests the doctor ran indicated a particularly high estrogen level. He wants me to go in for a sonogram as soon as I can."

"Schedule an appointment on my off day, so I can go with you," I volunteered. "I want to be as much a part of this as I can."

So not long afterward we found ourselves in Dr. Chihal's examination room, preparing for a sonogram. I was so amazed at this process. A sonogram is like baby radar. The doctor moved a rectangular box-like contraption-about the size of a small paperback book--called a transducer around Denise's belly and it bounced sound waves off her body. Thus, it could detect the shape of anything in the womb-like a baby! The mages appeared on a monitor for all of us to see.

The sonographer spread jelly-like goop all over Denise's midsection, explaining that this "goo" helped transmit the sound waves. The transducer was attached by a wire to the computer ... and that was attached to the monitor. Then we were all ready to go. Showtime!

Denise and I looked on excitedly as the doctor's transducer searched for our baby. It didn't take long for him to announce, "There's your baby!" as he pointed to the monitor's screen.

I squeezed Denise's hand as we both beamed from ear to ear. What an amazing moment. We were both so absorbed in this magic that we almost missed the doctor's next pronouncement.

"Well, look at that! Your baby has company! It appears to be TWINS!"

We were dumbfounded. In that split second, the doctor ceased talking about a baby, and started referring to Baby A and Baby B. Denise was ecstatic and I was shaky.

But before the reality of twins could sink in, the doctor had even more to share with us.

"Look at the monitor!" he advised excitedly. "I now see Baby A and Baby B ... joined by Baby C! You two are going to have TRIPLETS!"

Denise started to squeal and I started to panic. I don't know what came over me but before I knew it, I found myself screaming at the doctor: "TURN OFF THAT MACHINE BEFORE YOU FIND ANOTHER ONE IN THERE!"

I was completely overwhelmed. My face had turned white, and at one point I thought I was going to pass out. The sonographer instructed the nurse to have smelling salts ready ... just in case.

Was I happy? You bet I was!

But I was also quite taken by the enormity of the task

head of us. I guess it's a fairly typical response for the father to experience. Not too long after the good news, the dad finds his attention turned to things like:

Three cribs.

Three high chairs

Three strollers.

Three tricycles.

Three sets of braces.

Three separate college tuition bills.

No more table for two at restaurants-table for five! No wonder the doctor had smelling salts available!

It was an exhilarating time for us. We called family and friends who knew how we had struggled through our childless situation. They were all so happy for our "triple portion" from the Lord. As we settled in with our news, we became aware of two very important items that would affect us significantly.

1. Multiple births are high risk. We had to be very careful at every juncture.

2. Multiple births attract a lot of attention. We very quickly became items of curiosity in the Dallas area. This was cute for awhile-about seven minutes-then it became a nuisance. The media jumped on this story and became quite impossible at times.

"Can we have an interview with you and your wife?" "Can we be in the delivery room when the triplets are born?"

"Can we have the first interview after the birth?"

"Will you do TV?"

"Will you do radio?"

"Will you grant our newspaper an exclusive?"

It was obvious that my notoriety as a Cowboy was causing people to infringe on our private life as a family. For that reason, I made it very clear to the media that there would be no interviews or appearances until I said so. This announcement didn't endear me to the press, but there were more important endearments at the time ... my family. To the media this was just another story, but to us it was the most important facet of our lives.

A full-term pregnancy is forty weeks. When multiples are involved, the pregnancy is rarely carried to full term. Denise had set in her mind to carry the babies for thirty-four weeks. Obviously, the longer the mother carries them, the greater the chances for delivering strong, healthy babies without a lot of serious complications.

Eighteen weeks into her pregnancy, Denise was put to bed.

Her doctor wanted no needless risks, so bed rest was the prescription. Once again God's timing was so gracious. As these events unfolded, the '88 season concluded so I could once again give my total attention and focus to Denise without the distraction of football.

Bed rest worked for Denise for about seven weeks.

However, at the twenty-five-week point, the doctor wanted her in the hospital. She had experienced preterm labor along with toxemia. From this point on, every vital sign needed to be monitored in order to insure the health and safety of the babies and Denise.

Those were crazy days. I visited Denise every day at Medical City Dallas and actually spent the night with her every other evening. I'd sleep sitting up in those hospital chairs that are specially designed for discomfort. Then again, how can you complain when you're there to visit your wife who is really uncomfortable!

Denise would ask me to bring her things during her stay, and I would try my best to fulfill her every wish. Women get different cravings during pregnancies and I will always think of that time in our lives whenever I see a carton of Blue Bell Homemade Vanilla Ice Cream. Denise craved it, so I would sneak it into the hospital and she would chow down. (I'm not kidding-she gained seventy-two pounds during the pregnancy!)

One night before I left the hospital to go home, Denise had another odd request of me. "Honey, I forgot my iron at home. Would you bring it with you tomorrow?"

I couldn't imagine in my wildest dreams what Denise would need an iron for in the state she was in. But I had also learned that it was sheer lunacy to ever question a request. Just do as you're told, I said to myself and I promised Denise I would bring the iron in the morning.

When I arrived the next day with her steam iron, Denise let out a howl. She was laughing uncontrollably, but I didn't get the joke. Finally she let me in on it.

"Bill, I wanted you to bring my iron supplement tablets, not my steam iron! Why in the world would I need a steam iron in the hospital, you silly?"

I laughed along with her, but only because she was disadvantaged by her pregnancy. I truthfully didn't think it was that funny.

Six weeks into her hospital stay, Dr. Herzog was starting to show real concern over her physical condition. He took me aside at the beginning of her thirty-first week and spoke very frankly. "Denise has signs of developing toxemia. That concerns me. Also, as you know, she's been battling with severe high blood pressure the entire pregnancy."

"So what does this mean, Doc?" I asked.

"It means we can't risk Denise for the sake of the babies. We're going to have to go in and take them."

"But she wanted to go thirty-four weeks," I reminded him.

"I know," he replied. "But three more weeks are out of the question."

"Is there any way I can get you to reconsider?" I asked. "Look, Bill," he responded, "Denise is in a difficult situation. Her blood pressure is so high that it's beginning to affect her vision. We don't want to run any needless risks with her condition."

By now I was reeling. "I didn't realize how risky this was going to be," I admitted. "I guess there's really no question about it-it's time."

The doctor went in to share his decision with Denise. "Well, guess what?" Dr. Herzog said with all the cheeriness he could muster up.

"What?" Denise answered hesitantly. She had learned the doctor's techniques early on in their relationship.

"We're going to have babies tomorrow!"

"Oh, no we're not," Denise laughed back derisively. "It's still too early."

"No, it's not," the doctor answered.

"It's only thirty-one weeks. I want to get to thirty-four," she responded firmly.

"Denise, I'm afraid you'll be putting your own life in danger if we wait any longer, so I've arranged for the births to take place tomorrow."

By now Denise had exploded into tears. "No ... no ... we can't! It's still too early!"

"If you want to live to be their mother-it's tomorrow." With that, the doctor left Denise and me alone in her room. I felt so bad for Denise. She had spent the last seven months doing everything in her power to see this through. Now it was being taken out of her hands completely.

After we had some time together, Denise asked me if I would leave her alone in her room for a short time. I felt that I understood, so I went out for a walk around the hospital for some alone time myself.

Denise sat alone in her room, sobbing. This was to be one of the most pivotal times in her young life. From her sterile hospital bed, Denise cried out to the Lord. I've always admired her relationship with the Lord, but this incident brought it into a special focus.

Dear Lord, she prayed, You know I've done everything I could do over these last seven months to insure the safe arrival of our babies. And You also know that it has all been taken out of my hands now by the doctor's decision.

157

She continued, All of this has made me realize that the out- come of our triplets isn't really in my power anyway. I see now that this will all be a demonstration of Your power, Lord. So, I'm giving this whole matter to You. Please help me.

Still sobbing, she went on. I'm so scared, Lord. I want to trust You, but I have such fear. I know You can take away my fear if I trust You. Help me trust You, Lord. I want You to be proud of me because I trusted You. Help me, Lord. Please.

A sleepless night for both of us was ended with a gurney being wheeled into the delivery room on the morning of May 24, 1989. As Denise took that ride, I was right next to her in my hospital garb. I was head-to-foot ready for this event. Complete with hat, mask, gown, pants, and slippers, I looked like a big kid on Halloween. Fortunately, everyone else was wearing the same costume, so I felt less conspicuous.

The doctor's delivery team quickly assembled and it was quite a team! There were more people in that delivery room than we have on a football field on any given play!

Between twenty and twenty-five people were in that room to insure that all would go well. I don't remember them all, but it was a real "grocery list," believe me!

Two delivering obstetricians

Three neonatologists

Four scrub nurses

Six neonatal nurses

One anesthesiologist

Two nurses for Denise

Four to six more medical people doing other things

One pro football player feeling totally out of place

I remember gathering the whole team together for a "huddle." It was one of my better pregame inspirational talks. The thesis of my speech was simple: "Let's go out there and win this one for Denise!"

Everyone had a good laugh, helping to relieve some of the stress that accompanies an operation of this magnitude. Denise was remarkably calm. Her time alone with the Lord the night before had produced "the peace that passes all understanding."

The procedure began. The anesthesiologist gave Denise an epidural so she could be awake for the birth. Then the doctor cut her open for the Caesarean section. Once it started, it went quickly. The triplets were born one minute apart-an unforgettable three-minute joy ride.

First to arrive at 12:51 P.M. was the son we named Graham William. He weighed in at three pounds, nine ounces. The little kitten-like cry he produced brought cheers from the whole crowd. When a baby is that small at birth, often his lungs aren't strong enough to breathe on their own. So that tiny cry was a real victory yelp from our little guy.

One minute later, at 12:52, an even tinier figure came on to the scene. It was our daughter. We named her Brianna Gail. She weighed three pounds, one ounce, yet she astounded the delivery room by making the tiniest little squeak of a sound. The place erupted ... you'd have thought she won the Super Bowl!

Another minute went by and at 12:53, our third gift from God appeared. Another son! Weighing in at three pounds, six ounces, we named him Hunter James. Since he was the last one born, he was the baby in greatest "distress," as they referred to it in the delivery room. Because of the birthing procedure for the other two, Hunter had to go without oxygen for two minutes. Therefore, when he was born he didn't make any sounds, and the doctors immediately put him on a respirator.

I just wanted to be there to support my wife through this major ordeal I didn't do anything to embarrass myself, like passing out on the delivery room floor, but Denise can still recall how I looked during the triplets' birth.

Since my entire body was covered with sterilized garments, all that was really visible was a pair of eyes. According to her, every time a baby was about to be born, my eyes widened to the size of silver dollars! She could tell by my eyes that all was well. (Maybe she was applying the advice I had learned as a kid: you can tell if a person means business by the look in their eye!) Anyway, I was happy as a clam and so very proud of my beautiful wife.

Denise and I hugged each other more tightly than we had ever hugged previously. Triplets! God had answered our prayers ... all of them. Three healthy babies. We felt so much love and gratitude at that moment. It's one of those moments you wish you could freeze in time.

Once we were through the delivery, the roller coaster ride began. Denise was wheeled to the recovery room. Most moms stay there a few hours and then return to their regular room before being released. Denise was to remain in recovery for the next twenty-four hours.

The doctors started to run a whole series of tests on Denise.

Her blood pressure came in dangerously high, so they immediately put her on magnesium sulfate to lower it. Her kidneys started their task of moving through the twenty pounds of extra fluid she had kept for the triplets. That first night she didn't get a minute of the sleep she so keenly deserved. She was sick all night ... and there was nothing anyone could do.

The roller coaster took a downward plunge in the middle of the night, when we were visited by our neonatologist, Dr. Gary Burgess. He brought with him serious news.

"You need to be aware that two of your babies are struggling right now. They need blood. All three of them are on respirators, as it is vitally important that we keep their lungs inflated."

Part of the success in keeping them breathing had to do with an experimental medicine that they were using with our permission on the newborns. We had to sign all these extra forms from the hospital, releasing them from responsibility and such. But the medicine did its job, and we will be eternally grateful to the March of Dimes, who made that medicine available to us. It's a real testimony to God's hand on our lives.

During the last eight weeks in the mother's womb, the mother produces a hormone that goes to the babies so they can breathe when they are born. Therefore, babies who are born prematurely, like ours, are at a disadvantage. They need help in breathing. The March of Dimes in Dallas had three vials of a drug called Surfactant. The drug was developed specifically for this need-helping premature babies breathe. It had been put through all the rigorous tests and experiments necessary to insure its safety. A short time afterward, it was approved by the Food and Drug Administration.

But when we needed it, it had not yet been approved by the FDA. Thankfully, the March of Dimes came along. Denise and I had done a lot of volunteer work for this great charity, and it was as if they were paying us back for all we had given to them for their great cause.

Dr. Burgess agreed that Surfactant would be very helpful to the triplets, so we allowed them to administer it to them. It was amazing to watch the change in their little bodies. When they were born, all three were this pretty pink, new-born color. Twenty-four hours later, they were a pasty-yellow color. But twenty-four hours after the Surfactant they were back to their rosy-pink color. It was such a relief to see their color return.

We thank the Dallas March of Dimes so much for their wonderful work and how it has affected our lives.

http://www.marchofdimes.com/texas/texas.asp

When the sun finally peered over the horizon the next morning, the doctors allowed Denise and me to go upstairs to see our babies together. It was a strange and wonderful feeling for both of us. It was wonderful in that we were looking at the answers to our prayers. God had given us children.

But it was strange in that the babies were all on respirators . . . all covered with wires and tubes from head to heels. Denise said it well. "I feel so detached from them," she whispered from our side of the glass.

When Dr. Burgess came in for his morning visit, he made us aware of the situation with the triplets. "In multiple births, there is a very predictable pattern. Many times the babies do remarkably well for the first twenty-four hours after birth, but then they often take a serious nose dive. We will watch them carefully, night and day, for as long as it takes to get them out of the woods." We appreciated his thoroughness with our little treasures.

Eight days after the delivery, they released Denise from the hospital. She had been there for almost two months! It felt good to have her back home, yet it was difficult because part of her was still there in the hospital. Plus, she had been through so much!

As any mother can understand, it was hard to leave the babies behind. The "detached" feeling that Denise had mentioned only worsened. Because of all the tubes and wires on the babies, the hospital wouldn't even allow them to be clothed.

The one article of clothing that was permissible was a pair of booties. So the full extent of the gifts we could "lavish" on our kids was one stuffed animal and a pair of booties each. Also, as any mother can understand, Denise's hormones started acting up in a big way. She experienced severe hormone crashes that sent her into deep postpartum depression. Resulting from that depression were some horrible arguments. I just couldn't comprehend what was going on and consequently it caused some major misunderstandings. It was far from my finest hour as a sensitive husband.

I remember that at the time Denise was to be released, there were friends of ours staying in our house. We often had houseguests, so I didn't give it a second thought. Denise, on the other hand, was absolutely enraged over the prospect of returning home to share her house with others. She went to great pains to tell me that I was quite out of line for proposing this scenario. Foolishly, I said I didn't think it was a big deal. That only set her off more. She was wild and frantic worse than she had ever been.

Fortunately for me, Dr. Herzog took me aside and clued me in on what was going on. If he hadn't spelled out postpartum depression for me, we might have killed each other!

I tried to make Denise's homecoming as pleasant as possible. I went out and bought three great big signs and placed them in our front yard. Each sign was in the shape of a stork. One of them read, "It's a Girl!" and the other two read, "It's a Boy!"

We made daily visits to the hospital for the next six weeks.

By now we were into July. The scorching Texas heat was a daily reminder to me: Training camp was right around the corner.

On July 9, we were able to bring Graham, Brianna, and Hunter home. Part of our deal with the media had been that if they stayed away from us during the hospital stay, they could photograph the kids when they were released. So we prepared ourselves for a media circus. To an outsider, it may sound very glamorous, but it was a real pain to prepare a press release to correspond with the triplets going home.

With security police standing guard all over that floor of the hospital, the nurses wheeled our three bundles out into an ocean of bright lights, cameras, steno pads, and recorders. We all smiled, trying to look like we really wanted to be there. We didn't.

From the Dallas Morning News

When we arrived home, Brianna was still on oxygen and all three of them were on various medications. Part of the side effects of their medication caused them to sleep for only thirty minutes at a time. And they had to be fed every one-and-a-half hours.

We had some home nursing help at that time, but needless to say, we were overwhelmed. When we walked in the door with them that first day, we both looked at each other and said, "So what do we do now?" We felt lost and alone in this great adventure.

We weren't sleeping and there were no more doctors and nurses around the clock to help. It was a tough beginning. But Denise and I never forgot how we felt before we found out we were going to have the babies. We had yearned for children for so long, and God had been abundantly gracious in hearing and answering our request. We will be eternally grateful

Denise's mother came out and stayed with her during that time, and she was a big help. Talk to Denise today, and she'll tell you that the summer of '89 was a blur-she remembers very little. Time will do that to you when you don't get to sleep.

My life, on the other hand, once again had to refocus.

After having the triplets home for only one week, I was off to Thousand Oaks once again to meet another newcomer in my life ....

Jimmy Johnson.

"Don't Mess Up the Hair"

To fully appreciate July of 1989, it's important to understand February of 1989. On February 25, 1989 Jerry Jones bought the Dallas Cowboys Football Club. And it was on that day that Jerry Jones announced that his first business decision was to replace Tom Landry with the University of Miami's Jimmy Johnson.

Those outside of pro football often think the players have an exclusive "inside track" on information of this nature. Sometimes this is true, but it wasn't the case in this situation.

On February 25, 1989 I was sitting in my mother-in-law's house in Nashville, Tennessee when I heard the news over the radio ... just like most others received the information.

Needless to say, I was shocked to hear the announcement.

Back in Dallas, the public went into an outrage. "How could you fire Tom Landry?" the fans screamed. It didn't help matters any that Jones and Johnson were perceived as old friends from their days at the University of Arkansas. Being from Arkansas was not a plus to a Texas crowd.

Looking back, however, it's amazing to me how fickle the public can be. These same fans who were "outraged" at Jerry's decision to get rid of Coach Landry were the same fans who were "demanding" Coach's resignation just the previous December. Right around Christmas, people were calling a local call-in radio show hosted by my friend, Brad Sham, saying Landry should leave because "the game has passed him by."

Of course, nothing could be further from the truth. Coach Landry was and still is the most brilliant student of the game I have ever encountered. To say the game had passed him by was utterly ludicrous.

There were so many misconceptions during that cold winter of 1989. One misconception was that Jerry Jones had no respect for Coach Landry. That situation came out of people's misunderstanding of our new owner's personality. The truth is, he was a man who was absolutely ecstatic to be the new owner of the Cowboys. But much of the public thought his excitement looked like disrespect for what Coach had accomplished with the team. That was not the case. But it took the fans some time to get over that one.

To make matters even more tense, not only were the fans upset, but the media were hostile as well. Jimmy Johnson's first press conference was a demonstration of stress at work. Reporters jabbed and punched at Coach Johnson. But Coach held his own. The media quickly learned that Jimmy Johnson was a bright man who was also very shrewd when it came to the press. We saw numerous examples over the years of how Coach could actually manipulate situations with the media to his advantage. He always knew exactly what he was doing when it came to reporters.

Coach perceived immediately that he was being characterized as an outsider, not only to the Cowboys, but to pro football. But most significant was the fact that he was a non- Texan, which was unthinkable to true fans. "Listen, folks," Coach expressed in his opening remarks, "I'm a Texan. I was born and raised in Port Arthur." The other sentiment that Coach wanted to communicate was a simple one. "Just give me a chance, okay!"

Fortunately for him, after a little time Jimmy Johnson was no longer perceived as a villain. Unfortunately for him, Jerry Jones became the lightning rod for any and all criticism relating to the Cowboys.

Meanwhile, I was sitting in Nashville trying to ascertain how this coaching change was going to affect me. There were immediate rumblings about the difference in style between the two coaches. I decided that only time would tell. But I'd be kidding if I said I wasn't concerned.

The rumors were not encouraging to me. Rumor had it that Jimmy Johnson was in love with one attribute and one attribute only-speed. Coach Landry had always used a flex defense that demanded less speed from the players. Word had it that Coach Johnson favored a man-to-man defense on the receivers, requiring speed in his defensive secondary. Once again, it looked like I was in for the fight of my life just to make the team.

I felt bad for Coach Landry. Not knowing what else to do, I wrote him a letter expressing all he had meant to me and wishing him the best in any future endeavor. Promptly after receiving my letter, he wrote back this reply:

Dear Bill:

Thanks for your letter. I felt the warm understanding of your words and appreciate your taking time to write them. And my heartiest congratulations on the birth of your three children!

One of the nice by-products of getting released is the opportunity to get a letter from you guys. I really appreciate your concerns and the nice things you wrote about me personally. The one thing that I always tried to stress was the fact that life was going to present some crises. No one can escape that reality.

The things that I will remember will not be what happened to me this year, but the great years we had together. My best wishes to you and your family, and may the Lord bless you.

Sincerely,

Tom

A class guy in every sense of the word.

When I reported to Thousand Oaks in July of 1989, I discovered that the rumors about Jimmy Johnson were true. He worshiped the god of blazing speed. Regrettably, I was of a different religious persuasion.

The press jumped on this issue quickly. There were stories coming out of training camp about the "fierce competition" developing between Vince Albritton and me in the "battle for the strong safety job." It was frustrating, I'll admit. Here I was, the starter since 1986. I had even led the team in tackles the previous year with 124. But I was still fighting for my job. Newspapers were writing stories that included statements like, "Bates cannot compare with Albritton as far as speed, or size, or even strength." So once again, I was proving myself-something I had been doing my entire career.

That first mini-camp with Coach Johnson was very intense.

I was really concerned about making a great first impression, even if we were just in shorts and helmets. To me, the first impression should be engraved in the coach's mind forever.

It was a typical team drill . . . full offense against full defense, running plays full speed, but, of course, no tackling. We were told to tag off instead of tackling. I was getting my shot at strong safety when the ball was handed to Herschel Walker reacted quickly, remembering that you can't wait on Herschel. I hit the hole as quick as he did and BANG I tackled him!

Out of the corner of my eye I saw Coach Johnson heading my way. He was running, and he screamed at me, "I said no tackling!" Looking back, it wasn't very smart to make that kind of impression on Jimmy. And I now know I'm glad I didn't hurt Herschel if I had, we might not be wearing three Super Bowl rings.

I did like the competition. It brought out the best in me, as it always has. The reporters hounded me on this issue, but I told them in utter honesty how I felt: "After last season at 3-13, I can see why there might be a sense of needing to change people. It's only natural that the new coaches would

167

try to improve the team. So I don't take having to prove myself again negatively per se. I know the situation when you have to start anew."

"But," I added, "this is my seventh year in the NFL, and everybody knows I can play. I can make plays on the football field, not only at safety but on special teams. And if I continue to do that, I don't have any problems."

I worked hard that training camp, and I learned a great deal about the new regime. The contrasts between a Landry run team and a Johnson-run team became apparent. Coach Landry was a football genius who, consequently, ran every aspect of the game. But when it came to motivating his players, Coach Landry left that to the assistants. He also encouraged the older players to motivate the younger ones.

With Coach Johnson things flip-flopped. He allowed the assistant coaches to run the different aspects of the game while he, as head coach, majored on motivation. We soon saw that Coach Johnson was a master motivator of men. Before we even arrived at training camp, the coaches put us through some tests to assure them we were ready for camp.

With Coach Landry, camp always began with the "Landry Mile." You had to run the mile under a certain time. The toughness came because the "Landry Mile" was really a mile-and-a-half. It was a killer.

Coach Johnson had his own version of torture. The test involved running sixteen 110-yard dashes, back to back. If you were a lineman, you had to run each 110 in nineteen seconds or less. Everyone else on the team had to run all of them in seventeen seconds or less.

This test was met with absolute dread. It hurt. We actually trained for it because it was so painful. A lot of the guys buckled under this test. I thanked God for the fact that I had been exposed to the identical drill during my days at the University of Tennessee. Coincidentally, the trainer for the Cowboys at that time was the trainer for the Volunteers during my years in Knoxville. His name was Kevin O'Neal, and he had come in with Coach Johnson.

Preparing for that summer in Thousand Oaks produced some memorable moments. I remember a rookie in Dallas swooning during the sixteen 110's drill. Coach Johnson got right in his face. "What's your problem, boy?" he asked, knowing full well the television cameras were rolling.

"Coach," the poor guy squeaked out between gasps for breath, "I've got asthma."

"Asthma, my *!#*!" Coach screamed. "The asthma field is over there!" he added, pointing off the field. The player was cut that day.

Like I said, I did okay on that drill because I had been through it under Coach Majors. But most of the other guys felt like they had died that day. Coach Johnson was clear with the players on his code of requirements. As he described his rules, he would say, "Here's the line, guys. Step over it and you're gone." And he meant it.

Coach really likes to have fun, but not when it's time to work. He had an uncanny ability to develop tunnel vision when it came to football. If he was that focused, he expected his players to be the same way. I liked that.

The deeper we got into camp, the more obvious it became to me that I would not be returning to the strong safety position. Once that became clear, I shifted my focus, battling for playing time in other situations. I nailed down my spot on special teams and also went after the linebacker position in the Nickel Defense.

Hard work paid off because I landed both of those positions. Once again-to the surprise of my critics-it appeared that I was going to make the team. It took a lot of work to gain the confidence of Dave Campo, our secondary coach, and Dave Wahnstedt, our defensive coordinator, who are some of the most knowledgeable coaches around. With Coach Johnson's reputation for speed, making the team would become a real feather in my cap.

Camp still had its memorable moments. Nighttime snacks are very important to players--especially to the ones who are large men! Most guys had a good selection of treats, but Doug Cosbie was best known as the "King of the Late Night Snacks."

After many days of Tom Rafferty emptying Cosbie's snack bowls, Cosbie decided to retaliate. Doug filled his snack bowls with Puppy Chow. Tom found his way into Doug's room and began munching away without skipping a beat. He never missed a nighttime snack!

Our preseason games gave us some real optimism. Many coaches use preseason as an extension of practice. Consequently, the score isn't important. Not so with Coach Johnson. Every game, including preseason games, were there to be won.

We opened down the road in San Diego. We dominated them, walking away with a 20-3 victory. The next week we played the Los Angeles Raiders at the Coliseum. Once again we came out in front 27-20.

At 2-0, we traveled to Mile High Stadium in Denver to face John Elway and the Broncos. This team was geared more toward winning preseason games, so it proved to be a real contest. At the end of regulation, it was deadlocked 21-21. We were heartbroken when we lost in overtime 24-21. The plane trip home was like a wake at a funeral. Lighten up, Coach, I wanted to say. It's just a preseason game. It doesn't even count!

Our final preseason game brought us home to Texas Stadium ... at last. The local fans were finally able to get their first up-close look at the Jimmy Johnson version of the Dallas Cowboys. We were up against our interstate rival, the Houston Oilers.

Since it was the final preseason game, it was treated more like a regular season game. Like the game in Denver the week before, it was a close one. But when the gun signaled the game's conclusion, we were triumphant, winning 30-28.

You'd have thought we had just won the Super Bowl!

There was wild cheering from the stands and our side of the field. But by far the most memorable scene was one that we saw again on certain special occasions ... Jimmy Johnson and Jerry Jones hugging each other in jubilation as they strode off the field together amid all the pandemonium.

There was an excitement in the city of Dallas about the "new" Cowboys. The first nine days of September were sheer ecstasy. On September 10, we opened the regular season. We began on the road in New Orleans. To our dismay, the Saints beat us soundly 28-0. It was the first of many long plane rides back to Dallas.

If there was one word that characterized that first year with Coach Johnson, it would be change. The team was changing so much, it was barely recognizable from week to week. It wasn't uncommon to have three different starters in three consecutive weeks. This produced a lot of struggle within the team. In the NFL, you must have continuity in order to play like a team. We were lacking that quality during the '89 season.

After losing to the Saints, we lost to the Falcons, the Redskins, the Giants, and the Packers. In the loss to Green Bay, there was a good example of how mixed up things were that season. Because there was so much change occurring, we knew we had better do as we were told by the coaches or we'd be sitting on the bench.

We were on the road, playing in Milwaukee. With thirty seconds to go in the first half of our game against the Packers, we were on defense in our two-minute drill. The coaches called a man-to-man coverage, anticipating a short pass. We had the field covered short-middle and deep-middle. Before Green Bay lined up for the play, we knew they were going to Sterling Sharpe. We were in the wrong coverage. We were set up for plays to the middle of the field and he was set to run a deep corner pattern.

We considered calling off the coverage, and moving to a coverage that would have worked. But the truth was, we were all scared to call off the coverage the coach had sent in. If you went against his wishes and it didn't work, you could be history.

So the Packers ran the play. Sterling ran twenty yards, then cut to the sideline. He was wide open. Catching the pass, he continued to run for a total of eighty yards and a touchdown. All we could think of was, At least we didn't contradict the coaches.

With a 0-5 record, Coach Johnson decided to really shake things up. He traded Herschel Walker to the Minnesota Vikings. Hindsight is always 20-20, as they say, and looking back, it was a rather brilliant move on Coach's part. But at the time ... boy, did he ever have to take the flak! The trade didn't produce any immediate relief from our losing problems either. We went on to lose the next three games to the 49ers, the Chiefs, and the Cardinals.

After starting out 0-8, life was pretty miserable around the Cowboys ... and the whole Dallas area. The Dallas economy was going through the savings-and-loan scandals, and it seemed only fitting that their football team had the worst record in the NFL. Those were dark days in Dallas and they were especially dark for the Cowboys.

But even after a heartbreaking loss or an especially difficult practice, it all fell mute when I sat in the dark holding three beautiful babies . . . rocking them to sleep. Isn't it amazing how a guy can be so violent for two or three straight hours ... and then God puts everything in perspective as he holds his children in his arms? They didn't have a clue about how miserable my life was with the Cowboys at this time, and holding them close really seemed to erase much of my pain. It would soon get better ... at least for a little bit.

First Christmas

Our only win that season occurred the following week.

We were 0-8, going into the fierce rivalry between us and the Washington Redskins. To make matters worse, we were playing at RFK Stadium in Washington, D.C. Things didn't look too promising.

But to the surprise of every football fan in America, the Cowboys beat the Redskins that day 13-3. Our team was wild with jubilation! We were all out on the field, running around like chickens with their heads cut off. We were giving "high fives," hugging, smacking helmets, pads, tails ... anything! It had been so long in coming.

I ran smack into Coach Johnson midfield. In my reckless jubilation, I did something that I found out later was taboo. I reached out my hand, placed it on his head ... and messed up his hair!

That magic moment was to be the only magic we'd experience that season. Our best winning percentage was 1-8, since we went on to lose the rest of the games in 1989.

But many lessons were learned in that first season for Coach Johnson. Perhaps the most significant lesson was the need for continuity. At the end of the season Coach called us together for an important announcement. "We made some mistakes this past season. We're not gonna keep making changes. The people who are in this room right now are the nucleus of our team for next year. Start working now in order to make the team this fall. If you can make the grade, we want you."

That little pep talk proved to be very pivotal in the coming success of the Cowboys. It was as if Coach was saying, "The NFL is different from college. I've learned that now. So we'll form a team from what's here and not dink around with a lot of petty changes." That's exactly what we veterans wanted and needed to hear because it offered hope.

As training camp opened in July of 1990, I realized it was the same song ... next verse. I was going to have to prove myself all over again. Making the team was far from a given in my case.

The press was in a feeding frenzy, with most all of the reporters writing me off. Here's a sample article:

Bill Bates has seen the warning signs: Speed kills.

To clarify, Bates' lack of speed is hurting his chances of cracking the odds and making the Cowboys roster for an improbable eighth season. Bates, whose full-tilt playing style continues to make him a fan favorite, is no lock to make the forty-seven-man roster. Coach Jimmy Johnson brought in two Plan B free agent safeties, Antonio Gibson and James Washington. Both easily whip Bates in a footrace.

For Johnson, forty-yard speed is the measurable that surpasses all other factors. Among Dallas' defensive backs, Bates is the slowest 'poke around. Bates is in the option year of his contract and a new offer has not materialized. He's also a realist. As an eight-year veteran, he knows he's not in Johnson's five-year master plan.

Bates is painfully aware that his lack of speed hampers his chances of making the squad. His almost slavish adherence to his off-season conditioning program won't make him any faster or quicker. That's also frustrating. The Cowboy coaching staff is not even thinking of Bates as a possible starter. His slowness afoot would soon be exposed, they say. But Bates is a solid contributor as a linebacker in the Nickel Defense and his special-teams work remains first rate. Bates in 1984 became the first NFC player ever to be picked for the Pro Bowl based on special teams play.

"Bill's primary role is on special teams," Johnson said. "It comes down to how valuable he is on special teams. He can do some good things in the secondary. But we have other players who have more speed and really fit into the system a little better."

Bates still views himself as the obscure free agent from Tennessee who secured a roster spot against all odds in 1983. "Every year, I'm fighting for a job and it makes me proud of what I've accomplished, considering where I came from," Bates said. "If they don't think I bring enough, then I'll do it someplace else. But I'm proud to be a Cowboy. I want to finish my career here."

So, once again, it was time to shoot for the star.

I worked as hard as I could at training camp and nailed down my positions at linebacker for the Nickel and special teams. When the regular season opened at home against the San Diego Chargers, I was there. And it turned out to be a good game for me.

Opening at home is usually an advantage for the home team. But we were on a streak ... a losing streak. We had lost the last fourteen consecutive home games. We wanted to turn that around.

It began as a close game. Tied 7-7 at the end of the first quarter, we went in the locker room behind 14-7 at halftime. The third quarter was scoreless. Early in the fourth quarter we kicked a field goal, so it was 14-10.

Late in the fourth quarter, we made a noble attempt at driving the ball down the field but fell short, being forced to punt. San Diego took over possession and drove only to our forty-eight-yard line. With fourth down and six, the punt teams came on the field.

Coach Avezzano would have us play a really aggressive defense on punt situations. We would overload one side of the line with six guys in an attempt to block the punt, keeping only two on the other side of the line. I was lined up as one of the two men on the left side.

San Diego's head coach, Dan Henning, had decided to go for a fake punt in an attempt to gain the six yards necessary for the first down, and in so doing, hold onto the ball and eat up the clock. So when the ball was hiked, it wasn't hiked to the punter, but instead to Gary Plummer, a linebacker who had been put in to receive this short snap. He took the ball and ran ... right up my side of the field. Fortunately, I had sniffed out this possibility, so I was ready for him. This was my chance!

I tackled him before he could get the first down. We took over possession and momentum. With less than two minutes left in the game, Troy ran the ball in from the one-yard line and we won the game 17-14!

The locker room was mobbed with reporters who had previously put me down ... now they were ready to exalt me. They already had Coach Avezzano quoted as saying, "Bill Bates was the guy who made the play that enabled us to be in the position to win the game. You have to have knowledgeable players who can make the extra play for you and Bill did that. We had the proper defense called in case they did go for it. When they did go for it, they had a chance, but did not execute properly and Bates made the play."

Sitting in the locker room, tired and sweaty, I told the reporters my view of the play. "I had been blocked by the right tackle for the whole game, but not this time. So I knew something was up ... that I would either block the kick or it was going to the personal protector (Plummer). All of a sudden I saw it hit him in the chest, and all you do is react. Fortunately, my angle was enough so I could come back down inside and trip him up. It was just like in practice when our tackle didn't block me."

I became pretty overwhelmed in the locker room that afternoon. With tears in my eyes, I told the press, "I want to publicly thank the Lord for allowing me to even be playing this game."

I had worked so hard to overcome all of the public pressure about making the team. I was greatly relieved to go from the bubble to the hero. Even if it only lasted for a moment, it sure felt good.

I was honored to be the topic of Drew Pearson's column that week in the Dallas Cowboy Weekly. The former Cowboy great wrote:

This story has a happy ending. As you know, Bates not only made the team, but Coach Johnson rewarded him by naming Bill Special Teams Captain. And just as every story has a moral, this one is no different. The moral of the story is simple: Through hard work and a strong determination to succeed, you can overcome the toughest odds. The underdog doesn't always get the short end of the stick, and nice guys don't always finish last.

"Hopefully, Bates' teammates were observant of his personal experience and they will learn from it. Just because the Cowboys will be underdogs throughout the 1990 season doesn't mean they can't have a successful season. You can certainly count on Number 40 giving his all to make that happen.

Our team was an underdog throughout the entire season.

After the great win over the Chargers, we went on to lose the next three, before picking up a victory over Tampa Bay. Only one more win in the next five weeks put us at 3-7 in mid- November.

At that point things began to turn around for our team.

The successes that Jimmy Johnson was to enjoy started November 18, 1990 against the Rams in Anaheim. We beat them 24-21 in a confidence-builder. The following Thursday was Thanksgiving, on which we always played a game. This year it was against our archrivals, the Washington Redskins. On a roll from our new-found confidence, we were victors 27-17.

Now we were cooking! We defeated New Orleans and Phoenix-four straight wins to even us up at 7-7. Two days before Christmas, we traveled to Philadelphia with a new word in our vocabularies-the possibility of appearing in a playoff.

Very early in the game our confidence was shaken. Troy Aikman was injured on a play and the doctors said he was unable to return. We never brought ourselves back together that day, thus, losing to the Eagles 17-3.

But because of the results around the league that day, we were still in control of our own destiny. If we beat Atlanta next week, we were in the playoffs! We were still alive ... there was still hope.

The head coach for Atlanta in 1990 was Jerry Glanville.

The man notorious for leaving tickets at "will-call" for Elvis was just as crazy as a coach. The Falcons had been eliminated from playoff consideration weeks ago. So in order to fire up his team, Glanville was intent on beating us in Atlanta that final Sunday of the season.

He wanted to capitalize on the absence of Troy in our offense. He wanted to keep us out of the playoffs!

Going into Atlanta, we knew the Falcons wanted to play the role of spoiler; we just didn't know how badly they wanted it. After the game we found out how serious they were.

The game didn't go our way. Babe Laufenberg replaced Aikman, but was only able to produce one touchdown. The game ended 26-7 and with it ended our playoff hopes.

Down in the Falcon locker room there was pandemonium.

Before the game Jerry Glanville had shown the team what they could enjoy if they won. Since they won, he uncorked bottles of champagne from cases in the locker room ... just like it was a Super Bowl victory.

There was nothing wrong with what Coach Glanville did, but I'll have to admit, it sure hit me the wrong way. Being such a strong competitor, I was deeply disappointed that we missed the playoffs, especially since we came so close to making it.

But on the positive side, those last six games really set us in motion for the great days ahead. Finishing at 7-9 for the year was good-looking after the 1-15 season the year before.

So I turned my attention away from football as our season concluded the day before New Year's Eve. The year 1991 was at our doorstep ... it would turn out to be a good year for the Cowboys. It would also be a good year for the Bates' family because there's a little detail I neglected to mention ....

Denise was pregnant again.

"Call Me and Tell Me How Many There Are!"

Back in May of 1990 we threw a big birthday party, celebrating the first birthday of Graham, Brianna, and Hunter. We really wanted to do it up right. Our idea was to give this party as a "thank you" to all the people who had helped us with the arrival of the triplets the previous year.

Besides the usual invitations to family, friends, and neighbors, we also sent invitations to our obstetrician, our neonatologist, and others who were there in the delivery room. It was a big shindig. All the way through the party, however, I couldn't help noticing how tired Denise looked.

"Are you feeling okay?" I asked.

"Not really," she replied. "I feel sick."

"You're probably run down from all the work to pull off this party," I suggested. But I could tell by her look that she didn't agree with my diagnosis. The party was a resounding success, but even after it was over, Denise was still feeling crummy. This went on for a week after the party . . . two weeks ... four weeks.

Six weeks after the party Denise was no better. One night that week I threw out another suggestion: "Are you pregnant?"

Actually Denise had suspected that very thing for awhile. So I encouraged her to find out if she was or wasn't.

The next day she loaded up the triplets in the van to head off to the grocery store. As was her fashion, once she arrived at the grocery store, she grabbed two shopping carts-one for the groceries and one for the kids. She would push the kids while pulling the groceries in the cart behind her. It looked like the Bates Family Kiddie Train.

While she was at the grocery store, Denise saw some home pregnancy test kits and decided to purchase one. As she was about to throw it in the cart behind her, one of the kids grabbed it out of her hands-as a precocious one-year-old would be prone to do.

Rather than create a scene, she allowed the kids to play with the box. To onlookers at the grocery store, this was quite a comical sight. Here was this young mother, her hands full with three one-year-olds, who were playing catch with a home pregnancy test kit!

Once she made her way through the check-out line-with people staring in disbelief at what she was purchasing- Denise loaded kids and groceries in the van and headed home. Since this all occurred during the off-season, I was home when she arrived back.

After the groceries had been put away, Denise calmly went into the bathroom to administer the test. I waited curiously for the answer. I tried to be as patient as possible, but she didn't come out of the bathroom. After awhile I knew she had enough time to have administered the test to every woman in Dallas, so I softly knocked on the bathroom door.

"Denise? Can I come in?"

"Yes," she whispered.

I entered the bathroom to find her sitting on the floor between the sink and the toilet.

"Well?" I asked.

"It's positive." She spoke clearly and calmly .. Then she smiled and looked up at me with those crystal blue eyes, wet with tears.

"I want you to make an appointment to see the doctor right away," I added with true concern.

"Okay," she agreed.

Then I couldn't help but have a little fun with her.

"You go to the doctor," I said, "And after he examines you, call and tell me how many there are!"

We laughed. I helped her up and she went to the phone to call her obstetrician. "I'd like to make an appointment," she said into the phone. Because of the triplets, the entire office knew Denise and loved her.

"You need an appointment?" the voice asked over the line.

"Yes," she replied. "I'm pregnant."

In truly professional medical etiquette, the voice on the phone relayed the information to the rest of the office. And the result was fascinating. The entire office started laughing!

"You're pregnant ... again ... already?"

Once the laughter died down and the kidding subsided, the appointment was made and Denise visited their office.

The doctor administered his own pregnancy test, just to confirm Denise's findings. "You're right," he concluded. "You're pregnant."

"I told you so," Denise kidded.

"Well, let's see how many are in there," he suggested. So they set up the sonogram.

As he examined her, he made his assessment. "It appears that you are about fourteen weeks along," he estimated.

"How many are in there?" Denise asked nervously. The doctor smiled. "There's just one."

Sighing in relief, Denise got the word to me. I, too, was relieved. We were up for whatever God had in mind, but the unmistakable truth was clear: Even with one, it meant that in a few short months we were going to be the proud parents of four kids under the age of two!

Having gone through the ordeal of carrying triplets, this pregnancy was far more enjoyable for Denise. Thankfully, this pregnancy didn't demand bed rest, early hospitalization, or extended medication. It was simply a lot more fun ... if I dare describe pregnancy in that way.

The only restriction from the doctor came in Denise's fifth month. "No more lifting the kids," he announced. It was a protective measure which made perfect sense. The demands being made on Denise's life by three one-year-olds were pretty stiff.

So for a period of about five months, we hired a young girl named Tina to work as an au pair. She was just what we needed to assist Denise in some of the day-to-day routine that I couldn't help with because of my schedule. Tina helped take care of the kids, cleaned, cooked, and did other little domestic odds and ends around the house.

Thus, the pregnancy went along without a hitch. As delivery day drew closer, the doctor made us aware of the fact that Denise would have to have another Caesarean section.

"Because you had a C-section with the triplets, we cut you horizontally and vertically," the doctor explained. "I wouldn't want to take any unnecessary risk with those incisions."

So a week before the actual due date, our doctor scheduled a C-section. The date was February 18, 1991. Having a baby Caesarean section is much different than the stereotypical mad dash to the hospital. There is no running through red lights, no flagging down an officer for a police escort to the hospital, no "I almost had the baby in the back seat of a taxi- cab" sort of scenario.

It's quite the opposite. Early in the morning of February 18, the alarm went off. The operation was scheduled for 10:00 A.M., but the doctor wanted us there by 7:00 A.M. I knew I was in for a big day, so I started my morning with a hearty breakfast. I ate enough for two people, which was wise, since Denise was not allowed to eat before the operation. She sat across the breakfast table and watched me eat with a look of total disgust.

I grabbed her suitcase, threw it in the backseat, and put her in the car. We coolly and calmly drove off to the Medical City Dallas for the birth of our baby. To look at us in that car, we probably looked like a young married couple going off to work in their chosen careers.

Once we arrived at Medical City, the staff took over. As they prepped Denise, I donned my gown, mask, hat, and slippers . . . just as I had done twenty months previously. It seemed awfully quick to be back in this outfit!

We were pleased to see that many of the people who had helped us with the births of Graham, Brianna, and Hunter were going to assist us in this birth as well. It looked like a reunion of several of the nurses, doctors, obstetricians, and neonatologists.

One thing from the previous birth that wasn't present was fear. The whole atmosphere in the delivery room was far less tense and stressful. Giving birth can't really be described as "fun," but the difference in mood between the triplets' birth and this one was noticeable.

At 10:30 A.M. we watched as our son was born. This was no three-pound preemie. Tanner Forrest Bates weighed seven pounds, eight ounces. We were so proud as we got our first look at our newest addition. What a treat it was for Denise to be able to hold him soon after his birth. To see Tanner in her arms as she was wheeled out of the delivery room was even more special, since it had not been possible with the triplets.

Once again we were so grateful to the Lord for entrusting us with such a beautiful little life. Everything else pales in significance when you hold one of your babies in your arms. I would have five months to get to know Tanner before training camp started up again.

The year 1991 was a year for new beginnings. Along with our new son, we also started a new business. An opportunity presented itself that looked too good to pass by. Denise and I acquired a 386-acre ranch in McKinney, Texas, about thirty minutes outside of Dallas. We got it for a good price, and we also had a brainstorm of an idea on how to generate income from the property. Our goal was to turn it into a dude ranch, where groups of people could come and get a taste of western hospitality. The first project was to erect a huge, ten-thousand- square-foot pavilion that would hold hundreds of people. In the pavilion would be a bandstand on which live bands could perform. We also set up long, wooden, ranch-style tables and benches, so folks could enjoy a Texas barbecue-complete with all the trimmin's. There was also a mechanical horse for riding and a service area for cold drinks, nachos, popcorn, and various other treats.

Outside the pavilion were horses for horseback riding, several lakes for the best fishing around, two softball diamonds, horseshoe pits, volleyball courts, and a swimming pool. It had all the potential for a fabulous party place, and Denise and I were excited about the prospects.

We opened the Bill Bates Cowboy Ranch on the first of May that year for six hundred Pepsi Cola employees. We began experiencing moderate success. Since we had no heat in the pavilion at that point, we waited until the summer of '92 to reopen, and we did well. Then we added heat and air to the pavilion and hired a full-time ranch manager ... Katherine Schieb. She took over the day-to-day operations of the ranch, handling everything with speed and efficiency. She-better than anyone else we could have hired-knew what Denise and I wanted out of this ranch. Much of that understanding was due to the fact that she is Denise's mom!

"I'm Not Bullet-proof for a Reason"

When training camp time arrived in July of 1991, I reported to the campus of St. Edward's University in Austin, Texas, as did all my teammates. Once we were there, everyone knew three things:

Austin would be hotter than a stove top ... as always.

Training camp would be agony ... as always.

The big question would be, "Will Bates make the team this year?" ... as always.

All three of those statements proved to be true. The Cowboys had moved to Austin for training camp in Jimmy Johnson's second year as head coach. He preferred Austin to Thousand Oaks and, frankly, the only reason we were in Thousand Oaks his first year was because we were contractually bound to be there.

As one of the players, it didn't really matter where you held training camp because no matter where it was held, you hated it. That hatred knew no geographical boundaries. Camp was always horrible. The press had even quoted me one time saying, "If you didn't get hurt in training camp, you'd feel like you weren't doing anything." To further drive home my point, I had said, "Everybody's beat up to one extent or another."

I tried to bring the best attitude I could into camp. In terms of the location, I looked at it this way, in Austin, it was so hot that you couldn't practice for long. But those brutal practices in the scorching heat made you tougher. Likewise, in our days back in Thousand Oaks, we practiced longer since the heat wasn't as oppressive, and it was those long practices that made us tough. It was kind of a "name your poison" type of situation. Either way you looked at it, camp was a killer . . . but a toughener.

We brought a great deal of hope and anticipation into the camp of '91. The Cowboys had just completed a record-setting draft. Our leaders in the front office acquired seventeen picks from twelve rounds, thanks to deals with other clubs. After a pre-draft trade with the New England Patriots, we had the number one overall pick. We went for defensive tackle Russell Maryland, who had played for Coach Johnson at the University of Miami.

At six-foot-one, 274, he had won the Outland Trophy and demonstrated amazing potential for our defensive squad. He wouldn't let us down.

More specifically related to my situation was the fact that three of the draft picks were linebackers. Dixon Edwards from Michigan State, Godfrey Myles from Florida, and Darrick Brownlow from Illinois were all being touted as guys who could play the Nickel Defense, paving the way for my exit from the team. I needed to get up for a challenge once again.

To add further drama to training camp, there were three players conspicuous by their absence. Emmitt Smith, Michael Irvin, and Jay Novacek were all holding out for better contracts. We needed to get them signed. Contract negotiations are always delicate, so I knew they wouldn't hurry on our account. They needed to please both sides of the bargaining table.

In one of our team's little ironies, despite these three major players holding out, we had the best training camp out of the nine I had attended. There was a cohesiveness to the team that brought with it confidence and poise. Like whipped cream on top of the sundae, Emmitt, Michael, and Jay were finally signed to their contracts.

And once again I had successfully battled for a spot on the forty-seven-man roster. Reporters were asking me what I thought was ahead and I was widely quoted as saying, "This is the most together we've been as a team since I've been with the Dallas Cowboys."

Hopes ran high. Troy had suspected that these holdouts would be in the lineup by season's start, so that sneaky little quarterback had been faithfully faxing them plays from Austin to Dallas. They were as ready as they could have been without attending camp.

We opened on the road against the Cleveland Browns. In front of a huge crowd of Browns fans, we defeated them 26-14. We went on to lose the next two games ... to everyone's surprise. But by mid-October we had come back to win the next four in a row. So we were 5-2, after a win over Cincinnati at home. In one of my many journeys into the land of injuries, I fractured my left hand in the Bengals game and had to have it put in a cast. But it never kept me from playing a single game.

Our special teams were awesome that year. Coach Avezzano put together a team that ranked number one in the NFL ... as well as getting him named Special Teams Coach of the Year. I was so into all the aspects of special teams play, that I was thrilled to hear of our top rating. I felt I was making a real contribution to our success.

We ended up with an 11-5 record and for the first time since Coach Johnson had taken over the Cowboys, we were heading to the playoffs.

Four days after Christmas we were thrilled to be absolutely frozen stiff on Soldier Field in Chicago to face Mike Ditka's Chicago Bears. I didn't know it at the time, but I was in for a real memory-maker.

It was a close contest throughout the entire game. By late in the fourth quarter, we held a small lead at 17-13. It was a precarious position because the Bears had the ball and the momentum. Their quarterback, Jim Harbaugh, was brilliantly driving the ball downfield. Our defense was playing valiantly, but we were tired.

Late in the game, Harbaugh called a pass play that brought a receiver my direction. When he passed the ball, I reacted quickly and in a split-second the momentum shifted. I intercepted the pass!

I was ecstatic. I started running with the ball, much to the dismay of my teammates. "GET ON THE GROUND! GET ON THE GROUND!" they continued to advise me. They wanted no risk of me getting tackled in a way to create a fumble with a Bears recovery. So I went down with no incident. It was a Cowboys ball.

Sprinting off the field, I was swarmed by men in white jerseys with blue numbers. Everyone was hugging me, pounding my shoulder pads, or slapping my behind. When I was finally left to myself, I went down on one knee and began to cry. It was overwhelming. To be a part of this team, this game, this too-good-to-be-true life ... it was almost too much. I was the hero. It was the greatest moment in my life up to that point.

Beating Ditka's Bears on Soldier Field....wow!

Returning to Dallas, we were met by our fabulous fans.

They were all cheering and screaming for us. It was exhilarating. When I drove up to our house, even our neighbors joined in the celebration. The house was "ballooned." Helium-filled balloons of all colors surrounded the house and the yard, extending congratulations to me for my interception. Once again I had to hold back the tears of joy.

The victory over the Bears put us in line to travel to Detroit the next week for the divisional playoff against the Lions. I'm sure glad I had such a good feeling coming out of Chicago ... 'cause it wasn't going to happen coming out of Detroit. We went into the game with hopes.

If we could beat the Lions, we postulated, we'd go to Washington to play the Redskins for the NFC championship and then right on to play in the Super Bowl. We had beaten the 'Skins in Washington in late November and thought we could do it again, if given the opportunity. The opportunity never materialized. It was taken away by the Lions' sensational running back, Barry Sanders.

The Lions were absolutely incredible that day. As the gun sounded in the Silverdome, the end of the road had come for the Cowboys. We had been embarrassed 38-6. So it was the Lions who went on to Washington the next week. But the Redskins were too tough for Detroit. Washington won and went on to face Buffalo in the Super Bowl. It was the second of Buffalo's four straight Super Bowl losses.

As I made my tenth trek to training camp, the press took up right where it had left off in their continuing saga of "Will Bill Bates Make the Team?" The Dallas Cowboys Weekly wrote:

Once again, Bates is battling younger, faster, stronger players for a roster spot. Each year those who make their living covering this cutthroat game scratch Bates' name from the roster when they attempt to project final cuts.

And later in the summer Bates survives because of his full-tilt approach to special teams and his ability to make plays on pass defense.

"People have been trying to retire me for so long that I'm used to it," Bates said. "I'd hope that after nine years I wouldn't have to keep proving myself, but that's the nature of this game. You're never sure where you stand. Even though I've done some good things, it's what have you done for me lately? Even when I was starting, I didn't feel I was a lock. I put pressure on myself, no matter what. So I'm still paranoid about the situation."

This summer the Cowboys rolled a platoon of rookie defensive backs into camp in an effort to patch last year's woeful defense. Bates' primary competition for a role on special teams and as a linebacker in the Nickel Defense comes from free agent Reggie Cooper.

Cooper is ten pounds heavier, an inch taller, and seven years younger than the six-foot-one, 205-pound Bates, who's thirty-one. But Bates' history on the special teams, for which he served as a team captain and second leading tackler last year, gives him a huge advantage.

"Any coach in the history of football would love to coach a Bill Bates," said special teams coach Joe Avezzano.

So with the familiar "Go out and prove yourself all over again" scenario as the backdrop, it was off to work in Austin. Training camp was actually pretty upbeat that year. There was excitement about Emmitt Smith winning the rushing title in the previous season. The team set a goal to help him win it two years in a row. That goal included taking the team all the way to the Super Bowl. We set our sights for a January trip to Pasadena.

We were fairly confident about our chances. We had secured safety Thomas Everett in a trade that bolstered our defensive backfield. I had a good camp, once again securing a position on the forty-seven-man roster. Fortunately for me, there wasn't much question in Coach Johnson's mind about my contribution to the team. Being the number one special teams in the NFL created a positive impact with the coaches.

Coach Johnson put more emphasis on special teams than Coach Landry did. The addition of Coach Avezzano only served to strengthen that fact. There was even an unspoken maxim among the players: If you're a backup player on the Dallas Cowboys, you'd better be able to play special teams. It was an important part of our game.

Coach Avezzano, a class act and great coach

189

As the regular season began, it looked as if our confidence was not misplaced. We won three in a row over the Redskins, the Giants, and the Cardinals. We went to Veterans Stadium in Philadelphia and suffered our first loss. The next game was at home against the Seattle Seahawks. We were 3-1, and I was personally feeling good. But all that was to change on a routine kickoff coverage.

It happened on a second-quarter kickoff. I was running downfield, intent on making the tackle. I thought I had gotten by my blocker, so I got ready to make a cut. I planted my foot, and suddenly felt the weight of the Seahawks blocker pushing against my shoulder, putting all the weight of the hit on my left knee. I waited for the Astroturf to give.

It didn't.

My knee stung a little, but my body compensated with a massive flow of adrenaline. I finished the play and ran off the field with what I thought was a knee that was "a little wobbly" ... as I told Dr. Vandermeer, the team physician. Sadly, he didn't agree with my diagnosis.

"I think you may have torn something in there," the doctor replied, as he was feeling my knee on the sideline.

"No way," I barked back, rather rudely. "You don't know what you're talking about!"

"You may be right," Dr. Vandermeer replied, "but just to be safe, let's go x-ray the knee to be sure nothing's wrong."

I reluctantly agreed. To my delight, the x-ray showed no broken bones.

"See?" I sneered.

"I'm still not satisfied," said the doctor. "The knee is not stable. I'll schedule you for an MRI tomorrow morning to check for the possibility of any ligament damage."

"Fine," I snapped. "But when you get the results, you'll see.

I'm not hurt. I can run a couple of miles on this knee right now!"

"Don't," was all the doctor replied.

By now Denise had been ushered into the locker room. Dr. Vandermeer brought her up to speed with his speculations, and I watched as her eyes filled with tears. The look in her face was unmistakable. If the doctor was correct, this would be the toughest battle I'd ever fight.

The next morning I was taken in for a magnetic resonance imaging test (MRI). Afterward, I cornered the doctor who administered the test. I could see he was holding the results in his hand.

"Did I tear my ACL?" was my one simple question.

"Dr. Vandermeer will be with you shortly to discuss your test results," he replied in a rehearsed sort of manner.

"Come on, man, give me a break," I pleaded. "You've got the results right there. Just look at them real quickly."

Reluctantly, the doctor complied.

"Did I tear my ACL?" I repeated.

He just stared at the results.

"Did I?"

"Yes," he whispered, then continued down the hall. It turned out that I did one fine job on my knee. I had torn my anterior cruciate ligament-better known as the ACL. The ACL stabilizes the knee and keeps the lower leg from extending too far forward. To add to the severity of the injury, I had also tom my meniscus cartilage and my medial collateral ligament. The medial collateral ligament prevents the knee from moving side to side. It's the strongest ligament in the knee.

Deep down inside, I had known about the damage right when it occurred. 1 just didn't want to admit to it. "1 was into denial," 1 later told the press in an interview. "I got hurt doing what I've done for ten years. I've always wiggled, run around, made cuts, and not let guys block me. People say I'm not very fast, but 1 got pushed in the back when I got around the guy. So I'm not real surprised. 1 was going full bore. 1 got it when 1 planted my foot. If it had been grass, my shoe would have slipped and I would have just fallen. Artificial turf has caused more injuries than it's been worth.

"But every player knows the next play can be your last. It's a violent game. A lot of guys haven't gotten up, and I have. I've been blessed."

When I was asked to put it all into perspective, I was able to say publicly, "I have a tremendous amount of faith, and I know this injury is minor in relation to the big picture. I realize that I'm not bullet-proof for a reason. I'm shocked that I won't be lining up this Sunday when we beat Kansas City, but, as 'The Terminator' would say, 'I'll be back.'"

I meant all that I said, but the magnitude of the injury was staggering. I needed the normal reconstructive surgery and then a period of rehabilitation that could take from nine to twelve months.

My season was over.

That night Denise and I did the only thing we could think of. We both fell to our knees and asked God for the peace that only He could bring. "Lord," I cried, "You've been with us in our greatest hours and in our toughest hours. We're in a tough spot here, Lord. We need You. We need the comfort that only You can bring."

Like so many times before, the prayer helped quiet much of the trauma inside. God brought to my mind Romans 8:28, which explained God's perspective:

All things work together for good to them that love God . who are the called according to his purpose.

God had a reason for this injury. I vowed to do whatever the doctors told me to do in order to rehabilitate myself. But physically, I was in pain.

I didn't sleep at all that night. Between the pain and the agonizing reality that my good season was over, it was just too unsettling for sleep to come. When your knee hurts that bad, it's even difficult to toss and turn!

I was no stranger to injuries. In my college and professional career, I experienced well over two dozen injuries. To give a little overview, let's start at the toes and work up.

I've jammed both my big toes on different occasions. This injury is commonly referred to as "turf toe." It sounds innocent enough, but it's actually quite painful. Both my ankles have been twisted in games (I've already referred to the ankle twist in Denver, where it was intensified by the dry ice nitrogen bums up my leg).

During my freshman year at Tennessee, I had a partial tear of my medial collateral ligament-the same ligament I tore playing against Seattle-as well as the ACL and meniscus cartilage injury. I've had multiple tears of both groin muscles, and I've also pulled my stomach muscle.

Thigh bruises, a hip-pointer, and assorted broken ribs have also graced my life as an athlete. I've separated my right shoulder ... and I've separated my left shoulder. Working down the arms, I've broken my left wrist . . . and my left hand. I have a particular draw to finger damage. I've broken both my thumbs, dislocated both my pinkies, and broken my right ring finger on Phil Simms' New York Giants helmet. There have been a variety of skin bums on the turf.

I've had a stinger in my neck and stitches in my chin, lip, and eye. I've been poked in the left eye. Last, but not least, I experienced a concussion. (Remember "Tell my girlfriend I'm all right"?).

They informed me that they would conduct the surgery three-and-a-half weeks after the injury occurred. That would give the knee enough time to recover from the trauma and allow for the swelling to subside.

In that three-and-a-half-week period, my assignment was to get my quad muscle as strong as I could. By doing that strengthening, rehabilitation after the surgery would go along much quicker. I was interested in anything that would make this thing go quicker.

Meanwhile, the Cowboys had to go about the task of replacing me. In a move that was both honoring and rather humorous, it was announced that it would take five guys to replace me! The following list of substitutes was released to the press:

Middle linebacker-Ken Norton
Kickoff return-Darren Woodson
Kickoff coverage-Chad Hennings
Punt return-Tommy Agee
Punt coverage-Daryl Johnston

The twenty-five days between the injury and the surgery passed. To further illustrate the contrasts in my life, the day before the surgery I played eighteen holes of golf! Wearing a knee brace, I played against my buddy, Steve Beurlein. We always played competitive golf, and I wasn't going to let any- thing like some stupid major surgery on my knee get in my way. There was no question that I was hobbling around, but I shot a 79 that day. When we tallied up the score, I had beaten him.

When the day of the surgery arrived, I was ready. I had asked God to continue to give me His peace and I was as comfortable as I could be in that circumstance.

I have two very vivid memories of the surgery. The first memory is of the pain, which was excruciating. To ease the pain, I was given morphine every fifteen minutes, along with the other standard medications for a procedure of this nature. As a result of all the medications, it was common for the patient's bladder to tighten up ... which leads to my second vivid memory. I recall feeling like I had to go to the bathroom in a worse way than I had ever experienced. But I couldn't go! It was truly horrible.

After surgery Denise was right there. As I was wheeled into my room, she was there watching over me. That first night after the operation, I slept in little ten-minute catnaps, awakened often by the ongoing discomfort in my knee. Like the true champion she is, Denise was right there at my bedside to comfort me as best she could.

In a few days I was allowed to go home. The kids didn't know what to make of their daddy hobbling around on a pair of crutches.

I started rehab right away. I showed up at the Cowboys training facility at Valley Ranch. Waiting for me was Jim Maurer, who is the Cowboys assistant trainer in charge of the medical rehabilitation program. He immediately put me up on this odd-looking machine made of metal and black vinyl. I sat in the chair part of the machine with my left leg extended straight out in front of me. It felt awkward to be in this cold, sterile contraption. But nothing could fully prepare me for what was to happen on this machine-not even Jim's careful warning, "Now, this is going to hurt, Bill. So brace yourself."

The sole purpose of this machine was to get me to bend my knee. What was so distressing was that because of the operation, my knee did not want to bend ... so the end result was pain.

Bending the knee as soon as possible is necessary in order to break up any scar tissue that has developed. This makes rehab much easier. I'll have to admit that having someone deliberately bend my knee, knowing it would hurt, was something that went against my nature. But I knew there was a purpose. It was another real form of character testing.

A typical day would find me up early, showering, shaving, and driving off to Valley Ranch. First thing in the mornings, I attended the special teams meeting. From there I went to the training room for rehab on my knee for several hours. I rejoined the team for the noontime meal.

After lunch, while the team was out on the practice field, I would go into the weight room and put myself through the most strenuous upper-body workout I could endure. By about 2:00 P.M., I'd hobble out to the practice field and watch a little bit of practice. After observing a slice of their workout, I'd head for my pickup truck and drive home.

One of the saddest feelings I can recall is driving my truck out of the parking lot there at Valley Ranch. Because of the way the facility is laid out, you have to drive right by the practice field in order to exit the lot. I remember looking out the window of my truck ... yearning to be on that field with my teammates. Wanting to play and knowing I couldn't were two incompatible thoughts. If willing it could have made it happen, I would have been out there on the field giving it everything I had.

The Cowboys missed me. There were gaps, especially in special teams, that I knew I could have covered for them. But in spite of missing me, they kept on winning football games. After the Seattle Seahawks game-which we won- we were victorious in five of the next six games to put our record at 9-2 by Thanksgiving Day.

For home games I could stand on the sidelines with the team, or else the Cowboys could get me a press pass to sit upstairs at Texas Stadium with the writers. On Thanksgiving Day, my buddy Chris Wampler was in town, so we arranged with the front office to sit upstairs in the press section. My knee was really killing me that day. The only way I could get any relief was to extend my knee straight out. Doing that in the press area required sticking my leg out over a concrete wall, It definitely drew unwanted attention my way, but it did relieve some of the pain.

On away games I didn't travel with the team. It was horrible to sit at home in Dallas on game days. I would sit and watch the dock, thinking about what I'd be doing if I was playing that day. "I'd be in Chapel now," I'd murmur to myself. "I'd be listening to John Webber or Father Leo right now."

I'd carry this thought process through to kickoff. I'd be getting my ankles taped right now.

I'd be eating the pregame meal right now.

I'd be putting on my shoulder pads right now. I'd be lacing up my shoes.

I'd be out on the field warming up.

I was so into this mental torture that Denise began to worry. She thought I was going crazy. She was probably right too. Eventually I'd get so frustrated with my position that I'd get up from the chair, hobble over to my dog, Blitz, grab a leash, and take off for a walk. It was a pathetic sight to observe this beautiful Rottweiler dragging along this creaky old man. But I couldn't bear to sit there and watch what I was missing. Usually I could only walk Blitz for two quarters, which meant I was back in time to watch the second half.

The team continued to play well. By season's end the record was an incredible 13-3. The last regular season game was in Dallas against the Bears. We won 27-14. This meant that the playoffs were ahead for us one more time!

A personal highlight for me in an injured season has to be the Detroit game. The Cowboys were on the road, which meant I was relegated to watching it on TV. It was a blowout ... with the Lions getting embarrassed 37-3. After the game the television cameras went right into the Cowboys' locker room. As is our custom, game balls were presented for outstanding plays.

In a gesture of grace and class, Emmitt Smith and Michael Irvin stood on one of the benches in the dressing area and got the team to quiet down for one last presentation. In the midst of all the hoopla and in front of the TV cameras for all the world to see and hear-including me-they said: "For all that he has done all season to make a contribution to this team, we'd like to present this game ball to Bill Bates."

I cherished it.

"There's a Lot of Tape Left-You Can Still Tape Me!"

The Bill Bates Cowboy Ranch was doing well. Yet we still felt that if we had a little more exposure, the place would really explode. Well, out of the blue came an idea that was to provide the explosion we needed.

Since the Cowboys went 13-3 that year, we won our division. This meant, among other things, that we had a week off between the close of the regular season and the first play- off game. The schedule called for us to play the Philadelphia Eagles on January 10th in Dallas.

We had the week off, but the Eagles had to play that weekend. It was right after they won their game on our "off" weekend that Keller McCrary, a friend of mine, called me on the phone.

"The Eagles look pretty tough," he said. "Yeah, they do," I agreed.

"I think you're gonna need some serious excitement from the fans next Sunday," he continued.

"Right again," I said.

"Bill, I've got an idea. I think you should throw a gigantic pep rally out at your ranch next Friday night. Invite everybody in Dallas! It'll do a lot to build some excitement for the game on Sunday!"

As Keller was talking, I began to smile. This is a good idea! I thought.

"Let's do it!" I said.

A real Cowboy

And the plans were laid. Before we even had a minute to think, the word was out. A local television show, "Sunday Night Showtime," was made aware of our plans, and they announced it to the Dallas/Fort Worth Metroplex! They gave out the ranch's phone number to call for directions and immediately the phone started ringing ... and never stopped. It rang so much that we had to hire a temporary secretary just to handle phone calls.

I called my good friend, Tim Quintana, who is a lieutenant with the Collin County Sheriff's Department. When I told him what was planned, I asked if we could get two or three deputies out at the ranch for crowd control. "No problem!" he replied.

My initial expectation was a couple thousand people at the most. But because of the interest generated by the Sunday night TV show, forty-eight hours later I knew a couple thousand was a serious underestimation. I called back and asked Tim for a dozen deputies.

Next was the question, "How are we going to park all these cars?" We had plenty of space for the cars right there at the ranch, but we needed organization. I placed a call to Texas Stadium. They were more than happy to pitch in, so I hired the stadium's "car-parkers" to bring their crew out Friday night to keep the traffic under control.

Katherine took charge of the massive task of planning the food and drinks for the occasion. She ordered one hundred pounds of popcorn, eighty huge canisters of soft drinks, seventy-five kegs of beer, and cases and cases of nacho cheese with chips.

By Friday it appeared that we were as ready as we could be. It was time to wait for the people. We didn't have to wait very long. The pep rally was scheduled to begin at 7:00 P.M. At 5:00 P.M. the cars started to arrive. Radio stations were giving directions to the ranch on the air. Once the cars started pulling in, the steady stream of traffic remained constant for the next five-and-a-half hours! From 5:00 'til 10:30 that night, all you could see were headlights lined up for miles, waiting to get into the evening's festivities. It was like that scene out of Field of Dreams, where Kevin Costner "builds it" and the people come!

As much as we planned and prepared for the pep rally, we were overwhelmed with the results. The best estimates on our attendance for the evening were somewhere between 20,000 and 25,000 people! Tim estimated that we had to turn away one thousand cars!

It was crazy! We had a live band playing in the pavilion, and we topped off the evening with a huge bonfire. The highlight was burning a Philadelphia Eagle in effigy. The crowd went wild with enthusiasm.

At 2:00 A.M. Denise and I collapsed onto a couch out at the ranch house. In unison we looked at each other and through our exhaustion, said, "We'll never do this again!"

Little did we know that we'd turn right around and do it all over again for next year's postseason!

Anyway, all the effort paid off. By Sunday our fans were whipped into a heated frenzy. The Eagles came to town and they never had a chance. We beat them 34-10 in front of almost 64,000 screaming fanatics! Texas Stadium was really rocking that day.

The victory over Philadelphia gave us the chance to go to San Francisco for the NFC Championship Game. The assignment was clear ... beat the 49ers and go to the Super Bowl. Because of the magnitude of this game, the Cowboys allowed me to travel with the team, even though I was injured. I made the best of the trip . . . which included a California earthquake that shook my bed on the thirty-fifth floor of the hotel I tried to be an encourager to my teammates and help out wherever I could be of assistance. It was a wonderful trip for me ... I even snuck in a round of golf at the fabulous Olympic Club!

It was a rainy afternoon at Candlestick Park. The rain and wind whipped up the players and the fans. I stood helplessly on the sideline, wearing a rain slicker, but still soaked right through to the skin-wishing so badly that I could run out on the field to play.

Thanks to an unusually high amount of San Francisco turnovers, plus another 100+ yards game from Emmitt, we won the game. There was a tense moment for us in the fourth quarter. We had a fourth-and-one situation, where Coach Johnson decided to go for it. So we gambled ... and lost. The 49ers took over possession and promptly scored, bringing them to within four points. Thankfully, Troy connected with Kelvin Martin for a touchdown pass. We ended up winning the game 30-20.

The plane ride back to Dallas was a flying party! There was whooping and hollering and celebrating like I'd never seen before. The reality of the win was sinking in-we were going to the Super Bowl! The players were passing around the newly won NFC Championship trophy.

As it was moving from front to back, row to row, the excitement continued to mount. Jerry Jones, perhaps the happiest Cowboy of all, was in the rear of the plane, slapping backs and shaking hands. A group of players saw him and headed back to trap him.

"Hey, Mr. Jerry Jones, this is a great win, right?" they cheered.

"Yes, it is!" he replied.

"That's a great trophy there, isn't it?"

"That's true."

"Well, here's how we see it," they added. "It's a shame there's only one of those trophies. We can't all share it at the same time."

"Yeah?"

"Yeah. So we think, since you are the great owner that you are, that you should have replicas of that trophy made for each of us on the team so we can have our own personal trophy."

"So that's what you think, huh?" Jerry responded.

In the excitement of the moment, he agreed to get us all miniature replicas of the trophy. To make the situation even more delightful, he offered to wait until after the Super Bowl. If we won the Super Bowl, he would replace his offer by making us replicas of the Vince Lombardi Trophy! That's a lot of sterling silver, but we were more than willing to comply!

When the plane landed at Dallas/Fort Worth Airport, we were in for another surprise. Even though it was the middle of the night, and the plane landed over in a cargo area, we were shocked to see ten thousand fans waiting for our arrival. They were waving signs, screaming, and giving us the royal treatment. It felt good to be going to the Super Bowl, even if I couldn't play!

I never felt more like a "split-personality" than I did that week in January in Pasadena. Half of me was delighted to be a part of the team that was playing in the Super Bowl. That part of me pitched right in to do everything I could to support the team.

But I wanted to play so badly. This was an interesting point in my knee rehabilitation, in that the pain that I carried around for months was going away. The constant swelling that I had lived with all those months was also subsiding. I felt good physically!

The Cowboys flew to Los Angeles early that week.

Staying in Santa Monica, we used UCLA as our practice field. The Bills stayed in downtown L.A. and worked out at USC. I watched the team work out and tried to perfect my role as sideline cheerleader.

I needed a diversion from all the hype of the game in which I wasn't going to play. Fortunately for me, there was golf. My secret love is golf. I've loved and played the game since I was a kid. I'm a single-digit handicapper, and if I had my way, I'd figure out a way to join the pro tour after I retire from the NFL. I was recently asked what would be the perfect day for me? I quickly responded that I would get up at dawn and play golf 'til dusk.

If I can't play professionally, then I must live it vicariously through my friends who play on the tour. My good friend, Danny Briggs, has been playing professionally for as long as I have been in the NFL. He is a great player. He has bounced from the PGA Tour to the Nike Tour and continues to be successful. Seeing his struggle to make it makes me realize how tough the pro-golf tour has become. Thus, I know my dream of playing professionally is far-fetched ... but you have to keep a dream alive. Then again, when I see Fred Couples who belongs to my club, Glen Eagle, in Plano-it really makes my dream of playing shine even brighter.

I am a big fan of Fred Couples

That dream is living through my younger sister, Rachel. She played on the LPGA Futures Tour. Needless to say, we do not play competitive golf any longer.

Golf is good for me because it provides a way to get away from the focus I put on football. Since I am an extremely focused person, in order for me not to focus on football, there must be a diversion. Golf allows me to transfer my focus onto the little white ball. If you want to be a good golfer, concentration is essential. That's what golf brings to me. I've made a personal goal to never score above a 90. I have a hard enough time leaving the low 80s. If I don't stay in the low 80s, I get so angry at myself. It's not a pretty picture!

As I mentioned earlier, I felt very fortunate to be able to play at the prestigious Bel Air Country Club. But what I didn't mention is that I loved it so much, I worked out a way to play it twice while I was in southern California. Not only did the game divert my focus, but the course was so beautiful and rich in Hollywood history that it, too, took my mind off what I was missing.

The Cowboys allowed the players to bring their wives and children, which I really appreciated. The NFL had also set up all these side tours of southern California attractions we could take if we were interested. Denise and I took Graham, Brianna, Hunter, and Tanner for their first visit to Disneyland. We all had a great time for at least seven minutes ... before we were treated to a rare southern California rainstorm!

My most vivid memory of Disneyland was standing in a line (that was long enough to reach Vermont), waiting to purchase six bright yellow Mickey Mouse rain ponchos. Once we purchased them, we all put them on and looked as foolish as any family I've ever seen.

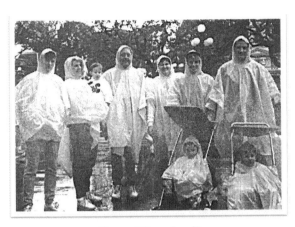

Fun at Disneyland?

Denise had her own adventure during Super Bowl week. We have a good friend in Dallas named John McGill.

John runs a very successful public relations firm, and he's been very instrumental in helping us with many of the charity events in which we participate. One of John's friends is Gary Collins, who at the time was hosting the Home show, along with Sarah Purcell, weekday mornings on ABC.

John came up with a fun idea that he passed on to Gary, who also thought it was great. "How about a Barbecue Recipe Cook-off on your TV show between the Dallas Cowboys wives and the San Francisco 49ers players?" John suggested to Gary and his staff.

"With the 49ers out of contention for the Super Bowl, they've got the time ... and I know they'd love it!"

Steve Young was chosen as the 49ers cook-off captain and Denise was captain for the Cowboys wives. Fortunately, through our contacts out at the Bill Bates Cowboy Ranch, Denise knew how to get her hands on the winning barbecue recipe. She called Arnold Sanchez, of "Arnold's Barbecue," whose barbecue was our favorite catered dish out at the ranch. He whipped together enough food to provide a complete meal for fifty people-and sent it out to L.A. He sent the recipe-along with the seventeen ingredients necessary to make the sauce to California with John McGill. The way the show would work is each team would make their barbecue sauce live on the air and then we would eat the food that had been prepared ahead of time. So we were ready to go!

The morning of the show, they came to get Denise at 4:30 A.M. I tried to be as supportive as I could from my spot under the covers.

"Do good, honey," I said in my sleep.

Once at the studio, they took the wives to the media room for coffee and donuts. Then it was off to makeup. Sitting in the makeup chair next to Sarah Purcell, Denise was having the time of her life. After meeting briefly with the hosts and producers, it was showtime.

Gary and Sarah introduced the players and the wives like it was a ballgame and they were running through the tunnel. "The captain for the Cowboy wives, Denise Bates!" ... and Denise ran out onto the stage. They introduced the other five wives who participated. "Pono Tuinei! (Mark's wife), Tammy Jeffcoat! (Jim's wife), Gina Gesekl (John's wife), Lisa Clayton! (Tony Casillas' wife), Secola Edwards! (Dixon's wife).

Then they did the same for the 49ers: "The captain for the 49ers, Steve Young!" ... and all the way through 'til all their players were out on the "field." Everyone was being such good sports, so it was really an enjoyable time for all involved. The Cowboys wives started making their sauce. Denise kept referring to a secret ingredient as "smoked buffalo" in a kidding reference to our Super Bowl foes. The wives quickly deduced they would win when the 49ers started making their sauce with about four ingredients-- mostly ketchup and sugar. They couldn't hold a candle to the seventeen ingredients from Dallas!

So Gary Collins and Steve Young were blindfolded and asked to taste from both plates to decide a winner. It was a good omen ... the Cowboys wives were victorious!

One of my diversions also involved television. Because of my injury, I had greater availability than the other players, so I was talked into doing a live broadcast back to Dallas every night for their local news and sports. Craig James from our CBS affiliate, Channel 4, persuaded me to share my views and general observations on our week in Pasadena. Once I finished his show, I'd also do guest shots on the other two networks, Channels 5 and 8. It felt like I was on the air all the time that week.

The day of the game finally arrived. The night before Coach Johnson had all the players move to another hotel to be away from family and friends. It wasn't necessary for me to move, but I chose to anyway. I was determined to be as much a part of this experience as I could.

Game day began, as always, with chapel. Father Leo and John Webber both spoke to us that day. I usually found chapel to be a powerful time, but this day was particularly moving. There in my seat in the hotel meeting room, I began to feel the tears welling up in my eyes. "Thank You, Lord," I silently prayed. "Thank You for giving me the opportunity to be here today."

I thought about what Dan Marino and John Elway had said to me earlier in the week on the Bel Air golf course. It was good to be here, no matter what part I played.

After chapel it was the pregame meal and then off to the Rose Bowl. As the guys began warming up, I assumed my position. As Mike Saxon, our punter, and Lin Elliott, our kicker, practiced their kicks, I was out there shagging balls for them. This allowed them more time to concentrate on kicking rather than chasing after footballs.

My knee had really improved in the last few weeks of rehab, and I was scurrying after balls effortlessly. It was a beautiful day in Pasadena, and I was so enjoying being on the field.

One by one the players went into the locker room to be taped up for the game. Eventually I ended up back in the trainer's room, watching my teammates prepare for the biggest game of their lives. When the last player had been taped, I looked around the room and saw miles and miles of tape still in rolls. The side of me that wanted to suit up could no longer restrain itself. I blurted out to one of the trainers:

"There's a lot of tape left here-you can still tape me!" He looked at me and, with one glance, knew I was serious.

"I don't think that's a very good idea, Bill," he replied, as kindly as he could. Deep down, I knew he was right.

Because that day's player roster didn't include my name, I couldn't have played anyway. But it didn't take away the desire.

Garth Brooks sang the national anthem that day, complete with air force jets flying over in perfect formation. It was a thrilling experience. I thought of my family, of course. Denise was in the stands, along with my two sisters, Rosemary and Rachel. The kids were back at the hotel, being watched over by one of Denise's good friends who came to California to help us with baby-sitting. My assignment was to be an extra set of eyes and an extra voice for Coach Avezzano. We wanted special teams to shine.

Unfortunately, it didn't start out that way. Early in the first quarter Buffalo's Steve Tasker blocked one of our punts. We were in shock. We hadn't allowed a blocked punt in four years. To make matters worse, the Bills took advantage of the block and used it to set up a Thurman Thomas touchdown. We were behind 7-0 at the game's beginning!

It proved to be a gut-check for us because we turned it around from that point, and the Bills never caught us again!

Troy was beyond description that day. He was a man on fire. He hit Jay Novacek for a passing score to tie it 7-7. Then Jimmy Jones intercepted Jim Kelly, and we scored again in less than a minute-14-7.

Michael Irvin got hot in the second quarter, catching two touchdown passes on successive drives. When halftime arrived, we were up 28-7. We appeared to be unstoppable!

As the team jogged into the tunnel of the Rose Bowl, I saw what was happening next and opted to remain on the field to see the extravaganza that had been planned. Since I didn't go into the locker room with the team, I was afforded a field-level view of the spectacular halftime show put on by Michael Jackson. It was unbelievable, especially since I was standing right there in front of all the action!

In the second half, we kicked a field goal right away to go up 31-7. For a few brief moments in the third quarter, there appeared to be a flicker of hope for the Bills. Jim Kelly had been replaced by Frank Reich, who engineered a touchdown and a field goal, so by third quarter's end it was 31-17. The Bills were only two touchdowns away.

But the fourth quarter proved to be a burial for the Bills.

With eight minutes left in the game, Emmitt scored to make it 45-17. The wheels started falling off for Buffalo. Leon Lett recovered a fumble and ran it in for a touchdown ... almost, that is.

As Leon approached the end zone, he started celebrating a little early. It was while he was showboating that Don Beebe came up from behind and knocked the ball out of his grasp before he could score. It was certainly an embarrassing moment for Leon, who is a great guy. The good news is that it didn't affect the outcome of the game. The bad news is that Leon would have a similar situation haunt him again next season!

With the game in its final minutes, Buffalo just couldn't get anything to happen for them. Another fumble occurred, and this time Ken Norton scooped it up and ran all the way into the end zone. We had totally demolished the Bills 52-17!

The sideline went berserk. A couple of our guys threw Gatorade all over Coach Johnson and then Emmitt went over to him to take his turn at messing up Coach's famous hair. Troy was given the Most Valuable Player award, which he justly deserved.

Once down in the locker room the pandemonium continued. The Vince Lombardi Trophy was presented by Commissioner Tagliabue to Jerry Jones and Coach Johnson. We passed it around, kissing it, getting pictures snapped with it, and hugging each other in triumphant jubilation.

When the locker room eventually calmed down, I went over to the cubicle I had been assigned to get my jacket. We had been given blue and white Cowboy jackets to wear on the sideline, but I had a beautiful leather jacket that I had been wearing previously. My good friend, Mike Hansen, had given it to me back at the pep rally. It had the Cowboy helmet emblazoned on the back, and I knew it had cost Mike well over a thousand dollars to buy it for me.

When I went to my cubicle, it was empty ... somebody had stolen my beautiful jacket! To this day, it's gone. I loved that jacket. If you're reading this and you are the thief, send it back, man ... no questions asked!

Perhaps one of the finest tributes to our championship season came from the pen of one of our devoted fans. Wanda Lampier from Lancaster, Texas wrote a poem to summarize the 1992 season from her perspective. I love the way she captured the goings-on of the year, so I asked her permission to include it in this book. She graciously consented.

My Tribute to the Dallas Cowboys by Wanda Lampier
'92 in Review
The road to the Super Bowl forever will stay an undertaking that will never be easy.

All kinds of detours are there, they say,

And bumps and grinds, which leave you queazy.

But the Cowboys continued on that narrow road,

Refusing to give up or stop,

Trusting all along, that they were traveling on A road that only led to one stop.

Training in Austin came, without a doubt,

But minus Michael, Step, and Jay.

Still they worked it out, and one by one,

They all came back to play.

Troy threw, and Emmitt scored;

Coach Johnson wore that famous frown.

But through it all, one thing was for sure-

"Da Boys were back in town!"

Some statistics were forgotten, not to linger,

And others made history.

I'll pen happenings as I remember,

Tho in sequence they may not be:

Irvin developed his very own show,

Probably seen throughout the nation.

And Troy Aikman wasted no time

In creating a special foundation.

Bill Bates' fate may have lessened the score;

Did your heart go out to him per chance?

Still his good spirits soared, and he proved it once more,
By the rally he threw at his ranch.
Russell Maryland made a touchdown!
And a mighty happy guy was he,
As he fell facedown and kissed the ground,
While he wondered, "Mom, did you see me?"
The postgame show was nothing to shun,
With Brad Sham, "The Voice," they say.
He'd grab 'em and pop those questions,
And announce the "Player of the Day!"
Hats off to Mr. Jerry Jones,
You did what you said you would do--
From selecting a coach, to scouting your team,
And that grand pep rally you threw!
Even with thirteen wins under their belt,
The playoffs seemed no lighter,
For like Santa said to his reindeer,
The coach said, "Gotta pull those reigns a bit tighter!"
From the very first game with Washington,
To Pasadena, which they ultimately won,
"How 'bout them Cowboys?" Johnson said.
They were downright sons of a gun!
It took a lot, but a smile they got;
In San Fran, the coach had no frown.
Yes, 10 and behold, Johnson literally beamed,
He even jumped up and down!
Well, the Cowboys now sport those Super Bowl rings,
Which makes them feel quite wealthy.
And lest we forget that Number 8,
Led them all the way and stayed healthy!
Maybe the time will quickly pass,
And the new season will soon be here,
When the Cowboys set out on their faithful task,
To win the Super Bowl next year!
Guess I'll end my story with this simple phrase,
But I think I might even frown,
'Cause the fans have to wait too many long days
Till "Da Boys are back in town!"
Like everyone else in Dallas,

I saw that the victory in Pasadena quickly led to the follow-up assignment Wanda referred to in her poem:

To win the Super Bowl again next year!

What Are Your Training Methods?

I had trained all my life for athletic competition. But no training was more significant and more helpful to me than the training regimen I went through to fully recover from my knee injury. From my earliest days as an athlete, I always trained hard. I feel that I beat a lot of criticism about my being too small or too slow because I worked harder than anyone else. If I had known back in high school what I know now, my life might have been different.

In high school and college, there was one key word for my training: strength. What I didn't know back then was that strength is not enough for a career in the National Football League. To make it in the NFL, you need to possess a combination of strength and speed.

There is a single acid test of any athlete's future in the NFL-the forty-yard dash. The faster you run that sprint, the greater your chances of playing professionally.

The agony I endured over not making the NFL draft could have been avoided if I had run a faster forty-yard dash. I believe that with all my heart. If I could have run a forty in 4.5 seconds instead of 4.7, free agency would have been unnecessary. If I were starting out in today's world, I would not only lift weights, but I would specifically train to run the forty. When I was just lifting weights, I concluded that I would run faster because my legs were getting stronger, That was true, but only to a certain extent.

In this chapter I want to talk very specifically about some excellent training methods that we use with the Cowboys. Before I get into those exercises, it's important to understand that I had to rehabilitate my knee to the point that I could participate in these methods. A typical week of rehab went like this:

Monday		
Warmup	Stretch	15 min
	Whirlpool	
Biodex		30 min

Upper body		45 min
Lower body		30 min

Tuesday

Warmup	Stretch	25 min
	Jump rope	
Upper body	Back/bicep/traps	45 min
Treatment		
Wednesday		

Wednesday

Warmup	Stretch	15 min
	Whirlpool	10 min
Biodex		10 min
Lower body		45 min
Aerobics	Bike/stepper	15 min

Thursday

Warmup	Stretch	25 min
	Whirlpool	
	Jump rope	
Upper body	Chest/shoulder/tricep	45 min
Treatment		

Friday

Warmup	Stretch	15 min
	Whirlpool	
Biodex		30 min
Upper-body	Back/bicep/traps	45 min
Lower body		30 min
Treatment		

As time went on, I was able to improve my strength. By April I was ready to participate in the standard Cowboys training program.

Speed can be defined as "the ability of an athlete to go from point A to point B in the shortest time." I learned an important formula: Running Speed = Stride Length x Stride Frequency. In other words, how far apart you move your legs and how often you move your legs.

There are stages of speed too. We break it down into six stages:

Reaction-this is movement of ball, man, or snap count.

Start-the ability to get your body moving from your stance.

Primary Acceleration-O-30M, achieving up to 92 percent of your maximum speed.

Secondary Acceleration-30-60M, up to 100 percent maximum speed.

Maximum Speed-60-7 SM, maintaining 100 percent maximum speed.

Deceleration-slowing down the rest of the way.

I always found these stages fascinating. By their own admission, when the NFL tests a player in the forty-yard dash, they are actually measuring his ability to start and accelerate because he doesn't run a long enough distance to test maximum speed!

When I train now, I break my forty-yard dash down into its four ten-yard components. With the help of my trainers, I discovered my 0-10 was slow, my 10-20 was okay, my 20-30 and my 30-40 were both fast. So to better my time, I needed to increase my effectiveness in the first half of the sprint. There are several issues that can produce improvement.

First of all, I needed to learn how to get out of the starting blocks with maximum speed. Not giving that much attention to it early in my career certainly added several hundredths or even tenths of seconds to my time. And as I've already stated, it can all boil down to a few hundredths of a second!

For me, I increased my speed early by increasing the length of my stride coming out of the blocks. Several drills were helpful here. One is called the Push-up Drill, where you actually start a race from a fingertip push-up position! This drill forces you to take fast-driving steps to keep from falling and to keep the body going forward. We also do one drill called a Ground Start, where you start by lying face down on the ground. Then, on command, you jump to your feet and sprint out for about ten yards. This drill teaches you to stay low and forward and get a good thrust in the start. I also discovered that if I moved my arms faster, my legs would automatically try to keep up with them.

Another maxim for running is so simple, it almost appears foolish: The only way you can run fast is to run fast. One way to achieve greater speed in training is to run downhill. By running down a hill with a seven, ten, or twelve-degree slant, your body is forced to run faster due to the decline. Practicing this way increases your stride frequency. The effects of running downhill can be duplicated by running with the assistance of a partner and a bungee cord or length of surgical tubing. With the cord attached to you and your partner, your partner's movement extends the pull of the cord, causing you to run faster. Players can run .3 -.4 seconds faster in the forty-yard dash with the assistance of this tubing!

Of course, running uphill is a good training method as well. Hill charges strengthen your drive off the ground, which is also vital in developing speed. Stride length can also be developed by resistive running. Once again, by using the surgical tubing, the athlete runs out of a sprint stance against a resistance provided by his partner, the harness, and the surgical tubing for a distance of twenty to thirty yards. This exercise forces the runner to get better drive on the push-off of each running stride, thus helping to develop stride length.

Another exercise is called Rope Releases. Here, the runner works with a partner who provides resistance by using a length of rope through the loop in the back of a belt we wear, called a sprint belt. The runner sprints out for ten to fifteen yards, held back by the partner. Then he is released for the final fifteen to twenty-five yards. In the initial part of the sprint, the athlete is overcoming a resistive overload and must pump his arms, drive his knees, and push off the ground more violently. Then, upon release, the athlete applies this stronger push and drives out for the rest of the sprint. If this is done correctly, the runner should feel an explosive burst when he is released from the rope.

Although these running drills are highly effective, they must always be conducted within the context of normal running. By spending time in normal running, we obtain the benefits of our assistive and resistive work. In other words, we apply what we have developed through those exercises, combining optimum stride length and stride frequency for maximum speed.

The Cowboys are very high on a model for training called The Pyramid of Physical Success. It's a diagram of a pyramid with strength at its base, power at the next level, movement next, and skill at the top. There are two side components- conditioning and flexibility. I've lifted the following from a handout we are given when we begin our off-season training:

The philosophy of our off-season conditioning program is predicated on your total development so that you can become a better football player. This means that we must take a serious look at the physical attributes necessary to play the game of football and strive to develop these during the conditioning process.

Strength is the base of the pyramid and is the foundation for everything that we try to do on the football field. All our on-field movements (i.e. running, jumping, blocking, tackling, kicking, throwing, etc.) require the application of force. Without force, there would be no movement! Thus, if we can strengthen the specific muscles that are responsible for these actions, we can improve the quality of these movements and make you a better football player. In addition to this, an athlete that completes an efficient weight training program will be less susceptible to injury.

In training for strength, we will utilize "cycle training," using a combination of free weight and machine exercises to ensure that we don't have any weak links. We will conduct testing to measure upper-body and lower-body strength to check your progress.

Power is the next level on our pyramid and is defined as the rate at which you can apply your strength (power = force x velocity). Most of us refer to this quality as explosiveness. This attribute is more important than "absolute strength" because a football player has only a very short time to apply force during the game.

A wide receiver in a full-speed sprint only has a ground contact time of .1 seconds! An offensive lineman, exploding forward into a drive block, has only about .25 seconds to create the momentum that will lead him into impact! A linebacker, executing a tackle from a breakdown position, has about .2 seconds to extend the legs and hips to stop the ball carrier! Many players are strong but the key is: Can they apply that strength on the field? This is why you must focus on this attribute in our off-season training if you really aspire to be the best you can be.

During the off-season we will use explosive exercises and drills to improve this all important aspect of power. We will monitor your progress with the vertical jump test.

Movement is the next level in our pyramid and includes the areas of speed and agility. It is during this type of training the athlete learns to apply his strength/power potential into actual movements that simulate what happens on the field.

Speed can be defined as the ability of an athlete to move his body or specific limbs at a high rate of velocity. Most people agree that this is the single most important attribute in the game of football. If you can improve in this area, you will be a better player!

During the off-season program we will utilize form drills, resistive running, assistive running, and special drills to improve speed and acceleration. In the past many believed that speed was genetic and could not be improved upon. However, experience has indicated that this is not true! If you can improve leg strength, power, flexibility, stride length, and/or frequency, you will run faster. We will monitor progress in this area by testing your speed and acceleration over ten, twenty, thirty, and forty yards.

Agility can be defined as the ability to move in multi- directions, to stop and go from a variety of starting positions (back, belly, two-point, etc.)

that simulate those performed on the football field. Many athletes can run fast, but they don't have this multi-directional capability which allows other athletes, who are slower, to play faster than them on the football field.

During the off-season program we will utilize a variety of different foot-quickness and agility drills to improve this area. You should see your positional coach to identify areas of weakness that you need to work on. We will use the pro agility test to monitor your development for this attribute.

Skill is the peak of the pyramid and is when the athlete applies his strength, power, speed, and agility in the actual skills of playing his position. Athletes should stay in touch with their specific skills during the off-season training .. As training camp gets closer, you should do more in this area to get ready to play the game.

Flexibility is one of the side components of our pyramid and is defined as the range of motion an athlete has at a particular joint or a group of joints. Having sufficient flexibility is an important prerequisite to efficient on-field movement. An athlete who is inflexible has to fight against his own internal resistances while he moves. This results in less-coordinated, herky-jerky movements and injury.

During the off-season program we will stretch on a daily basis. We will use the stand-and-reach flexibility test to monitor your progress in this area. Work at this area. It may keep you on the field!

Conditioning for the on-field demands of football is the final component of our pyramid of physical success. An athlete can be fast, strong, explosive, agile, and flexible, but if he is out of shape, he will never be an effective football player. What good is it if you can run a 4.6 second forty but in the fourth quarter of the game you are playing at 4.8? As you slow down a step, you will be less effective on the field and more likely to get injured.

During the off-season program we will first start with some distance running to develop the cardiovascular system and develop an "aerobic base." Then we will switch to long and short speed-endurance workouts to get into "football shape."

You will be tested in the sixteen 110's prior to camp to measure your level of fitness going into the season.

A final comment: In looking at this pyramid, you can see why all these areas are important to making you a better player. You will only be as strong as your weakest link. You can have great strength and power but if you can't apply it with speed and agility, you will not reach your potential. You can have all of these physical attributes but if, due to inflexibility, you get injured, you will not be productive. If you are out of shape, you cannot be a great player.

PYRAMID OF PHYSICAL SUCCESS

During the off-season training we will gradually progress from general to specific types of training with the objective of making you the best possible player ....

Another key aspect of training is working on agility and quickness. Agility is defined as the ability to move well in various directions (front, back, lateral, etc.) and change directions in a rapid fashion with combination movements (front to back, side to side, ere). Quickness can be defined as the ability to move the feet with speed in a variety of patterns.

At the Cowboys Valley Ranch training facility, we use a variety of methods to train for agility and quickness. One of the devices that proves to be helpful is the bungee cord/surgical tubing. We strap on a belt that has hooks on front, back, and both sides. Hooking the bungee cord to the front hook, our trainer hooks himself to the other end. The cord is about ten yards long relaxed, but it can stretch to about thirty-five yards.

With the cord attached, the player takes off for a sprint.

The trainer back-pedals from his end and once the cord fully extends, it ends up pulling the player along at a faster speed than he would normally run. Since the only way to run fast is to run fast, this is another effective way of producing that additional speed.

Our strength and conditioning coach is Mike Woicik. Mike is a good buddy. Both of us share a love for fishing. Many an afternoon, Mike can be found out by one of the lakes at my ranch, casting a line for a big old bass while enjoying a cigar. Besides being a close friend, Mike is exceptional at what he does.

The 1992 Super Bowl season is a great example of Coach Woicik's effectiveness. On offense, nine of the eleven Cowboy starters were healthy and on the field for all nineteen of the regular and postseason games. Offensive linemen

Mark Tuinei and Nate Newton only missed one start each due to injury. That's impressive. On defense, six of the eleven starters played every ball game that season. Coach Woicik was chosen by his peers to be Strength Coach of the Year for producing such amazing results.

During the off-season many of the players continue to train with Coach Woicik, so that once training camp arrives, it's not such a shock to the system. In terms of running, we have a set conditioning regimen the coaches put us through each week.

Typical Monday and Thursday mornings can for speed drills. This is how they work: It begins with three thirty-yard, downhill sprints. Between each sprint there is a rest period in order to achieve complete recovery. Becoming faster demands full recovery; otherwise you cannot work on maximizing your speed after each run.

After the downhill runs we turn it around and run three twenty-yard, uphill sprints, each with full recovery. The speed drill concludes with two forty-yard sprints, again with complete recovery in between.

On Tuesdays Coach Woicik puts us through an endurance drill. Knowing that training camp will start with Coach's six- teen 110s, we start right in on preparing for that test. We begin with eight of those dreaded 110-yard sprints, each with a one-minute rest period in between. It's one difficult test of endurance. Since off-season training begins about eight weeks before training camp, we add one more 110 each week. Thus, at the end of the eight weeks we're running sixteen 110s-just like we will in camp.

Friday mornings are set aside for a metabolic workout.

Coach Woicik explains metabolic training this way: "The concept behind this type of conditioning is to simulate actual movements that are made on the football field with short recoveries. The best way to get in shape for football is to play the game. Keeping this in mind, the coaches work with me to develop specific workouts for each positional group on the team.

This exercise involves three series of ten drills with a two- minute rest between each series. A series will include things you will be doing out on the football field, so in that sense, it's a running drill and a football drill. Here's an actual set from a linebacker's metabolic workout. Remember, it's ten consecutive movements with a walk back recovery.

Five-yard sprint.

Five-yard back-pedal; sprint forward five yards.

Back-pedal ten yards; break left on forty-five-degree angle forward for five yards.

Back-pedal ten yards; break right on forty-five-degree angle forward for five yards.

Twelve-yard drop to the right.

Twelve-yard drop to the left.

Shuffle to the left for ten yards, plant, and then shuffle to the right for five yards.

Shuffle to the right for ten yards, plant, and then shuffle to the left for five yards.

Run a twenty-yard sprint.

Run a forty-yard sprint.

That's one set. This exercise also increases in the eight weeks before camp. It starts with three of these series, but by training camp time it's built up all the way to five grueling series.

A potential danger with a great deal of weight training is losing your flexibility. Therefore, you need to learn how to maintain a flexible body. If you want to improve your speed and efficiency of movement and reduce injuries, you must learn how to stretch. Stretching is important before and after working out to ensure that full amplitude of movement is not lost.

The biggest lesson to learn about stretching is the difference between right and wrong. The right way to stretch is a relaxed, sustained stretch with your attention focused on the muscles being stretched. The wrong way (unfortunately practiced by many people) is to bounce up and down, or to stretch to the point of pain; these methods can actually do more harm than good.

When you begin a stretch, spend ten to thirty seconds in an easy stretch. No bouncing! Move to the point where you feel mild tension, and relax as you hold the stretch. The feeling of tension should subside as you hold the position. After the easy stretch, move a fraction of an inch further until you again feel a mild tension. Hold it for ten to thirty seconds. Again the tension should subside. This type of stretching fine-tunes the muscles and increases flexibility.

I lift weights a lot. How do I offset all that weight training? Golf. I find that playing golf forces me to relax, stretch, and stay flexible. You can't be any good at golf if you're not flexible. I've lifted weights and played golf together for years, and it's worked out perfectly for me.

I've discussed the long speed endurance runs (the sixteen 110s) and the short speed endurance runs (training for the forty-yard dash), so I should also mention cardiovascular endurance runs. This type of running involves distance runs of one to three miles or ten to thirty minutes in duration. An alternate activity would be an exercise bike, treadmill, or stepper. Even though football is not an aerobic activity in itself, cardiovascular fitness is essential for recovery between and during workouts. Aerobic training allows the athlete to recover more quickly between bouts of high-intensity exercise with rests of short duration, exactly like a real foot- ball game!

A combination of cardiovascular endurance, long-speed endurance, and short-speed endurance will develop the necessary level of conditioning for the long, hard double sessions that we face each summer in Austin. Being in great condition allows us to tolerate and acclimate to the heat, thus having productive and intensive practices.

Another note on training: One component of sports conditioning that many programs overlook is nutrition. Your diet should provide sufficient nutrients and energy for intense physical activity. Applied nutrition is the key, for this process has a positive effect on body composition and maximizes the benefits of physical training.

Lower body fat increases mobility. Excess weight, in the form of fat, reduces speed and endurance. Nutrition is one of the key factors in lowering fat and stabilizing or increasing muscle tissue. A balanced diet is achieved by modifying your current eating habits. The football player's diet should look like this:

60 percent complex carbohydrates 20-25 percent fat

12-15 percent protein

Like most athletes, I find it necessary to supplement what I eat with a dietary supplement. Working my body as hard as I do, I need vitamins and nutrients quickly. I use Met-Rex dietary supplement first thing in the morning, right after I work out in the afternoon, and before I go to bed. It's a great product that really works for me.

Of course, simple nutrition boils down to the basics I try to abide by: Live right and eat right!

Without question, the best football drill I've ever seen is what we call "The Viper." To conduct this drill, you need to return to the bungee cords. This time you attach two of them to either side of your waist-belt. The other ends of the cords are attached to something stationary-poles, posts, or players who will stand still during the drill.

Stand in the middle with these cords stretching you from both sides. Ahead Of you are three plastic cones (like those fluorescent orange tubes you try not to run over when you take your driver's test). The cones are lined up so that the center cone is about seven yards straight ahead of you. The other two cones are placed on either side of the center cone, making them about ten yards away from you at a diagonal.

At Coach Woicik's command, you run to the cone of his choice. Because of the bungee cords attached, it takes more strength to make this run. Running straight tests strength, but the runs to the side cones produce additional positive effects. When running to the left cone, you feel the push of the one side and the pull of the other.

The reason I feel this is the best football drill I've ever seen is that it produces balance, speed, and quickness like nothing else I've ever seen in all my years of training. All the Cowboys are really high on "The Viper," and I believe I'm the biggest cheerleader on the team.

After my knee injury, the first question I had was, Can I run and cut on that knee? If I couldn't change directions, my football career would be over. It simply boiled down to running and cutting. It would be a real challenge on a reconstructed knee.

I began to run early in my rehab. Back at the Super Bowl in Pasadena I was running sprints at the Rose Bowl, which is part of the reason I wanted to be taped up to play.

But in order to insure the greatest possibility of making cuts on my knee, I became a slave to "The Viper." I was determined to come back. My career was not to be ended yet. Coach Woicik put me through "The Viper" all of March, April, May, June, and midway through July-which was when training camp began down in Austin.

Even in training camp, I was obsessed with "The Viper."

When the defensive coaches began working on specific plays, they would break them down into first-down plays, second- down plays, third-down plays, and fourth-down plays. Since my position in the Nickel was exclusively third- and fourth- down participation, I would go over to another part of the practice field and do "The Viper" while the coaches were going through first and second down drills. It was a killer drill, but I couldn't get enough of it.

All through the rehabilitation of my knee I continued to lift weights to build up the strength in my entire body. I could feel it-I was not only faster, I was stronger!

Thanks to God's grace and a lot of hard work, I was able to. fully rehabilitate my knee. Not only did I come back, but I actually improved! It was emotionally overwhelming to me to run my forty-yard dash at training camp. The best time I had ever run as a Cowboy was 4.6 seconds. What was I going to run on this first test after coming back?

To everyone's amazement I ran a 4.58! It was the best time I ever recorded. The coaches were all scratching their heads, checking and double-checking their stopwatches. But the watches didn't lie-I really had run my fastest forty ever. Incredible!

My improved time in the forty and a league rule change that expanded the roster count from forty-seven to fifty-three put me in position to beat the odds one more time.

Even Coach Johnson was flabbergasted. He told the press, "Three weeks ago I would have given you ten-to-one odds that Bill Bates wouldn't have a chance to make the team. But he's an amazing person. It really is incredible what he has done."

"Now I'd say with the expanded roster, there's no way he won't make the team. He's too valuable on special teams."

Coach Johnson's sentiments pretty much summarized how everyone felt. No one really gave me any chance of coming back. Having lived so long with "too small" and "too slow," now I was having to hear "too old" and "too beat-up" to return to the NFL.

But, as has been the case for my entire life, beating the odds was a challenge that brought out the best in me. My trainers and doctors had assisted me in every way they knew how. But in the final analysis, it was all up to me to make a comeback happen.

Tanner's 1ˢᵗ Camp

I told the press my feelings in a preseason interview:

"I worked harder than I ever worked in the off-season. I was in a position where I could really focus on my body getting as healthy as I possibly could. My body responded well. Once you're over thirty and playing in the NFL, you want to see how your body responds. That's what determined whether I would come back and play. Mentally I wanted to play all along, but physically I wanted to see how things went. My coming back had a lot to do with nine months of training. Not too many people have the luxury of training for an event for nine months. Normally you point to something like that for four months.

"I always work hard anyway. But my legs are stronger, and my upper body's stronger, I'm bigger and faster. And I feel as quick.

"I wouldn't be out there if I didn't realistically feel I was going to be a part of the team. And I don't think Jimmy would have me waste my time, either.

"The expanded roster also helps. But I don't want to be one of fifty-three. I want to be out there on the field. I don't want to be just sitting around.

"I can't wait."

"Once I Make That First Hit, I'm Back!"

It was no big deal to anyone else.

It was a simple fourth-down punt situation. It was a scrim- mage under the scorching Austin sun. I was in my position as personal protector. My assignment was to keep the defenders from blocking the punt. The ball was hiked, the offense lineman did his job keeping guys out, but a defender snuck through anyway. It was up to me to keep him from blocking the punt. So, in a play I had executed hundreds of times before, I hit the guy. And my block kept him from the punter's foot.

The punt was successful, the play was called, twenty-one men stood on the field, waiting for further instructions ... while the twenty-second man on the field awkwardly wiped tears from his eyes. That twenty-second player was me.

I had just accomplished a dream I had visualized for nine months. I even spoke about it. I told people throughout my rehabilitation, "Once I make that first hit, I'm back!" It had been so long since I had hit someone on the football field. And on this very routine play, I had done just that. Once again, I was shooting for the stars and they were coming my way!

If that first hit felt good, my first tackle felt even better!

Our first preseason game was at home against the Vikings. We were kicking off to them, so I was on the field. Once the ball was kicked, I sprinted down the field. The kick returner ran to his right, forcing me to cut to my left. I planted my left foot and successfully made the cut on my newly reconstructed left knee. The cut was fast enough that I was able to get to him before any of my teammates-so I made the tackle!

I couldn't believe how good I felt. The speed I used to get to the kick returner amazed me. I felt like I was on "The Viper," being pulled to the ball with speed beyond my own! I was pumped.

The events that led up to the opening of the 1993 season have been well-documented, since we were the Super Bowl champs. What really put us under the microscope by so many people was the notion that we could actually put together a team that could do the same thing this season. An idea like that will either get you attention or get you written off as being cocky. I'm sure it sounded arrogant to some-but truthfully, we got a lot of attention.

During the off-season Troy had gone under the knife and was coming back from his back surgery quite nicely. He was to be 100 percent by our opener with the Redskins.

But the biggest news of all surrounded Jerry Jones and Emmitt Smith. The two of them could not agree on a new contract for Emmitt, so he elected to hold out, missing training camp in its entirety. But as training camp wore on, the rumor around Texas was that Emmitt would continue to hold out into the beginning of the regular season.

WEEK 1

The Cowboy season began on Monday night, September 6, 1993. Once again, we were in Washington, D.C. to play our conference archrivals, the Redskins. To our dismay, Emmitt was still holding out. That fact, coupled with the fact that Washington had prepared the entire off-season for this one game, proved to be too much for us.

The evening before the game, the team was taken over to RFK Stadium to get the feel of the field. Players ran imaginary pass patterns or practiced kicking, blocking, or any number of things. That evening at RFK was a strangely symbolic experience for me.

First of all, coming back from my injury was a feeling of great joy. Second, to be coming back at RFK, where my pro career had begun eleven years before, was an incredible coincidence.

When we arrived at the stadium the groundskeepers were still working on the playing field, so we were asked to remain on the sideline for a few extra minutes. It was while I was waiting on the sideline that a small object on the ground caught my attention. Bending over to pick it up, I saw that it was a small feather, no more than four or five inches long. It may have come directly off a bird, but my hunch was that it had come from an Indian headdress found in the stadium during game day.

After I picked it up, the groundskeepers allowed us permission to walk on the field. I walked out to the center of the field, in a spot where I would be alone, and laid down on the grass. Even with some movement from our players on different parts of the field, the overwhelming feeling was of quiet, peaceful serenity. I thought to myself, Twenty-four hours from now this place will be packed with screaming people, anticipating a great contest. The two evenings were in such vivid contrast. It's the calm before the storm, I concluded. It all starts up again tomorrow.

I got up off the ground and walked into the locker room. I placed the feather in my locker, deciding it was a symbol worth hanging on to. I kept that feather all season ... right on through to the Super Bowl. That feather came to symbolize my comeback ... my recovery. At the writing of this book, I am planning to frame my game jersey from this year's Super Bowl. I'll leave a little extra room in the frame to include that feather.

It's said to have been the most watched "Monday Night Football" game ever. By the end of the game, I wished more people had gone shopping that night. Despite the fact that we scored first and closed out- the first quarter leading 6-0, the rest of the evening was horrible.

It was the first time since our 1-15 season of 1989 that we allowed five touchdowns in one game, including an incredible ninety-nine-yard drive in the third quarter. We were embarrassed 35-16.

I began to keep a journal of my thoughts during the football season. I wrote in my journal after the thrashing:

No Emmitt. Jerry offered him a five-year deal, but Emmitt didn't know about it. Jimmy is starting to apply the pressure. We need to practice good habits. Good habits make winners. Publicly, Coach Johnson was quoted as saying, "I'm tired of talking about Emmitt Smith."

WEEK 2

We hoped to turn things around for week two. Our home opener at Texas Stadium would be a rematch with our Super Bowl foes, the Buffalo Bills. The deeper we got into practice that week, the greater the probability that we would once again be Emmitt-less. I wrote in my journal that week about an ongoing joke that I had with Coach Avezzano, concerning this year's rookies and their inability to make it to meetings on time. I wrote: I told Coach Avezzano, "When I was a rookie, if there was a 10:00 A.M. meeting, we were there at 9:45, just to play it safe. This rookie class has been late for all the meetings concerning Buffalo."

The game was sweet revenge for the Bills. Up 10-3 at halftime, they were taking advantage of every weakness they could find. Emmitt's replacement, Derrick Lassie, a rookie, could only manage fifty-two yards on nineteen carries. We had four turnovers.

After a scoreless third quarter, we were able to put a touchdown on the board eight minutes into the fourth quarter to tie it 10-10. With a chance to go ahead late in the game, Troy threw to Jay Novacek, but Buffalo safety Matt Darby was there to pick it off.

With twelve seconds remaining, the Bills kicked a field goal to go ahead 13-10. We lost ... 0-2 as reigning Super Bowl champs.

The press noted the disturbing feeling in the stands that day. The Dallas Morning News wrote:

Sensing public sentiment against him, Cowboys owner Jerry Jones stayed in the end zone tunnel in the fourth quarter instead of taking his customary sideline stroll.

After the game we followed our customary pattern, which included gathering together in the locker room to say the Lord's Prayer. The last player into the locker room was a discouraged Charles Haley. Once inside, Charles winged his helmet completely across the locker room. Its final destination put a huge hole in the locker room wall. Now that he had everyone's attention, including Jerry Jones', he said loud enough for all of us to hear, "We need Emmitt!" Most of the players resisted the temptation to look over at Jerry so instead, we simply hung our heads in frustration'.

After the game I wrote in my journal one sentence:

Emmitt's hold-out seems to be a bigger thing than anyone thought.

WEEK 3

The third week brought with it some great news for Cowboy fans everywhere: Emmitt ended his battle with Jerry Jones and signed a contract! Beyond what his skill brought to our team, there was a strong psychological effect as well. We felt like a complete team again.

Since Emmitt signed in the middle of the week, he practiced only one day before we headed off to Phoenix. He ended up sitting out the first half, but saw some limited action in the second half. Derrick Lassie ended up having a pretty good game, so we were ahead 10-0 by halftime. Emmitt ran the ball eight times in the second half for forty- five yards, and Troy was twenty-one of twenty-seven for 281 yards on the day. We won our first game of the season 17-10.

After the game we went back into the locker room for our postgame rituals. After the Lord's Prayer, Coach Johnson gave us an inspiring speech. The basic message was that we were back and he was grateful. He continued on in his talk by thanking different people who made important contributions to the team over the last few weeks. For his final thank you, Coach Johnson turned to Jerry Jones and publicly thanked him for being such a great owner (with an obvious reference to signing Emmitt)! Jerry capitalized on the moment by reaching down to grab one of our helmets. He then proceeded to throw the helmet completely across the room!

Looking at Charles Haley, Jerry erupted into a huge laugh that brought the house down.

On the plane trip home, I wrote in my journal:

We've lifted morale by cementing team unity.

It really felt good too.

WEEK 4

We would win seven straight games before losing one. Our next opponents were the Green Bay Packers ... played in Dallas. The old flame had returned for this game. Michael Irvin had a sixty-one-yard touchdown in the first quarter to light our fires! Emmitt scored his first touchdown of the season on a twenty-two-yard run in the third quarter. We were able to hold Green Bay's ace receiver, Sterling Sharpe, to only four catches. Cap it all off with a record day for our field goal kicker, Eddie Murray (five field goals, including forty-eight- and fifty-yarders) and you can feel the jubilation in a 36-14 win.

WEEK 5

Now we were back even with a .500 record. Our next game was in Indianapolis with the Colts. The press called this game, "Emmitt Smith's coming out party," since he exploded for 104 yards on twenty-five- carries. It was also a defensive extravaganza for us. Thomas Everett had two interceptions, Ken Norton had one, and Kevin Smith had one.

We were expected to go out there and dominate. That's what we did. We won 27-3.

I wrote in my journal concerning a funny event involving Michael Irvin, who also had a great game:

Back at the hotel, Michael sees a video camera pointed at him, so he starts hamming it up, having a good time. Once he finishes his little dance, he starts walking away. While he's walking, he accidently trips on the carpet in the hotel.

He's unaware that the camera is still rolling.

The reason we know about this is Coach Johnson showed the film to the whole team when he showed us the game films. It's the funniest thing you've ever seen!

WEEK 6

After fairly easy games with the Packers and the Colts, a true test was ahead as we traveled to Candlestick Park for a rematch of the NFC Championship Game against the 49ers.

229

The game started tenuously for us as Emmitt uncharacteristically fumbled a ball that San Francisco recovered and ran in for a forty-seven-yard touchdown. But Emmitt came back to score in the second quarter, and Eddie Murray kicked three field goals in the first half. We went into the locker room at halftime, clutching a 16-10 lead.

The game had been touted as a duel between two all-pro wide receivers, Michael Irvin and Jerry Rice. While Jerry was contained by our defense, Michael had twelve catches for 168 yards, including a thirty-six-yard touchdown reception from Troy.

We won our fourth in a row by a 26-17 margin. It was an exceptional game for the defense and the special teams. Still basking in the glow of a great performance, I wrote:

We have a Pro Bowl kickoff team! Especially since we added Elvis Patterson from the Raiders, Matt Vanderbeek from the Colts, and Joe Fishback from the Falcons.

Our defense gave up some yards, but forced turnovers that killed San Francisco. Game balls were given to Charles Haley and Russell Maryland, and deservedly so.

I am so glad to be playing the game!

"Can We Repeat?"

The pressure was on. The question, "Can we repeat?" was now being mumbled far beyond the city of Dallas. Football fans all around the country were beginning to ask the same thing. With a record of 4-2, we had the players and the momentum to give it our best shot.

Super Bowl Helmet – a season of hits

WEEK 7

Week seven took us to the City of Brotherly Love to play the Eagles." It was one of those games out of the archives of the National Football League. Halloween day was a dark, dismal, rainy day in Philadelphia. By game time it was really pouring.

Therefore, it wasn't a day for the pass. Troy could only manage nine completions on nineteen attempts for a measly ninety-six yards. The message from the weatherman was clear ... find yourself a running back, give him the ball, and let him fly.

The Cowboys' rushing record for a single game was set by Tony Dorsett with 206 yards.

Until Halloween.

Emmitt Smith was the rocketeer that day. He ran like he was jet-propelled, carrying the ball thirty times for a new record-237 yards! That was nine more yards than the Eagles had in total offense.

In the beginning of the game the Eagles had been unsuccessful in driving the ball, so they were going to punt on fourth down. I ran onto the field to assume my special teams position. As soon as the ball was snapped, I rushed in for the block. With no regard for my body, I threw myself in the way of the punt. But miraculously, it got into the air.

As I descended to the ground, my fall was broken by landing on the punter's personal protector. Once on top of this fellow, I made no swift attempt to get up, much to his dismay. He felt I was holding him (which I was) from running down field to make a tackle. He finally squirmed his way out from under me, but the play was already over. Angry and frustrated, he grabbed my face mask and began to wrestle me. In all honesty, I did nothing to diminish his feelings of anger. Instead, I joined right in and we started going at it. It took quite a few players and officials to break us up. When the smoke cleared, we had both been slapped with personal fouls, resulting in off-setting penalties.

Surrounded by my teammates, I was escorted over to the sideline. I don't like to be called for penalties, but this event was so full of emotion, I was high on an adrenaline rush. I'm not sure why I became so charged up about that particular play, but I do have a guess.

The Eagles player I had my little tussle with was Herschel Walker!

We beat the Eagles 23-10 that wet afternoon at Veteran's Stadium, winning our fifth in a row.

WEEK 8

After three weeks on the road, it was good to get back to the friendly surroundings of Texas Stadium. The battle for NFC East supremacy was slated for Sunday, November 7, as we faced the New York Giants. We had identical records of 5-2, but once the game got under way, any similarities between the two teams were minor.

Alvin Harper had a great game for us, catching two passes for touchdowns in the first half. We were leading 17-6 at halftime-the Giants unable to produce a touchdown.

The second half was a tough one for a quarterback. Troy pulled his left hamstring and had to sit out the rest of the game. In the fourth quarter we knocked Phil Simms out of the game also. Emmitt had 117 yards rushing and we handed the Giants a 31-9 trouncing.

For me, one of the real highlights of the day was the half time ceremony when Coach Landry was added to the Cowboy Ring of Honor in Texas Stadium. Of course, we were in the locker room while it was going on, but on our way into the tunnel at halftime, I connected with Coach. I put it in my journal this way:

As we were going back to the locker room I saw Coach Landry getting ready to be escorted onto the field. I just had to go over and congratulate him. It was such appropriate timing, since he not only coached the Cowboys, but he had also played for the Giants.

I went over and gave him a hug.

WEEK 9

Events were unfolding in other parts of the National Football League that would have impact on the Dallas Cowboys. After the victory over the Giants, it was announced that Troy would be out of action for approximately two more weeks.

What were we going to do? Our backup quarterback, Jason Garrett, was only in his second year and it would be a stretch for him to come up to the level of play that we needed.

Jason is from a football family. His father was a long time scout for the Cowboys and he is now the Head Coach. He was a fine young man with a great mind for the game. Now he has taken over the task of making the Cowboys into a winner again. I have no doubt of his ability make them America's Team once more.

At the time I thought it was absolutely amazing that in Cleveland that very week, Art Modell released Bernie Kosar from the Browns. To me, it was unthinkable to cut Bernie. The man was a leader, a legend ... but no matter. In a few short days he was on the circuit, shopping for a new home.

We picked up Bernie almost immediately. It proved to be a great investment in our future. What I didn't realize at the time was that Jason would stick it out, continue to play for the Cowboys and eventually become the Head Coach.

Since Bernie had only three days to practice and-more significantly-try to digest the Cowboy playbook, Coach Johnson decided to start Jason Garrett. But by the second quarter of game nine against the Phoenix Cardinals, Kosar was in the driver's seat.

It was to be a pretty one-sided first half, with us scoring seventeen unanswered points by halftime. But Phoenix did come back, scoring fifteen points in the second half. We added a field goal to put the final score at 20-15. Bernie was thirteen of twenty-one for 199 yards and one touchdown.

I made a note in my journal concerning a defensive highlight in the game:

Kenny Gant finally makes an interception!!

WEEK 10

Seven straight wins would end in Atlanta's Georgia Dome. Maybe we were getting a little overconfident, but we never suspected what was waiting for us the Sunday before Thanksgiving.

The surprising Falcons dominated us from the start.

When the gun sounded to end the first half, the score was in Atlanta's favor 13-0, plus they had fifteen first downs to our one and 245 yards to our twenty-five. Troy-still out with the hamstring injury-wasn't playing. The downward spiral continued when Emmitt suffered a thigh bruise. He left the game after only one rush for one yard and four catches for nine yards.

Bernie tried to rally the offense as best he could, but it just wasn't our day. We had gotten a little lethargic. Even Coach Johnson was quoted as saying, "We kind of saw it coming. That's about the way we practiced last Thursday."

By the game's conclusion it was Falcons 27, Cowboys 14.

Atlanta had 400 total yards. We were embarrassed.

A bright spot for me was recovering an onside kick in the game. But personal achievements always dim when the team experiences a loss.

I was angry. I wrote harshly in my journal that night:

We had nineteen missed tackles. We had eight mental errors.

Our preparation was not good. Our practice was not good.

It's time to separate ourselves from the other teams in the NFL

The loss to Atlanta put us in a tie with the New York Giants for first place in the NFC East.

WEEK 11

It was to be a Thanksgiving game we'd never forget. The game was filled with rarities. We rarely saw the Miami Dolphins here at home. We rarely had such a bizarre game. We rarely had the weather we experienced that day in Texas Stadium.

It was snowing! I don't believe it had ever snowed and sleeted during a game in Dallas. It was a big factor in the game's outcome.

The game was a 3:00 P.M. start. By kickoff, the snow had not let up. It was like ice hockey/football out there on the field. Dan Marino was sidelined, so the Dolphins turned to veteran Steve DeBerg for its quarterbacking assignments.

DeBerg handed off to Keith Byars, who ran for seventy seven yards and the first touchdown of the game.

Down 7-0, Troy Aikman was back. He hit Kevin Williams for our first score, and then Kevin returned a punt sixty-four yards for our second touchdown. By halftime it was our lead 14-7.

Miami scored a field goal in the third quarter to come within four points. I had some important contributions in the snow ... I forced a fumble and intercepted a pass!

It was the last quarter that produced the truly bizarre.

Midway through the fourth quarter, Pete Stoyanovich kicked a thirty-one-yard field goal to limit our lead to one point, 14-13.

Late in the game, Stoyanovich tried a forty-four-yarder in the snow. We were ready to mix it up. As the ball was hiked, we penetrated their line and blocked the kick. The ball started rolling around in the snow. If we simply left the ball alone, we would take over possession. There was so little time left, we could easily sit on it and eat up the remainder of the clock. Appearing to be all sewn up, the entire scene changed in a millisecond.

Despite all of the Cowboys screaming to each other to stay away from the ball, one of our guys-in his own personal enthusiasm-didn't get the message. Leon Lett went after the ball. In the snow, he ended up sliding into it. Unfortunately, he touched it but didn't come up with it. Jeff Dellenbach, of the Dolphins, was there to pounce on the ball.

With the ball in Miami's possession, the Dolphins quickly set up Pete Stoyanovich for a nineteen-yard chip shot at the gun. We were standing out in a field of snow and ice in utter shock. We lost 16-14. Why was this happening to us?

We went into the locker room and I started looking for Leon, like most of the other players. We knew how terrible he must feel and we wanted to tell him it was okay. But Leon, or "Big Cat," as we nicknamed him, was nowhere to be found. He was hiding. Later we would find out where he was. I was deeply affected by how he must have felt. I wrote about it that night in my journal:

Wow! What a fiasco!

It was the worst snow I have ever been in. Until the end it was also the most fun I've had!

Poor Big Cat! I feel so bad for him. We were all yelling, "Peter, Peter, Peter!" which was our code for "Stay away from the ball!" Obviously, he didn't hear us.

After the game he wouldn't talk to anyone.

He went into the training room and cried like a baby for a long time.

Everyone makes mistakes, Leon.

Why did Leon do it? I don't know for sure, but I imagine it was a combination of things. He's young and in the excitement of the moment, I'm certain he thought he was doing the right thing.

Leon Lett is a great guy. He's quiet and shy by nature. He was a major player in the National Football League for years to come. This one event so moved the people in our area that the kids in Dallas started a Leon Lett Fan Club. They wrote him letters of encouragement and support. It was great to see this occur.

One letter was rather ironic, however. A well-meaning eight-year-old kid sent this letter to Leon:

Dear Leon Lett:

Please don't feel bad. Everyone makes mistakes. Last year a player on the Cowboys had a ball taken away from him as he was getting ready to score a touchdown in the Super Bowl. So don't let it bother you. Everyone makes mistakes.

The little kid signed his name to the bottom of the letter.

This sincere child used Leon's own mistake in last year's Super Bowl as his example of other peoples' mistakes!

WEEK 12

Playing on Thanksgiving Day gave us a little extra time to rest up for our next contest. The Philadelphia Eagles were coming to town. It was scheduled for a Monday night, so we ended up with eleven days between our loss to Miami and this battle.

After suffering two straight losses, we came out with great intensity. Emmitt was ready for another good showing against Philadelphia. He ended up with 172 yards on twenty-three carries, which gave him more than 400 rushing yards in the two regular season games with the Eagles.

I had one of my best games on special teams. Once again, I had the opportunity to face my old friend and rival, Herschel Walker. It was a good meeting.

I wrote in my journal that night: .

I put the biggest hit on Herschel Walker I ever have!

We ended up beating the Eagles 23-17, but not without a fourth-quarter scare. Philadelphia was moving the ball under the direction of their quarterback, Bubby Brister. They appeared to have the momentum as they picked our defense apart. I was in my linebacker slot in the Nickel when Bubby threw one my direction. Instinctively, I moved toward the ball and made the interception! It turned out to save the game!

I ran with the ball past the Eagles' offensive receivers and linemen. I almost broke it through all the way, but was stopped by Bubby himself at the Cowboy sideline. As I rolled out of bounds, I realized I was right near where Denise sits in the stadium!

Denise and her game ball

My eye spotted her right away. I rolled over, got up, and ran to where she was located. By now, she was standing and cheering like the entire stadium. Once I arrived at her spot, she leaned down, while I stretched up on my tiptoes to give her a big Ol' kiss! I handed her the ball to keep as a memento of a great game. What a thrill for both of us!

The victory put us at 8-4. We were one game behind the New York Giants with four weeks to go.

WEEK 13

We went to Minnesota to play the Vikings in a strange contest. It was strange in that we beat them handily, but came away from the game feeling like we had lost.

Emmitt had 104 yards, but the amazing feats were saved for our field-goal kicker, Eddie Murray. He nailed three -three pointers, two of them for over fifty yards! We won the game 37-20, but you'd never have guessed it by Coach Johnson's performance in the locker room after the game. He exploded.

I recorded in my journal:

We got to Minnesota and really kicked their tails!

Jimmy Johnson blew up after the game. He really laid into the defense. He wasn't happy. I think he was setting the tone for the next game. We won, but it wasn't good enough for future opponents.

Jimmy was a real motivator.

Eddie Murray kicked two 50+ yarders-who says he's old? We must stay together.

We paid a dear price in that game. Our all-pro center, Mark Stepnoski, went out of the game with a scenario I knew all too well. He injured his ACL. "Step," as we nicknamed him, was in the exact situation I had been in a little over a year before. I took him aside and tried to encourage him about the road ahead. As it turned out, he followed the exact program of surgery and rehabilitation that I had experienced. Step told me later that I was a real help to him during that difficult time.

"Bill gave me something to shoot for," Step said later. "He had people amazed at his rehabilitation and recovery. By the time he recovered to 100 percent, he ran the fastest forty of his life. That really inspired me!"

"I know it sounds corny," Step continued, "but I really do look up to Bill Bates. He was playing for the Dallas Cowboys while I was still in high school. He brings experience and knowledge to our team. You can learn a lot just by watching him or talking to him. I benefit from Bill because of all he's experienced going before me."

I was glad to be as much support for Step as I could. I knew the road back would be rough. But by encouraging him to "shoot for his star," I wanted him to see that total rehab was certainly possible.

"Put It In Three-inch Letters-We Will Win The Game!"

As we came down to the last three regular season games, it was an odd schedule that put us in Dallas one of those three weeks. But the other two weeks, we'd be at the Meadowlands.

We played the Jets and the Giants on their home turf.

WEEK 14

We needed a victory in New York against the Jets. Our biggest concern about the game was the playing conditions. On the way up there on the plane, I scribbled in my journal:

What will the weather be?

It was a great game for Troy. He had 252 yards, completing twenty-one of twenty-seven passes. He also rushed for twenty yards on a key third and sixteen play in the third quarter. We were up 21-0 at the beginning of the fourth quarter and were clearly in charge.

It was not an error-free game, however. We turned the ball over five times and the Jets turned it over four. We both scored touchdowns in the last quarter to make the final score 28-7. But it was what happened immediately after the game that had everybody talking. The head coach of the Jets, Bruce Coslet, approached Coach Johnson in the tunnel after the game and chewed him out for sending blitzes on his quarterback, Boomer Esiason, so late in the fourth quarter while maintaining such a big lead. It got pretty hot there for a few minutes. Coach Johnson-who is so much like me on issues like this-thought the whole thing was incredulous. He looked Coach Coslet straight in the eye and exclaimed, "If you would stop trying to score, then I would stop blitzing!"

Before they could get into too much of a scuffle, a man in a finely tailored suit stepped in between them to break it up. It seems like Jerry Jones is always around when you need him.

By the time we got into the locker room, Coach Johnson was in a lather. He had some choice words for us ... even in victory. He singled out one of our running backs (not Emmitt) and screamed at him, "If you fumble the ball again, I will cut you!"

When the dust settled, the good news was-we had clinched a spot in the playoffs!

WEEK 15

We had to keep winning games in order to procure the best possible position for the playoffs. Our final regular season game at home was hosting the Washington Redskins. There was so much talk around the team practices during the week about what the 'Skins had done to us in the season opener. We wanted to get them back ... and good.

This rivalry affected me personally as well. Writing in my journal during the week, I penciled in:

The 'Skins get at me like no other team!

There's something about the extra intensity of the matchups, the long history between our two teams, and the richness of the contests that bring additional bursts of adrenaline to me.

By game day it was obvious that many of my teammates
shared identical feelings. We went out on the field and handed Washington their heads on a platter. It was the most one-sided game in the entire sixty-eight-game history of Cowboy-Redskin contests.

Chip Lohmiller put the Redskins on the board first with a thirty-two-yard field goal. We came right back with a touchdown, Emmitt running in from one yard out. The first quarter ended 7-3. That was the last time it was even close. Troy threw two touchdown passes in the second quarter-one to Michael Irvin and the other to Alvin Harper.

Zeroing in on a ball carrier

At the half, it was 21-3. In the third quarter, we had even more fun! We scored two more touchdowns in the third, including one by our special teams. Kevin Williams returned a punt for a sixty-two-yard touchdown. We went on to put three more on the board in the final minutes of the game, so the victory was decisive at 38-3. The Dallas Morning News wrote: "The only good move Washington made was general manager Charley Casserly's introducing himself to offensive coordinator Norv Turner before the game." As a result, Coach Turner left us and moved on to become the head coach for Washington.

Although he didn't score, Emmitt had 153 yards and took over first place in the NFL rushing lead. The setup for the next week's game was right out of a movie script. We were tied with the New York Giants, our records being 11-4. We would face them at the Meadowlands in seven days.

If we could manage a win, the NFC East title would be ours. Along with it came a week off, and for the first time in fourteen years, we would have home field advantage throughout the playoffs.

WEEK 16

This game ended up like a champion staring at himself in the mirror. We put three points on the board, then seven more. Reciprocating, the Giants put up seven and then followed it with three. The game reached the conclusion of regulation tied at 13.

In the second quarter Emmitt suffered an injury. He separated his right shoulder, which is the kind of injury that causes excruciating pain. A lot of guys would have remained on the sideline with that kind of pain, but not Emmitt. This game was far too important. He's too much of a competitor to sit by and watch. He ended up with 168 yards for the day and, in doing so, he won the NFL rushing title for the third year in a row. This is even more meaningful when you consider how hard it was to play in such pain and that the Giants were the top-ranked scoring defense in the league!

Watching Emmitt play was inspiring to all who saw him, including me. I wrote in my journal after the game:

The most courageous afternoon I've ever witnessed.

He was that good.

Meanwhile, since we were mirroring each other's efforts, the game ended in a tie at 13. In preparing for an overtime period, it's handled like the start of a new game. The captains go out for the coin toss and play begins with the kickoff teams. I had been captain of the special teams for the last few years, so I knew I'd be one of the guys to go out on the field for the overtime coin toss. What I didn't realize was that no one else was going to join me. I would be going out there alone to call the toss against the legendary Lawrence Taylor. It figured. Nobody wanted to face Number 56 on the field in any situation!

Coach Johnson called me over to talk with me before the toss. "Bill, we want the wind with us," he told me. "If we win the coin toss, take the field position. I don't care if we kick or receive ... I want the wind with us. Do you understand what I'm saying?"

"Yes, sir," I replied.

I thought through how I would handle this transaction. I knew if I won the toss, I'd never say, "We'll kick off." I'd say,

"We'll defend this goal." That way, the Giants still would have the chance to choose if they wanted to kick or receive. And you never knew what they'd choose. Stranger things have happened.

I walked out to Jerry Markbrite, the referee, who was waiting for me. I looked at L.T., acknowledging his presence on the field, and went about my business. Since we were visitors, I was to make the call. And as always, as the coin was tossed, I yelled, "TAILS!"

It came down "heads," and the crowd erupted in raucous approval. The Giants had a different game plan than we did because once they knew they had won the toss, Lawrence asked for the ball.

I immediately responded by saying we wanted the side of the field with the wind, which Jerry gave us. So, in one of those strange twists of events, I lost the coin toss but got exactly what I had been sent out there to get!

The Giants tried their best, but they could not move the ball. We got our chance and capitalized on it. We put together a drive of fifty-two yards, forty-one of them achieved by Emmitt. Eddie Murray came in and successfully split the uprights for a forty-one-yard winning field goal. We won 16-13 in overtime!

As we were running off the field Phil Simms, the Giants quarterback, caught up to me. After he congratulated me on the victory, he said, "Can I ask you a question?"

"Sure," I said.

"If you guys had won the coin toss in overtime, you were going take the field position anyway, weren't you?"

I nodded and grinned.

"I thought so," he mused, shaking his head. "Well, good luck!"

The week off that this win provided was much appreciated.

We needed to get Emmitt back as strong as he could be. An extra week's rest was always therapeutic.

Plus, I had another pep rally to run!

Friday, January 14, 1994, we held our second pep rally out at the ranch. We had learned a great deal from last year's rally, so we were better able to handle things the second time around. The biggest hitch the first time was access into the ranch by car. In the year in between, we created more entrances to the ranch so cars could come in and park with greater ease.

We also braced ourselves for a much larger crowd than the previous year. We secured thirty parking attendants, thirty security guards, and tons of food and drink. It appeared that our opponents were to be the Green Bay Packers. In order to drum up support for our team and to vent some hostility toward the Pack, we found an old Mercury Bobcat that we painted green and white. On the doors we brushed on the letter "G", to represent our competition. We placed the car right in the center of all the pep rally's activity.

243

People lined up to buy tickets for $2.00 apiece. With that ticket, they were given the opportunity to use a sledgehammer to hit the "Packer Car" wherever they wanted to hurt it. The money we raised was turned over to charity, and the car looked like a child's lunch box at the evening's end.

At different intervals during the evening, players got up on stage to cheer on the crowd ... or we played pre-shot videos of players who were unable to attend.

It was such a zoo! It was a smaller turnout than the previous year, but it was just as rowdy. I made my little speech to the folks and decided I'd better leave early before I got trampled to death by well-meaning fans. I drove back to Dallas a little before 10:00 P.M.

At 10:00 P.M., the pep rally featured a giant bonfire, like we had lit the previous year. When I got home, I flipped on the television set to see that the local TV stations were covering the bonfire as a "live" event!

I was quoted the next day in the newspaper, explaining what the pep rally was all about:

"A lot of these people can't be at the stadium. They'll be watching on television. This pep rally gives them a chance to participate. Plus the hype from a rally like this rubs off on the players. They see the fans pumped up and they get pumped up too. We'll make the pep rally an annual affair as long as we keep winning playoffs and Super Bowls!"

The press would call our victory over the Packers "ugly but efficient." But a win is a win. Green Bay led 3-0 at the end of the first quarter, but that was be the end of their time on top.

Emmitt was still hurting from the shoulder injury he had received at the Meadowlands two weeks earlier. He was limited to sixty yards on thirteen carries. Fortunately, it was of little consequence since Troy had a colossal day. For the second time that season, he passed for over 300 yards. By halftime we were up 17-3.

It was an awesome day for our defense, as well. We had four takeaways, plus we held Green Bay to a mere thirty-one yards on the ground. We had a fake punt situation ready for this game that Coach Johnson decided to use. As the personal protector for the punter, the ball was to be snapped to me for a run. We tried it, but the Packers were onto it. I took the ball and ran straight ahead, but I came up short. They took over possession but, thankfully, couldn't move it, so we quickly had the ball back.

We scored 10 in the second half to their 14. Thus, the game ended with us triumphant 27-17.

Focus

In the locker room after the game, Coach Johnson gave his opinions on our victory. Eventually a reporter asked him about the fake punt play, where I ran the ball but got stopped. "How did it happen?" they wanted to know. With a smile on his face and a twinkle in his eye, Coach Johnson looked over in my direction and said, "I think Bates' mind was still cloudy from that big pep rally at his ranch the other night!"

We laughed but knew inside ourselves that we would need to play much better if we wanted to beat San Francisco next week.

There is no finer illustration of Jimmy Johnson's ability to use the media for his advantage than the incident that took place the week before the NFC Championship Game against the San Francisco 49ers. Coach was looking for a way to ignite the fans, especially those who would attend the game that Sunday in Texas Stadium. He wanted noise on the level of jet engines and rock concerts.

So, one evening in the middle of the week, the Dallas radio talk shows were yakking up a storm about who would win the game, by how much, who would be in the Super Bowl, etc. Right smack in the middle of a sports talk show on local station WBAP, a familiar voice came over the air as a phone-caller. He had a simple message for the fans:

We will win the ballgame!

"Can we quote you on that, Coach?"

"Put it in three-inch letters--we will win the game!"

Everyone went bonkers. The 49ers were livid at the arrogance of the prediction. The fans were ecstatic! Our team was filled with a new-found confidence, based on Coach's belief in us.

When the two teams first met on game day, the Niners, who are usually more reserved and businesslike, came out pushing, shoving, and fighting. This was going to be a showdown.

But Coach did get the crowd into it. The noise was more deafening than any time in recent Cowboys history. So Coach got his noise ... now, would he get his victory?

Emmitt ran in for his first score midway into the first quarter. It was the second quarter that proved explosive for us. We scored three touchdowns in the second quarter to their single TD. By halftime, we were firmly in control of the game 28-7.

Two plays into the second half, Troy ran into the knee of 49ers defensive end, Dennis Brown. He suffered a concussion and was taken to Baylor University Medical Center, where he stayed overnight for observation. The poor guy really got his bell rung. He didn't know where he was. He kept thinking he was in a high school game in Henryetta, Oklahoma. It reminded me so much of my concussion, when I asked friends to tell Denise that I was all right ... the time I referred to her as my "girlfriend" instead of my wife. Troy would be okay.

During the whole second half, San Francisco tried to get back in the game. This meant a lot of passing, which also meant I saw a lot of playing time. The Niners couldn't make it happen for themselves. We were up 38-21 with about thirty seconds left in the game. I was on the field, playing linebacker in the Nickel. There were so many pass plays, I felt like I was doing wind sprints from one side of the field to another. I was completely exhausted.

Looking over to the sideline, I was trying to get the attention of my backup, Ken Norton, to see if he would play this final play for me. I was in the defensive huddle ... throwing up-for the first time since my days at Tennessee. I didn't want to cost us the game.

When I finally found Ken on the sideline, I could see that he was occupied and I would need to finish out the game ... which I did.

What was Ken doing?

He and Charles Haley were busy pouring Gatorade all over Coach Johnson!

It's all in a day's work.

Next assignment: Win the Super Bowl in Atlanta!

"Who's Gonna Win the Super Bowl? Daddy Is!"

The day after we beat the San Francisco 49ers, the Dallas Morning News ran a headline in inch-high, bold, all-capital letters:

HE TOLD YOU SO!

"Jimmy Johnson predicted a win and got a blowout. He asked for noise and got a sonic boom. If Texas Stadium hadn't already had a hole in the roof, fans would have blasted one on Sunday."

The next week was a flurry of activity almost beyond comprehension. Friends we hadn't heard from in twenty years suddenly left messages on the answering machine, ask- ing for any extra Super Bowl tickets that we might have. Denise was trying to get everything prepared for a week away from home with Graham, Brianna, Hunter, and Tanner.

But one of the most demanding aspects of a Super Bowl experience are the media. There were reporters everywhere ... coming out of the woodwork, the plumbing, the glove compartment, all looking for the same thing-that unique angle to make their story stand out among the thousands of stories that would be filed in covering the game.

The Cowboys decided the team would travel to Atlanta early in the week with family members asked to wait until Thursday to arrive. Coach Johnson wanted as distraction- free an environment as he could get for as long as he could get it.

But "distraction free" and "Super Bowl week" are opposites. The press was everywhere. Usually it's guys like Emmitt and Troy who are swamped, but with the Super Bowl hype, anyone on the Cowboys roster was a fair target. I got my share of hounding because I'd been around so long. Here's the kind of article that would appear in newspapers all over the world that week:

Cowboys' Bates Battered but Happy

(Knight-Ridder News Service)

A 1983 walk-on with the Cowboys, Bill Bates had endured the five straight losing seasons (1986-1990), including the 3-13 and 1-15 years at rock bottom. When it came time for him to celebrate his first Super Bowl championship, it seemed unfair that he had to do so as an injured spectator.

Not this time. Bates, the second oldest (defensive end Jim Jeffcoat is two months older) and perhaps the most popular and inspirational Cowboy, has been given a chance he thought he might not get. He is as excited as a kid flying to Disney World, knowing that Sunday--despite the longest of odds-he finally will play in his first Super Bowl.

"This is the greatest," he said. "Compared to last year, this is such a wonderful feeling. I guess because of what it took to get here. It's something I wish every ten or eleven-year veteran could experience in his career, because I think when you work that hard and keep making it and producing for ten or eleven years, you deserve a Super Bowl."

"1 jumped and hollered and enjoyed the celebration after we won last year, and felt a part of the team, but it's definitely much sweeter this year. And if we win, you bet, it's going to be a completely different feeling, because I know I had a part in it on the field."

One of the more amazing facts about this young, incredibly fast, deep Cowboys team is that Bates again led the special teams he captains in tackles this season, with twenty-five solos on punt and kickoff coverage. Most Cowboy observers thought his career was finished after knee surgery so late in his brilliant career.

"It makes this even more rewarding, I think, because I never stopped working to get here, and to finally be here, it's indescribable," said Bates.

"If (Coach Jimmy Johnson) wants me back and the owner (Jerry Jones) wants me back, I'll go to work and maybe be faster than I've been."

It was a real circus, to say the least. Reporters were turning into neurosurgeons, giving expert advice on how Troy's concussion would affect him in the game. Beyond expert opinion on brain function, they were also ace weathermen, fashion consultants, tour guides, and family counselors. They even did an article that featured comparison and contrast on what the Cowboys and Bills eat for breakfast!

I was so glad when Thursday rolled around, so I could be with Denise and the kids, if only for a little bit. Of course, as soon as their plane hit the ground in Atlanta, the press mobbed them as well. By Saturday, even our families were the stuff of headlines:

Players' Families Enjoy Super Visit
(Fort Worth Star-Telegram)

Sometime around 3:00 P.M. today, Denise Bates' husband, Bill, will disappear to a clandestine spot, and she won't speak to him again until late Sunday. She and the other wives of

Dallas Cowboys players and coaches say they have no clue where there husbands will be-a situation Coach Jimmy Johnson hopes will alleviate distractions and help the team to focus on its Super Bowl rematch with the Buffalo Bills.

In fact, 'Denise said Johnson didn't want players' family and friends in town until Thursday, so that's when the team's chartered jets for loved ones arrived.

"He didn't want the distraction," she said.

Despite their short stay, the Bates family and scores of other wives, children, parents, and friends have had plenty to do in Atlanta. Yesterday, while players were running plays, family members were running up charge-card bills as they stocked up on Super Bowl XXVIII souvenirs. Many of them visited a special stand at the team's hotel that offered a 40 percent discount for players' relatives and friends.

Because the Super Bowl comes just a week after the NFC Championship Game, the team had little time to make elaborate preparations. That means that special events held last year in connection with Super Bowl XXVII in Los Angeles such as the team dinner and a fashion show for wives-were not repeated.

But families stayed busy seeing the sites of Atlanta, and they praised the city for its cleanliness and friendliness.

"This place has a Southern hospitality that was lacking in LA.," said Denise Bates, who lived in Atlanta for two years.

Many families hit the malls adjacent to the team's hotel in Atlanta's northern suburbs, while others visited Super Bowl related events such as the NFL Experience, a 500,000-square-foot football theme park that let them kick field goals, make their own trading card, and suit up in game-day gear.

While Bill Bates was on the practice field yesterday, his wife climbed into a white stretch limousine and toured the interactive exhibit with the couple's four-year-old triplets, Graham, Brianna, and Hunter, and three-year-old son, Tanner. They were joined by their neighbors in North Dallas.

One burly Chicago Bears fan asked the children if they were Bears fans. Graham shook his head, responding, "No way. My dad's a Cowboy."

Denise laughed at the fans' bemused expression.

"They don't think they're unusual," she said of her children. "They think everybody's dad is a football player."

251

I expected to pick up a newspaper and see a headline that a Cowboy or a Bill blew his nose that day. These people wrote about anything!

They even got a game prediction from my kids. A bunch of reporters surrounded the triplets and asked them, "Who's gonna win the Super Bowl?"

Without missing a beat, the kids responded, "My daddy is!" Denise had her hands full that week. We are very protective of our kids and this whole zoo-like atmosphere of interviews, tape recorders, and TV cameras was a bit much. In order to keep our kids out of the public eye and also to keep their lives a little more on the normal side, we don't give many interviews as a family. We don't want "child stars." We want happy, healthy kids. With all the family that came in for the game, we also had a couple of baby-sitters come along to watch over the kids on game day. That way Denise could attend the game without worrying about the children.

As the article stated, the team went to another hotel for a little seclusion. By Saturday night we needed it.

As I walked off the field following the coin toss, in the midst of all the emotions and memories flooding my mind, I knew it was time to settle in and play football.

Within the first three minutes of play, we put points on the board with Eddie Murray's forty-one-yard field goal. Before we had a chance to feel too good about that, Buffalo kicked their own field goal to tie us. This particular field goal by Bills kicker, Steve Christie, was fifty-four yards ... a new record as the longest in Super Bowl history.

We were tentative the entire first half. I don't know if it was nerves or all the hype surrounding the game or what, but we were tight for two entire quarters. We scored another field goal to end the first quarter leading 6-3. But the Bills opened the second quarter with a drive that capped off with a four-yard scamper by Thurman Thomas into the end zone-10-6.

As the gun ended the second quarter, Christie hit another field goal to put the halftime score at 13-6. Coach Johnson told the press after the game, "I wasn't upset at halftime. It (the seven-point deficit) wasn't that big a thing. I knew we'd be okay. I told the guys to hang in there, that we made some mistakes, but that we'd be fine."

He had told us from the start that we would win this thing in the fourth quarter, so he was consistent with his game plan. Coach calmed us down in the locker room while the crowd was whipped into a frenzy by the fabulous country western halftime show. Being a serious country-western fan, it broke my heart to miss the festivities, believe me!

Because it was the Super Bowl, the halftime was much longer than normal, which can make the players really antsy downstairs. It was ironic, however, how our team responded. I wrote in my journal afterwards about our halftime state of mind:

I've never seen as much confidence in a team that was behind.

We returned to the field, but it was all to change in the second half. Our team was in complete oneness. When the offense was on the field, the defense was cheering them on from the sidelines like never before. And when the defense was out there, our offense was pulling for them with a zest never before seen.

The momentum of the game changed in the first six-and-a half minutes of the second half. James Washington recovered a Thurman Thomas fumble (set up by Leon Lett-hurray!) and ran it forty-six yards for a touchdown in the opening seconds of the third quarter. This was immediately followed by Emmitt scoring off a fifteen-yard run. With six minutes and eighteen seconds gone from the second half, it went from 13-6 to 20-13.

As the fourth quarter opened, James Washington was at it again. This time he intercepted the ball and set up another touchdown run by Emmitt Smith. Now it was 27-13 and hope was fading fast for Bills fans.

Emmitt personally saw to it that the Bills would be denied a Super Bowl victory. With a total of 132 yards on the day, Emmitt had ninety-one of those yards in the second half. He set up one final Eddie Murray field goal, sealing Cowboy victory at 30-13.

Once again, in the final seconds of the game, I was out on the field. Buffalo was in a no-huddle offense, throwing the ball with reckless abandon. As a result, I was doing another series of wind-sprints on the field. I thought I was going to throw up.

Just like in the NFC Championship Game, I looked over to the sidelines for Ken Norton. And just like in the NFC Championship Game, he was hamming it up for the television cameras, pouring Gatorade all over Coach Johnson!

Super Bowl Nickel Defense

To cap off a valiant season of personal triumph, Emmitt was named Most Valuable Player of the Super Bowl. He also won the rushing title and was named Most Valuable Player in the National Football League ... all well-deserved by an amazing athlete.

The locker room was Christmas morning, New Year's Eve, and the Fourth of July all rolled into one. It's all the stuff you see on TV-and then some! Champagne was being sprayed everywhere and guys were hugging each other. Specially made hats and T-shirts were being passed around. Cameras were everywhere.

Whether we win or lose, I am usually one of the last guys to leave the clubhouse after a game. I think it's a combination of factors, but not the least of which is that I'm completely and utterly exhausted after a game-I barely have the strength to shower, dress, and leave.

The Super Bowl was no exception. I wanted to squeeze every moment of joy from this experience. Here I was-the kid who was always too small or too slow. Now I was the one who was too old to play. Now it was me who was injured beyond the expectation of return. I'm the guy who had to fight for a slot on the roster every year ... and now I was the guy standing in the locker room, kissing the Super Bowl trophy. That was me, actually experiencing the culmination of a dream that began with a boy in a Headhunters uniform. This was my moment- the one I visualized back at Farragut High School . . . the moment I dreamed of all through the years at the University of Tennessee. It was the vision that propelled me past my difficulties with Coach Majors, "The Play," not getting drafted, and all the injuries. It was the sweetest feeling on earth.

Sweet!

But I had my head on straight enough to realize that it was all because of God's grace that I was standing where I was standing. Sure, I worked harder than anyone I knew, but that in itself wasn't enough. It was my deep trust in the Lord that brought me to where I was. Early on I had decided to trust Him and shoot for the star.

The locker room was almost empty when a voice cried out, "Is Bill Bates here?"

"I'm over here," I replied.

"Well, hurry up and meet me at the police car in front of the locker room door." The voice was coming from Larry Lacewell, our head scout.

"Why?" I inquired. "What's up?"

"Jerry Jones wants to see you right away."

It turned out that I was in for a special little getaway.

While the whole team was filing back onto the bus that brought us here, there were two helicopters waiting a little further up the road.

One helicopter was reserved for Jerry Jones and his son, Steven. Larry was riding in the other helicopter and the extra seat was reserved for me. I was put in the helicopter and flown back to the hotel after a breathtaking ride through the beauty of downtown Atlanta at night.

But I should mention one last thing. Before I left the locker room there was one final photo opportunity I couldn't pass up. This gentleman and I had made a promise to each other a year ago in Pasadena that if we won the Super Bowl again the next year, we would have our picture taken together holding the Vince Lombardi trophy.

By this time the trophy had already been placed back in its box. As the box was being carried to the bus I screamed, "STOP! I need one more picture with that trophy."

At first the handlers were unwilling, but I persuaded them it was vital for me to have a few more pictures with the trophy. I eventually wore them down, and they hauled the trophy back into the locker room.

I searched the team area and spotted my friend. I invited him over for a picture and in doing so, reminded him of our promise to each other the year before. He had not forgotten and was more than willing to pose with me.

In my mind it was so fitting that the last item of business for me at the Georgia Dome, before boarding the helicopter, was to have my picture taken with the Vince Lombardi trophy and my good friend, Father Leo.

It will help me to always remember.

24 - Epilogue

It was an overcast day in Baltimore in the middle of March's cold winter. The sun had not shown its face that day, and the weatherman said the rain would be turning into snow very soon. I was warm-sweating, in fact-in my hotel room right downtown in the city. I was fumbling around with the bow tie I needed to wear with my tuxedo.

In a few short hours I would be driven to an awards ceremony where I would be presented with the Ed Block Courage Award. The award is given every year to the player on each NFL team who best exemplifies courage in coming back from some sort of major setback, usually an injury. It's one of those awards you hope you never get because you hope you'll never get injured. But if you do get hurt, it's a real honor to receive it.

By the time I arrived at the hall, the rain had turned to snow. Yet the room was filled with people swarming around like a hive of bees, searching out their favorite players for a handshake or an autograph.

I took my seat at the prearranged table. Art Monk from the Redskins was seated next to me. We small-talked for a second before the crowd spotted us and immediately circled the table. I signed programs, footballs, football cards, jerseys, helmets, photos, wristbands, and napkins. After each signature I'd hand the autographed item back to its owner. At that point they usually noticed my Super Bowl ring. "Wow, can I look at your ring?" they'd coo, usually in complete awe.

"Sure," I'd reply. "This is last year's ring. We haven't got this year's yet. It'll be even better!"

"Better?" they gasped. "How can you top this-it's huge!" Then they would notice the hand the ring was attached to.

"That's quite a hand you've got there!" was about the nicest thing a person could say. With all my broken fingers and swollen knuckles, my hands are unique, indeed. I've got fingers that point left when my hand faces right. I've got knuckles big enough to belong to Paul Bunyan. Juxtaposed with that hand is this ring of diamonds ... this ring of champions.

The evening's program was delightful. Former NFL greats like Paul Hornung and Doak Walker made speeches. A video was shown from a visit we had made earlier that day to St. Vincent's Center for Abused Children. As the tape captured us playing games with the young kids, the sounds of "Hero" by Mariah Carey were heard in the background.

When it eventually came time for me to receive my award, I thanked the people who were responsible for it, letting them know how symbolic it was to me. Coming back from adversity had become a constant theme in my life. Yet the most important thing, I told them, was the opportunity it provided to do things like cheer up those kids over at St. Vincent's that morning. People helping other people, that's what life is all about.

The Ed Block Courage Award – Quite an honor

They handed me a beautiful award, a solid silver, full-size Cowboy helmet resting on a silver urn. I thanked them again and returned to my seat. I stared down at the award and thought of some of the other awards I had received in my career. I've been honored to receive the Bob Lilly Award for three of the last four years. The plaque says, "For demonstrating the highest standards of sportsmanship, dedication, leadership, and achievement as exemplified by Bob Lilly during his fourteen-year Hall of Fame career with the Dallas Cowboys." The thing that's really great about that award is that it's voted on by the fans.

As the program continued, my mind kept returning to those abused kids. I'm sure it sounded corny up on the platform, but I meant every word. In God's grand scheme of things, the most important reason for me to be in Baltimore that snowy March day was to be a little bit of an encouragement to some kids who are far less fortunate than myself.

There is no doubt that I am a fortunate fellow. The Lord smiled down on me and made my life a dream come true in so many ways.

"Have you seen this quote from your old friend, John Madden?" a friend of mine asked as he jammed a piece of paper under my nose. He showed me a statement I had not previously seen.

"Bill Bates has covered kicks better, with more enthusiasm, and for more seasons than any other player I've ever seen. Every game starts with a kick, but when Bates is on the field, every game begins with a Bang!"
-John Madden
Sportscaster and Former NFL Coach

I just stared at the page. This was all so joyously overwhelming to me. My friend smiled as he saw my reaction. He knew how meaningful this sort of praise was to me, and he was glad to be the bearer of glad tidings.

Seeing how the Madden quote affected me, my friend pushed a little further. "I talked with Brad Sham the other day-you know, the Voice of the Cowboys."

"Sure, I know Brad. He's a good friend," I responded.

"He was so glad you were getting this award. You really deserve it."

"Brad's a great guy."

"Well, he sure likes you," my friend went on. "He said to me, 'I'd describe Bill Bates with one word-intense-but that word is inadequate. There's so much more to him than that. He is a great human being, a husband, a father, a public servant, a doer of good deeds."

My head was spinning. Sitting at this table, horribly uncomfortable in this straightjacket of a tuxedo, listening to friends tell me what a great guy I am-it was all kind of eerie. It felt good, but I never really did stuff just for the praise of other people.

As the driver plodded along on Baltimore's snowy streets that night, I looked out the window, completely lost in thought. So much had happened in my life, the two Super Bowls capping it all off. What's ahead for Bill Bates? I certainly had been asked that a lot in the recent weeks.

In a few short days the question would take on even greater depth. Before March was ended, Jimmy Johnson would be finished with his responsibilities as head coach of the Cowboys.

There was lots of speculation on why Jimmy Johnson left Dallas. As one of his players, I saw firsthand the hours and the commitment it took for him to take the Dallas Cowboys to the first Super Bowl in Pasadena. It is obvious to anyone who knows him that Coach Johnson is a man driven to succeed in any endeavor in which he participates.

So after the win in Pasadena, the big question was, "What's the next challenge?" The answer was to win back-to-back Super Bowls, of course. To do that, you had to have good systems, naturally. But-more importantly-for this to happen, good players were a necessity.

The strain on Coach Johnson must have been incredible, especially at the beginning of the '93 season. Emmitt was holding out, we got murdered by a Redskin team that had prepared the entire off-season for our Monday night contest, we went on to lose to Buffalo ... and suddenly you're the head coach of the championship team that's 0-2.

Despite turning around the record, the pressure was still there. By the end of the season, while we were preparing for the Giants in New York, a reporter asked Coach Johnson if he was interested in the head coaching job for the expansion team in Jacksonville, Florida. Instead of just saying "no," Coach Johnson scratched his chin and responded,' "Hmmm, That's interesting. Maybe I'd have to consider that."

His response became big news nationwide. And, naturally, it had an impact on Jerry Jones.

"I've got Jimmy Johnson under contract," Jerry countered to the press.

The battle intensified and it is well-chronicled for everyone to know. It was only a matter of time before Coach Johnson would leave, and time was up on the last day of March.

With the classic speed Jerry Jones is known for, no sooner was Coach Johnson out than Barry Switzer was in.

Who's Barry Switzer? I only knew of Barry Switzer as the head coach of the Oklahoma Sooners. I knew he won the national championship. But that's all I knew. Once he was hired, the team hastily called a meeting for all the players who were in town during this off-season break. Coach Switzer was introduced to us, and he made a few brief comments to the team. My initial impression was of a man who was excited. Not only was he excited, but more importantly to me, he showed it! I looked forward to playing under a man who is so energetic and excited about his job.

Another impression I came away with was his knowledge of the game of football. He knows what he's doing. He also gets along with his players-all of his players. It's hard to find anyone who has played for Coach Switzer who isn't positive about him, and I feel that says a lot about his ability and his character. I'm impressed.

I was the Cowboys' player representative for the National Football League Player's Association (NFLPA). I was voted in by default, since no one else wanted the position. Our union has had its good times and its bad times. The strike of 1987 was especially bad.

At this time we are at peace with the owners. A number of people and players feel this new collective bargaining agreement is bad for the players, yet others think it's good. No matter how you feel we are now living with free agency and a salary cap. Many people say the players were bought out for a $200 million settlement. It definitely has affected my situation as an older player.

The owners and the players will live with this agreement for seven years with salaries and benefits continuing to grow. I hope the fans will continue to crave the NFL and especially the Cowboys!

As for my future, the story will proceed with the similarity of former chapters. I'll play again this year for the Cowboys. Everyone will write me off during training camp, saying I don't have what it takes to make the team. I'll work harder than I've ever worked and-to everyone's amazement-I will somehow make the final cut.

It's just not going to be easy to get rid of me. Our whole family loves Dallas, and we plan to make it our home for a long time. Once I do get too old to play, perhaps coaching will be the next item on the agenda. I look forward to the chance to coach my sons.

Wherever we are, we want to give back to those who have given so much to us. Someone once shared with me a poem that has come to typify what I want to do with my life. ruse it in my speeches when I talk to people around the country about what is really important.

Count your blessings,
Instead of your crosses,
Count your gains,
Instead of your losses.
Count your yeses,
Instead of your nos,
Count your friends,
Instead of your foes.
Count the full years,
Instead of the lean,
Count your deeds,
Instead of your mean,
Count your health,
Instead of your wealth,
Count on God,
Instead of yourself.

25 - Living the Dream!

We won Super Bowl XXX in Tempe, Arizona on Sunday, January 28, 1996, but it wasn't until the middle of April that we could gather the team together for some very important congratulations. Oh sure, there were parades, parties, media falling over each other, a meeting with the president at the White House, and all the other hoopla that accompanies winning the World Championship. But when our mini-camp convened in April, it was the first time we were together as a full team since the Super Bowl win.

Coach Barry Switzer used this spring day at our training facility in Valley Ranch as an opportunity to personally congratulate all of us, since there had been no time for this after the game. He went on to talk about the players we had already lost in the off-season. Kindly, he pointed out how we would miss each and every one of those guys. But he quickly moved to the excitement he had for the new players, assuring us that we still had what was necessary to be champions.

Coach Switzer is not one to sit back and rest on his accomplishments, and he will not allow us to fall into that position either. "Now is the time to work to get better!" he urged. It was just what we needed to hear. I've been around the Dallas Cowboys long enough to know that we actually win our Super Bowls in the off-season with our training.

Before too long our owner, Jerry Jones, stepped to the front of the room to make a few remarks. He, too, was congratulatory regarding our accomplishments over the preceding year. The statements he made that meant the most to me went something like this:

"We are a family. In a family you have times when you get upset with one another, but you fight for one another. We've been through a lot, both good and bad, but don't ever forget-we are a family."

It's such a great feeling for a player to feel that sort of support from the club's owner. I couldn't help but sit back and think of some of the events that had taken place in my life over the last couple of years. There were some pretty amazing things!

April 1994

When I first finished Shoot for the Star, the Cowboys had just come through the head coaching transition from Jimmy Johnson to Barry Switzer. My initial impression of Coach Switzer was positive, and I continue to maintain that position. Barry Switzer is exactly what this team needs. We have players at a place where they know what their job is, and how to get that job done. Thus, we don't need a lot of the prodding that we needed during the team's earlier days with Coach Landry and Coach Johnson.

Coach Switzer manages us well and keeps a smile on our faces. Granted, he represents a new school of coaching-but for where I am in my career, it is a genuine breath of fresh air to have a coach who believes in me.

July 1994

It's nice to have an owner like Jerry Jones, as well. It doesn't get into the newspapers a great deal, but this man has a tremendous heart. A personal example of this giving spirit occurred during our training camp two years ago, the summer after we had won the Super Bowl in Atlanta. On a warm summer day in the middle of July 1994, I was working out with the team down in Austin. Word had reached the training camp that my cousin and dear friend, John Graham, had been killed in an ATV accident back in our home state of Tennessee.

It was such a tragedy. Just months earlier John was in Atlanta with us, enjoying our Super Bowl victory. Now he was gone. In the midst of this turmoil, the Cowboys excused me from camp for a few days in order for me to attend John's funeral. Jerry Jones made arrangements for me to use his private jet to fly to Tennessee. I left Austin, stopped in Dallas to pick up Denise, flew to Newport, Tennessee, and home again. Denise and I were so grateful for this wonderful gesture on Jerry's part. He truly is a remarkable person.

I still think about John a great deal. We miss him so much.

August 1994

I remember when our Super Bowl rings arrived from the victory over the Bills in Atlanta. We were invited to a very formal, very private team dinner in Dallas. No media were allowed past the doors of the beautifully decorated room where the players and their wives gathered for the Super Bowl XXVIII celebration.

At our places on the table were gift-wrapped boxes, and we knew that our rings were inside. In order to heighten the anticipation, we were asked to wait until after dinner before opening our presents.

The rings were breathtaking. In another classy act by the Jones family, Jerry's daughter, Charlotte, asked me if I would offer a prayer of thanks for this festive occasion. I stood at the lectern, asked everyone in the room to bow their heads, and prayed:

> Our Heavenly Father:
> Thank You for this time to celebrate the accomplishments of our past. Thank You for the many friends we have made through this journey, which we will always hold dear to our hearts. And in this time of celebrating great accomplishments, help us to be humble and not forget that our greatest accomplishment lies ahead!
> In Jesus Name, Amen.

November 1994

We traveled to San Francisco to face the 49ers in Candlestick Park on November 13. It was the classic confrontation between two front-runners in the NFC, and we knew we were in for a tough game. When we came up on the short end of the score, naturally I was disappointed and discouraged.

When we arrived back in Dallas, I found my group of encouragers waiting for me .... my kids. Graham, Brianna, Hunter, and Tanner couldn't have cared less whether I won or lost. They just loved their daddy! Sitting around the dinner table, we were all laughing and cutting up. I couldn't help but notice that Denise was a little more quiet than usual. She seemed a bit preoccupied, and that just wasn't like her. I decided to tease her a little to see if that would bring her back to life.

"Okay Denise, tell me, what have you done?" I scolded her in a kidding way.

"It's not what I've done; it's what we've done," she replied with a sly grin on her face.

"What are you talking about?" I asked.

"I'M PREGNANT!!" she declared in a tone of voice that reminded me of her days as a cheerleader.

I must have looked as surprised as I felt, for she immediately added, "Don't worry, I've already made a visit to the doctor and he gave me a sonogram."

"And?"

"It's ONE!"

We both sighed in relief, not sure whether we could have handled a second set of triplets.

It was the thought of another little Bates running around the house, and the four little fireballs already in our home, that gave me the perspective I needed to get through a very difficult season.

January 1995

Our season ended on January 15, 1995, when we lost the NFC Championship Game to the 49ers in San Francisco. The 49ers came to play, jumping on us early. We never could recover. As a result of that loss, all we could feel was pain. The 49ers earned Super Bowl XXIX. After that game and throughout the off-season, I would be asked over and over to assess our loss in that critical game. Here's my response:

"We lost the NFC Championship Game in the first four minutes of the game. It was 21-0 before we knew it! Take away four minutes of the 1994 season, and it might have ended up another way. This next season we won't come up four minutes short!"

The Cowboys were committed to going back to the Super Bowl First, we had to talk Charles Haley out of retiring, but perhaps the strongest indication was demonstrated by the fact that we all began training in the off-season immediately after our loss in San Francisco. We didn't want this situation to occur again.

April 1995

One of our picks in the NFL draft was a cornerback out of Mississippi named Alundis Bryce. When I first met Alundis, we made small-talk about my alma mater, Tennessee, and his, Ol' Miss. Eventually we got into a conversation that was far from small-talk.

He shared with me how he had been hanging out with some of his buddies one night not too long ago. There was a lot of laughing and kidding around, but for some reason, the scene turned ugly. One of the guys picked a fight with another guy, and Alundis stepped in and attempted to break it up. Suddenly a gun was pulled. A shot rang out. Alundis was hit by a bullet at point-blank range. The shot entered his chest just to the right of his heart.

"It's okay, it's okay-I wasn't even hit" Alundis told his friends. He walked a few steps before collapsing. He was rushed to the emergency room of the hospital, where the doctors miraculously saved his life.

Nothing was going to keep Alundis from realizing his dream of playing in the National Football League, not even a life-threatening injury. I was fascinated by this story he was telling me, but Alundis had a personal note for me. He went on:

"During my stay in the hospital, someone gave me a copy of your book, Shoot for the Star. I wanted you to know that book gave me great inspiration in my recovery. I just wanted to say thanks."

I didn't know what to say. I had received nice comments and notes from folks who enjoyed the book, but to hear a guy say these things who would be lining up with me on the football field was something very special to me. Alundis did make a full recovery. We drafted him, he made the team, and he's making a real contribution to the Dallas Cowboys.

July 1995

Graham, Brianna, Hunter, and Tanner proudly announced the newest rookie on the Bates team. Our "nickel back," Dillon Timothy Bates, was born on July 5 at 8:22 A.M. At almost twenty inches long, he weighed in at eight pounds. Mother and child came through everything in championship fashion! When we sent out the birth announcements, we wrote at the bottom:

SCORE: Kids 5

Denise and Bill 2

(Mom and Dad are definitely outnumbered now!)

It's a non-stop circus at our house with five little ones.

Their energy knows no boundaries. Between the thousands of questions they ask, the numerous activities they are involved in, and the constant supervision required, Denise has a full-time job-all day, every day.

One afternoon I was feeling especially sorry for Denise, who was utterly exhausted. In a spurt of newfound bravery, I offered to do the grocery shopping for her. She quickly agreed with my plan. With a sense of invincibility, I also suggested that I take the five kids with me, allowing Denise an opportunity for some rest. A brief glimpse of fear entered her eyes, but relief won out. So that's how I ended up with all five kids at the grocery store.

The kids hit the store at full speed. I placed Dillon in the shopping cart, getting him strapped into his little infant seat. By the time I got him settled, I looked up to discover that the older kids were running up and down the aisles, knocking over cans, displays, and anything else in their way. Dillon had been quiet long enough so, as if on cue, he started screaming at the top of his lungs.

I unstrapped him, picked him up, and tried my best to calm him down. With as soothing a voice as I could generate, I kept repeating, "Don't cry, Billy! Don't scream, Billy!"

A woman who had been observing this entire scene walked up to me and politely commented, "Excuse me, young man, but I couldn't help but notice how well you take care of your family. I certainly respect you for it. I especially like how you talk to your baby, Billy, to calm him down." I swallowed hard and told her the truth. "Lady, his name is Dillon; I'm Billy!"

September 1995

The first of the month was an exciting day for the Bates family. A new season upon us, another chance to show the world that the Cowboys had the stuff to be world champions. We had worked harder during the off-season than most of us could remember. Our goal was clear: Go to Tempe, Arizona in January and win Super Bowl XXX.

On another front, there was additional excitement in our family. After months of planning and preparation, my partner Ric Levit and I opened The Bill Bates Cowboy Grill in Dallas on September 1. A family restaurant with the best food around, it opened with a bang! The menu featured all kinds of fun items like a "Souper Bowl of Soup" to start out with, or "Linebackers" (jalapenos stuffed with chicken and jack cheese) for an appetizer. Then there were championship main courses like "Bill Bates Crack Back Ribs" or "Cowboy Smoked Chicken Fried Steak" (the house specialty) or the "Bates Burger," topped off with a piece of "Cowboys Cheesecake." A feast fit for royalty!

I also saw to it that the restaurant was decorated with plenty of memorabilia from my playing days-game balls, trophies, jerseys, photographs-and of course, big-screen televisions for the viewing of Cowboys games!

We opened the season on the road. Labor Day evening, the Cowboys were in the Meadowlands to face the always tough New York Giants for the premiere of "Monday Night Football" It was doubly exciting for me, feeling the anticipation in the stadium and also knowing that back home in Dallas, the restaurant was packed to capacity with fans glued to the big screens, cheering us on at every play.

The stadium was filled to capacity with 77,454 fans. The noise level quickly diminished as Emmitt Smith exploded up the middle of the field for a sixty-yard touchdown run the very first time he carried the ball. Little did we know at that time that it was a sign of things to come. We won big-35-0, our first shutout since 1992.

Personally, I played a good game. Later I was told there were quite a few instances where I was the focus of the TV camera, which sent the restaurant crowd into orbit!

On one particular play, I made a tackle against the Giants rookie running back, Keith Elias. We were both in this massive pile of bodies on the field. As we're getting back to our feet, he turned to me, saying, "Bill Bates! I want you to know that I really respect you!"

I smiled, but he wasn't finished. "Yeah ... I've been watching you play football since I was about eight years old!"

Sincerity was written all over this kid's face. I responded curtly, "That's not something you do in the middle of an NFL game .... telling a guy how old he is!" We both chuckled and made our way back to our respective teams.

Someone I had been watching and playing against for years joined our team-Deion Sanders. As everyone knows, he truly is a great player. When you play against him you want to smash him, because of his ability and especially the image he portrays.

But I soon discovered that he really is a great guy. He's funny, a great locker room presence, a hard worker, and a teacher of other players. Unfortunately, images are created that cause people to make judgments without really knowing a person. I know; I used to see Deion through different eyes. Now, I really like him and can call him a friend.

December 1995

Christmas night the Cowboys were in need of some cheer. So did my family! Being away on Christmas made it difficult for kids. They were so worried about missing out on all their presents that they wrote Santa to remind him to come a day late!

The last three weeks had been difficult ones. After Thanksgiving we had the best record in the NFL at 10-2. But the next three weeks were traumatic. We lost to the Redskins again.

Then it was on to Philadelphia. Playing in Philly is always very difficult for our team. Coach Ray Rhodes had his team ready to play, and they took it to us! The game was tied late in the second half. We were up against a fourth-and-one situation. Almost everyone on the sideline was saying, "Go for it!" We did. Emmitt was stuffed twice by their defense. Basically, that was the game. From that moment on, Coach Switzer would be unduly hammered by the fans.

We were back in Texas Stadium the next week. We squeaked by the New York Giants, winning with a Chris Bonoil field goal at the gun. Final score: 21-20.

We needed three events to take place in order to regain home field advantage throughout the playoffs: Chicago had to beat Philadelphia,

Atlanta needed to upend San Francisco, and we had to beat the Cardinals on Monday night.

On Sunday, December 24, Santa delivered a victory against the Bears as well as the Falcons. That evening, as we went about our walk-through on the field at Sun Devil Stadium, I found myself looking up at the clear night sky. I was looking for the jet that carried the 49ers back from Atlanta. I remember thinking, "This is our chance! We don't want to put smiles back on the faces of the 49ers Tuesday morning!"

We controlled our own destiny on a warm Christmas night in Tempe. It was a little strange, working on Christmas, but that's life in the NFL. Coach Switzer's pregame talk was straight and to the point: "We want to be back here in Tempe in a month for the Super Bowl!"

The Cardinals were no match for us that evening.

Nothing seemed to be going their way. Even at halftime, as the two teams ran off together into the tunnel, I was jogging behind Arizona quarterback Dave Krieg, when suddenly he slipped on the concrete, falling flat on his back right in front of Deion Sanders. Poor Dave! He was heard to mutter, "This isn't gonna be my night!"

We won the game 37-13, beating Arizona for the eleventh straight time. Homefield advantage was ours!

January 1996

Our first playoff foes were the Philadelphia Eagles. The Friday night before the Sunday afternoon game, we once again held a pep rally out at the Bill Bates Cowboy Ranch. Why is the temperature always so cold at these Rallies? I guess we can't be choosy! Twenty thousand cheering fans made the evening a screaming success.

Sunday wasn't too shabby either. We had some unfinished business with the Eagles. When we were through, it was Cowboys 30, Eagles 11, including a score by Deion Sanders that sent the crowd through the hole in the roof of Texas Stadium!

The victory over the Eagles brought us to the NFC Championship once again, but this year our opponent was the Green Bay Packers. A lot of people were picking the Packers to go all the way, so there was some pride on the line. Since the 49ers game we had worked so hard to get here. The first four minutes weren't stopping us this time! Troy threw to Michael Irvin for two touchdowns in the first quarter. Emmitt had three touchdowns of his own. Tack on a field goal and the final score was Dallas 38, Green Bay 27.

Next stop ... Tempe. I'll cover the Super Bowl in a later chapter. Here is what happened in the following months.

March 1996

What did I feel after winning this latest Super Bowl? Relief. This year there was so much pressure surrounding all of us in the Cowboys organization-from Jerry Jones all the way down to the lowest position on the totem pole. We had something to prove .... we were still champions. So, mixed with relief was the thrill of living on Cloud Nine during the off-season again.

A lot has happened during this off-season-not all of it good. But every person on this team makes his own decisions that affect his personal life. I try to do what the Lord wants me to do, trusting Him to show me the way. He opens many different doors, and it's my job to have enough faith to walk through the right ones.

A good example of this principle occurred in my life during the off-season. After thirteen years of working and scrapping like a junkyard dog to make the team, I was approached by another team in their effort to sign me as a free agent. must admit, I was flattered to be sought after by the Oakland Raiders, but in God's timing I had no sooner finished my conversation with the Raiders people when the Cowboys signed me for my fourteenth year. I guess you can't read this book with seeing loud and clear that our whole family loves Dallas. I feel like 1 am exactly where God wants me to be.

He continues to use me. The Fellowship of Christian Athletes passed on to me a copy of an application to one of their summer camps that had come in from a twenty-one- year-old college junior. One of the questions asked of the applicants is, "Explain when and how your walk with Christ began." This young man wrote, "1 was saved while in junior high school, but my Christian walk didn't kick in until my sophomore year in high school. Bill Bates spoke to my church and ever since then I have been walking on solid ground."

On March 8, I flew to Washington D.C. to be honored at the twenty-third annual NFL Players Awards Banquet as one of the thirty Unsung Heroes of the 1995 Season. Gene Upshaw, executive director of the NFL Players Association, explained the award this way: "We are honoring thirty NFL players, voted 'Unsung Heroes' of the 1995 season by their teammates and fans. These players best exemplify dedication, commitment, and love of professional football. Every NFL team had at least one. The guy who really came to play every week, in the mud, blood, for the love of the competition and the game."

I was thrilled to receive an award of this nature. When the voting includes the fans, it is especially significant to me. The ballots for this award not only had a space for the name of the player who should receive this honor, but it also had a place to write in the reason why each person voted as they did. At the banquet we received our awards, as well as sets of "Unsung Heroes Trading Cards." Our pictures were on the front, and the back side had comments about each player made by fans who voted for him.

My card read:
Bill Bates
Bates epitomizes the concept of an unsung hero.
A few samples:
"His intensity is unmatched and sparks his Dallas teammates."
"He reminds me of the Eveready Bunny.
He just keeps going and going!"

I cherish this award because it came from the fans. It will always be a wonderful reminder of that great group of people.

My young son, Tanner, thought the whole adventure was pretty cool too. He was asked where his daddy was and he responded, "Daddy is in Washington, DC. He is receiving a reward for being the oldest player in the NFL! My daddy has been playing for one hundred years!"

I was recently inspired to press on in my playing career by receiving a wonderful letter from a young girl here in the Dallas area. She writes:

Dear Mr. Bates:

I read your book, Shoot for the Star. That was the best book I ever read. Reading it helped me to be much closer to God. You are my idol, not just because you are the best player on the Cowboys, but also because you are the godliest man and I can tell that God lives in your heart. In your book you said to dream big. Well, I had given up all hope in ever getting to play football on a team because I am a girl. But now, although most of my classmates make fun of me, I'm still going to dream big. I'm never going to give up on my football fantasy. I always dream that one day I'll be able to play football on a team. I've always wanted to play football. I go out as often as I can and just throw the football around with my dad, and at recess I throw with my best friend, Christi. Most everyone says I can't play football because I'm short and weak, and most of all, because I am a girl. It really hurts when people make fun of me, but I just have to block out their voices, which is very hard to do. But reading your book put hope back into my life that I can dream big and shoot for the stars. You said that is what you did, and now you're the best player on the Cowboys.

Everyone says that I'm just going through a tomboy stage, but I don't think it's just a stage. As stupid as this may sound, I want to spend the rest of my life playing football and hear people ask me questions like "So Meredith, how do you do it?" I would say, "God has blessed me with this talent so that I can glorify Him." I just wish I was a boy so badly, because I would be allowed to pursue what I love doing the most. Well, I know you get a lot of fan mail, and I bet you're really busy, but if you want to, do you think that you could write me back?

Love in Christ,
Meredith Lins (signed with a hand-drawn football)

What a treat to receive a letter like Meredith's! When I was younger I had things that I wanted to accomplish. It's important to keep our dreams alive, but also accept who we are. God made each of us in a unique way in order to fulfill His plan. Maybe God's plan for Meredith will be to fulfill her life- long desire to play football. Maybe she can realize a piece of her dream at this young age as her dreams blend in with the reality of today's world.

In terms of my future in professional football, my thoughts are simple and straightforward. I'm living the dream for as long as I can live it! When I feel I can't keep up with these younger players, I'll retire. But until then, I feel good as a player and I still feel like I am making a contribution to the Dallas Cowboys.

26 - Super Bowl XXX

We were a great football team. I go back to this Super Bowl because there are memories I didn't share in the original writing of the book. Back then I was on top of the world and now I can look back and really appreciate the accomplishment.

First of all, I wonder how in the world a 35 year-old was able to play in the National Football League? When I was playing, everyone talked about how an old man like me was able to make the team year after year. I just kept my focus and every day I put my heart and soul into making the team. It had worked for me all those years before, so I didn't try to do anything new. I feel fortunate that my body held up to the rigors and that the knee injury was the only major injury I sustained besides various strains, muscle pulls, broken fingers and a few concussions.

Throughout the original book I told of the hit Hershel Walker put on me in college. Sometimes I think that hit is what propelled my career. On that day, on that five yard line and in front of a stadium full of people, and a TV audience, Hershel gave me an incredible gift. Over the years it was something that motivated me like no other and I teach it to my players today. It became my secret weapon on the field and I only realized it years later.

Hershel was coming at me at full speed and man did he have speed. When I stopped and set up, he had the momentum and the results are still being played on YouTube around the world. I vowed to myself then and there to never breakdown like that again. In a hit like that you are either the bullet or the target. From that point on I was the bullet not the target and because I was always hitting people at full speed, my career was long and rewarding.

Winning my third Super Bowl ring was incredibly satisfying and being a Cowboy during this run of Super Bowl wins will always be looked back on as a highlight in my life. What it took to get us to the point where we were once again a winning team was a journey that helped shape me into the man I am today.

It wasn't easy being a Cowboy. The highs were sweet, the lows were excruciating. I appreciated it more than many of the other players who had not suffered through the changing of the coaches and those horrible 3-13 and 1-15 seasons. Had we not gone through that deep valley, I doubt that we could have ever been a great team. It took a lot of faith and fortune to make the Super Bowl runs. It took a total team effort from Jerry Jones, Jimmy Johnson, Barry Switzer, the Cowboys front office and a group of the most talented athletes in the world.

Looking back now, these are the things I remember most about Super Bowl XXX:

I sat in front of my locker. I wasn't going to lose another Dallas Cowboys leather jacket like at the last Super Bowl so I was wearing only Cowboy issued garb. They had given us great sweat suits to wear before and after our workouts on Super Bowl week and the weather in Phoenix was nice and warm.

It was about midmorning and I wanted to be in the locker room by myself before the game. It would give me time to reflect on those who would helped me become a Cowboy and to take in all of the sites and trappings of this wonderful building they called Sun Devil Stadium. I needed to be out of the hustle and bustle of the Super Bowl buildup for just a little while so that I could get my head together and focus on the game.

I checked my shoulder pads and mouthpiece and placed them back inside the locker. I slowly put the hip and butt pads in my girdle and gave a little pull to loosen it up then hung it on the hook inside the locker. Pulling out my pants I was struck by just how silver they looked in the low light of the locker. They looked just like the pants I had worn at Farragut High School in Tennessee nearly 20 years before.

Just sitting there holding those pants brought back a rush of memories for me. A feeling of warmth welled up inside me as I thought about my teammates on that championship team my senior year. We had quite a crew back then and I knew that they would all be pulling for me today in the Super Bowl. I relished in the thought that they would be sitting around televisions with their families and friends and telling stories about all the games that we won together. Here I was before one of the biggest games of my career and I was thinking about those special people who were my friends back then. I truly hoped they realized what a special part of my life they were and that today, wearing the same uniform, I was still one of them.

There are pockets on the inside of football pants that hold the thigh and knee pads. I slipped my hand down inside the leg and opened up the pocket to put in my right knee pad. It has a flap over to make sure they stay in place, so putting the pad in securely can be a bit tedious at times. Then I grabbed the other kneepad from the shelf. It was a little larger and thicker than my right one because I chose to protect my left knee a little more. I recalled all of the hours, and months it took to rehabilitate my left knee after surgery and now I was bigger, faster and stronger than before. The transformation of my body was incredible. I had picked up over ten pounds and it was all in my legs and arms. I knew that if I could not play at 100% that my time as a Dallas Cowboy would be over. I worked my knee hard and was elated when it held up to the rigors of running and cutting at full speed without limitation. What I once viewed as torture, running full out sprints, was now a pleasure and something I relished. I was still the Cowboys nickel linebacker and special teams captain just like the Super Bowl XXVIII in Atlanta. It was going to take more than a knee injury to pry me out of the lineup.

The thigh pads were easier to place in the pockets as they slip right in. I remembered how proud I was as a freshman at Farragut to get to suit up for a game. I would still get the same thrill when I slid the pants on and could see the tight material stretch over the pads and around my legs. Since the knee surgery I had really focused on working my legs even harder than ever in my career. I saw a little more bulk in them but the difference in strength was incredible. I spent a lot of time stretching to keep them limber and loose. The combined strength and stretching had increased my speed, which as one of the older guys on the team, was a surprise that gave me an edge.

My friends back at Farragut High Jeff York, Jack DeMatteo, Tim Beeler and my Vols teammates Brad White, Tim Irwin, John Cook, Willie Gault and Reggie White knew how hard I had worked to make it to the NFL. They had worked hard and long beside me and I knew that without them I would have never made it this far. I thought back about our games, the runs, the blocks, the passes and catches and of course the tackles. I took a piece of each of them on the field for every game and today I would need every bit of them.

Standing up, I walked over to mirror in the corner to take a look at how well the pants fit and make sure the pads were positioned right. I did a couple of squats to stretch out the material. Then I slid them off. When I picked them up off the floor, I saw the reflection of myself in the mirror. My gray T-shirt and shorts cover the finely honed body of a professional athlete. My face was not that of a young stud that was ready to go out and take on the world. Instead I saw in my eyes, the look of a seasoned veteran. Looking into that mirror closer I saw the eyes of B.R. Pruett, Bobby Henry, Conrad McCreary, Johnny Majors, Tom Landry, Jimmy Johnson, Barry Switzer, Dave Campo, Mike Zimmer, Joe Avezzano, Ken Sparks, and of course the best coach a man could ever have, Dan Bates, my Dad. I stood there looking into those eyes and gave thanks for each of those men and thought about what they meant to me.

One of the younger equipment managers came by it startled me as he asked if I needed anything. No, standing in front of that mirror I knew that I had everything. I walked back to my locker got down on my knees and gave thanks. I gave thanks for the inspiration of all of these men. I gave thanks because they picked me out of a crowd. I gave thanks because they gave me the confidence to shoot for my STAR. I chuckled to myself and thought about the banner Coach Bobby Henry had hung at Farragut Middle School that simply read:

Dream and shoot for the stars
you never know .... You may reach your star.

Well, I had reached my STAR. It was bigger and brighter than I could have ever imagined. On my knees in the locker room before the Super Bowl, I gave thanks for the blessings that had been bestowed on me by our Creator. I was ready to play football, but the game was more than six hours away.

I had to keep myself calm so that I wouldn't create too much adrenaline and have nothing left for the game. I remember that the stadium had been spruced up a lot before being awarded the Super Bowl. Sun Devil Stadium is on the campus of Arizona State University. I had played there several times but now, it would forever hold a special place in my past. It would also be the last Super Bowl in a college stadium. In the calmness of the pregame locker room I found space in a corner where I could lay down and think.

During the next couple of hours, I lay there in silence. I thought back to every play that I had seen of the Steelers. Their tendencies had been charted for our defense to memorize. I had studied them so much that I didn't need to memorize a thing. If they stuck to their tendencies, which we anticipated, I knew every play that they were likely to call in every situation. I also knew that their wily Head Coach Bill Cowher would have a few tricks up his sleeve.

I thought about the plays they might run on first down and ten from the 20 or second down and four from the 40. Coach Cowher had a cadre of weapons at his disposal. Neil O'Donnell had thrown for nearly 3,000 yards and 17 touchdowns. He was throwing to Pro Bowl wide receiver Yancey Thigpen, a swift Andre Hastings and Ernie Mills. I was so glad that we had picked up four-time Pro bowl cornerback Deion Sanders in the off season to go along with Larry Brown, the eventual Super Bowl MVP, Darren Woodson and Brock Marion to help handle this talented group of Steelers receivers.

There had been a lot of talk that Barry Switzer was the recipient of a well-oiled Jimmy Johnson team full of super stars. I didn't think too much of it back then because I knew how great of a coach Barry was. It was pointed out to me some years later that the Super Bowl XXX has only 30% of the players still on it from the Super Bowl XXVIII team. Barry had done his own house cleaning and while keeping the core of the team together, he built his own version of the Cowboys.

The locker room was still quiet as I continued to think about the plays that would happen later that day. Lying with my back on the floor and my feet up on the stool, I envisioned myself making a tackle on each of those plays. Covering a back in the flat or taking on the tight end to prevent a back from getting around the corner, I saw myself doing it all. In my mind I was jumping in front of receivers and intercepting passes at full speed. I saw myself scooping up fumbles. I saw myself blitzing up the middle and sacking Neil O'Donnell. I saw myself slicing behind the line and catching Kordell Stewart in the backfield. I saw myself running down the field and making the tackle on the kickoff team. I saw myself dodging blockers and leveling the punt returner. I even saw myself recovering an onside kick even though during the game, they tried the surprise onside kick to Dixon Edwards the other side of the line. It was the same page from the playbook that Shawn Peyton used to help win Super Bowl XLIV.

No matter the situation I saw myself making the play that was expected of me not only by myself but by the coaches, other players, Cowboy fans and the 95 million Americans who were watching it on TV with my friends from Farragut and Tennessee.

There was some bustling around the locker room but I maintained my meditation knowing that when I did get up I would begin to get excited about the game. I wanted to stay as calm as possible until right before game time. There was no talking but I could hear someone close by. When I looked over, there seated in front of his locker was Deion Sanders. For the next half hour I watched as he laid out every piece of his uniform on the floor in front of his locker. When he finished, his uniform was laid out perfectly with no wrinkles from top to bottom on the floor. He was sitting on a stool admiring it with a big grin on his face. It was something special that he did before every game, and I believe that just like me he used it to calm and focus himself.

I got up and refilled my cup with water, quickly downed it and drank another. It was not unusual for me or any player for that matter to lose 5% to 10% of their body weight during a game. It was a warm day, so I knew I had to hydrate properly or I would be in trouble by halftime. I had learned through the years of playing in the hot Texas sun that if I wasn't hydrated properly, they would be pumping fluids through a needle into my arm at half time. I would keep drinking until I started to urinate frequently. Then I would know I was ready to play.

Understanding this hydration issue and how important it is to the health of all football players, from grade school on up, I have built a company called Temperature Management System, which deals with preventing heat related illness and death. Our most successful product is our air conditioned shoulder pads. It is amazing how well players compete when their core is kept at optimum temperature.

The Field

I felt calm after going through the game at least four times in my head as I lay on the floor of the locker room. In another hour we would take the field for walk-through with the whole team. I wanted to go out beforehand and walk the field to help myself remain calm. Slipping into my new Cowboy sweats and my favorite game shoes, I walked out the door and down the tunnel to the field. Security had tightened and they weren't just letting anyone on the field. I guess it was the sound of my cleats clicking on the concrete that alerted them that I wasn't just an ordinary guy trying to get on the field.

Getting out into the sunshine felt good. I walked across the end zone, and then started to jog around the perimeter. Cameras were being set up. Chairs for the bands were being unfolded along the sideline and end zone. Rounding the corner at the far end zone, I could see a flurry of action taking place near the tunnel, which I had just come out of only moments before. I kept jogging, hoping not to be noticed and asked to leave the field.

On my second trip around the field, a young lady walked out to the 50 yard line. People were working on the sidelines and in the stands when all of the sudden the national anthem started on the loudspeakers. I came to a halt and looked around and found the flag. Placing my hand over my heart, I could see that the workers around the stadium also noticed and were now standing with hats off and hands over their hearts. I didn't know who the young lady singing, but she had an amazing voice and pride welled up inside me, even though this was just a practice for her. As she closed out the final notes I snuck a look at her and began to clap along with the rest of the workers in the stadium.

Before the game started later that day I found out the name of the young lady was Vanessa Williams. She once again made me proud as she sang the national anthem to the 76,347 fans in the stands and at that time the most watched sporting event ever on American TV. It was second only to the final episode of M*A*S*H as the most watched program of all time until Super Bowl XLV. Just a thirty second TV commercial for the game cost over a million dollars.

I was glad to get my little run in before our pregame meetings. All of the Super Bowl parties, appearances and events were wonderful but had wreaked havoc on my own personal schedule. Not having to be anywhere, interviewed by anyone or in a team meeting allowed me to shake out the cobwebs while loosening up my 35-year-old body. It had been a grueling 20 game preseason and regular season schedule. Add the playoffs and now the Super Bowl for a total of 23 games. Everyone was nicked up but I was physically and mentally ready.

The Cowboys were America's team. We had appeared in eight Super Bowls and had won two of the last three. We were on a roll. Our successive Super Bowl wins had been stopped by the San Francisco 49ers the year before, in the NFC championship game. They went on to win Super Bowl XXIX. We were determined to reach our goal of another Super Bowl victory.

America's Team was back on top and playing in the Super Bowl once again. And by the grace of God I was on that team. This four-year period had more ups and downs with injuries and success than any period in my career. Looking back now it is clear to me that I would have never made it without Denise and my growing family. When I got back to the locker room, I hit my knees again, and gave thanks for my family. How could she ever know how much my success depended on her?

The Season

We came out hot and heavy winning eight of our first ten games. Our 10th game was at home against those stubborn 49ers, who had knocked us off the previous year in the playoffs. Their left-handed Hall of Fame quarterback Steve Young was out of the game due to injuries. They proceed to put 31 points on us in the first half and our balloon started to deflate with a 38 - 20 loss. Although we lost two of the next four games, our fans stood

281

behind us and helped bring us back. Our next win was a close one as we were able to score 3 touchdowns while holding the Giants to 20 points in a 21 - 20 victory. It wasn't pretty but it got us back on the right track. My knee was holding up as I pushed it to the max and it responded.

The final game of the season was held here at Sun Devil Stadium against the Arizona Cardinals. Our 11-4 record would get us into the playoffs. We had come to Tempe with the goal of winning the game. On the airplane to Phoenix we found out that San Francisco had lost 27-28 to Atlanta giving us home-field advantage throughout the playoffs. We were determined to bring our fans two more games at home. They had stood by us through the tough times in the middle of the season. We knew that any team coming into Texas Stadium would feel the wrath of our fans, giving us an edge.

So we delivered a Christmas present to the fans by winning the Christmas night, Monday Night Football game over the Cardinals 37-13.

We were in the playoffs with home field advantage. Our first game was against the Eagles, who played strong for the first quarter. We scored first on a Chris Boniol field goal, before they tied it up in the second quarter.

We were well into the quarter when Deion Sanders took the field as a wide-out. Looping behind the line, he ran a reverse 21 yards for a touchdown. We felt the win early and the offense was clicking on a seventy-nine yard drive when Emmitt Smith dove in from 1 yard right before half to take a 14 point lead.

Barry Switzer would soon become the first coach in the history of the NFL to win a Super Bowl in his second coaching season. We as a team were out to prove to America that we could win without Jimmy Johnson. The off-season acquisition of Deion Sanders added a little spice to the mix. Deion was an excellent cornerback who was as smooth and fast as anyone I have ever witnessed in the NFL except Willie Gault. Just his presences on the field, made teams throw to the other side.

Deion handled the attention with style. There were plenty of other superstars on the team that would also make pro football's Hall of Fame, specifically, Troy Aikman, Michael Irvin and Emmitt Smith. Getting Deion on the Cowboys roster was an incredible move by Jerry Jones. Deion got it, the it being that playing for the STAR got him a $12.99 million dollar signing bonus on top of a $35 Million contract. There was a bidding war for Deion at the time and I believe his relationship with Michael Irvin was the key to getting him into our locker room. I liked to think he figured out that he couldn't cover Irvin, so it was best to join him.

The National Football Conference Championship game came back to Texas Stadium. Only a year before the San Francisco 49ers knocked us out of our chance for a three-peat of the Super Bowl. Dion Sanders had been a 49er and now he was on our sideline as we hosted Brett Favre and the Green Bay Packers who knocked off the 49ers the week before.

The game started with a bang as we posted a 14-3 lead. Troy was hot and Michael Irvin was catching everything. It was the big stage and they came to play. So did Brett Favre. Although we held the Packers to just a field goal in the first quarter, they came flaming back with Favre throwing a 73 yarder to Robert Brooks and followed it with a 25 yard strike to Keith Jackson. We were suddenly down by three points. Defensively we were shell shocked. Favre's two touchdowns in the second quarter were the most scored on us in a quarter that year.

This Dallas team was special though. We had people step up and make plays all year long, on both sides of the ball. Now it was time for Troy and the offense to take control and they did it with style. On our next possession Chris Boniol knotted the score at 17 with another field goal.

Green Bay came storming back. Favre was making plays to the left and right before we stopped them. Green Bay punted and the ball was eventually downed at the one yard line.

I think everyone in the Texas Stadium thought like me. Just get the ball away from the end zone and give John Jett some room to boot it. Then we would throw our defense at Favre and hope to stay even at the half. Normally I would be sitting on the bench back with the defensive team and coaches getting ready for the next series. On this drive I was standing near mid-field, preparing myself to make a play when we would were sure to punt.

I was wrong. The Cowboys offense had other ideas. When you have a back like Emmitt Smith, sometimes you just have to get on his back and ride him. Starting at the one yard line, Troy handed off to Emmitt behind one of the best offensive lines in the history of the NFL, in my opinion. Emmitt found the hole between Erik Williams and Larry Allen for a 25 yard gain. I kept watching as Coach Switzer continued pounding the ball up the field, sending Emmitt into the line play after play. This was football at its finest. The Cowboys faithful were being treated to some rough and ruckus ball and they were showing their appreciation loudly. The final play was fitting as Emmitt took the ball in from the one yard line. Our defense held on the next series and we took a 7 point lead into the locker room.

Emmitt had an amazing day scoring 3 touchdowns. His 86 yards in the first half alone helped us keep the ball out of the hands of a dangerous Brett

283

Favre. By the time the game was over Emmitt had run the ball 35 times for 150 yards.

We found out in the third quarter just how dangerous Favre was. On Green Bay's first two possessions, he backed us up to the twenty yard line before we stopped him. Chris Jacke knocked in a 37 yarder and our lead was cut to 4 points.

Our offense was yet to find its footing in the second half and when we gave the ball back to Green Bay, they were only 56 yards away from a score. Favre got the ball back into Jackson's hands and he took it down to the two yard line. The Packers caught us off-guard on the next play as we manned up in our goal line defense expecting Edgar Bennett to take it up the middle. Instead they slipped Robert Brooks into the huddle late and he ran a curl route out of backfield. It was a boom-boom play and just like that, the Packers were back in the lead.

Down 27-24 our defense was a little embarrassed. It wouldn't last for long though as we closed the third quarter with an offensive drive and Emmitt scored again from the 5 yard line. He was well on his way to a final quarter total of 50 yards. Midway through the quarter he scored again, putting us up 38-27 and icing the game. The thing I remember most about that game was how proud I was that every time that Green Bay would fight its way back into the game and regain the momentum, we took it away from them. It truly showed our character

We were going to Tempe looking for a fight and the Steelers were ready for us. From the beginning, I felt this was our game to win.

January 28, 1996-Super Bowl XXX

It was the sort of feeling that was a bit unreal. A third Super Bowl in four years! People often ask me to compare and contrast the three separate appearances we made in those Super Bowls, which is fairly easy for me.

Like most guys, the first Super Bowl is the best. I had played ten years in the NFL before we went to the Rose Bowl for Super Bowl XXVII. We had come close a few times, but we had never done it. It's something I'll never forget.

The second Super Bowl was a different feeling of excitement for me, because it was the first Super Bowl in which I actually played. No injuries kept me from the Georgia Dome for Super Bowl XXVIII. Yet that was the year the NFL decided to hold the game one week after the last playoff game, instead of the usual two weeks. I can remember feeling somewhat rushed as we won the NFC championship in San Francisco, only to find ourselves immediately in Atlanta preparing for the Buffalo Bills.

Having an extra week before the Super Bowl is one of the reasons I enjoyed going to Tempe for Super Bowl XXX. It was quite a family affair for the whole Bates clan. Graham, Brianna, Hunter, Tanner, and even Dillon not only accompanied Mom and Dad to Phoenix-they actually attended the game! That was incredibly meaningful to me.

It was nice to be back outdoors, as well. The Georgia Dome was nice, but I appreciated the natural beauty of the Valley of the Sun.

Forgive me for such an obvious statement, but the National Football League does the Super Bowl right. There are parties, fireworks, jets flying overhead, world-famous musicians. The whole thing is one classy event to be a part of. Most of all was gratitude to the Lord for making all this possible once again.

As I had done before, I was again one of the Cowboy players chosen to go out to midfield for the coin toss with our AFC rivals, the Pittsburgh Steelers. But this year there were a lot more guys out on the field, and most of them were Cowboys! It was still pretty exciting for me as I walked to the fifty-yard line to shake hands with the man asked to flip the coin. He was a boyhood hero of mine, Bart Starr. Troy Aikman made the call for us.

It was time.

We wanted to take control right from the start, so that's what we did. We scored on our first three possessions; including an Aikman-to-Novacek TD pass. At the end of the first quarter the score was 10-0. We'd make it 13-7 at the half.

In the third quarter we held Pittsburgh scoreless, while Emmitt Smith ran for his first touchdown of the day, making the score 20-7 by the end of three.

The Steelers tried desperately to make it a game. They scored a field goal. Then they did something unexpected an on-side kick. I was ready for it, but I neglected to tell Dixon Edwards to be prepared for it. The kick worked perfectly. Bam Morris ran in for a touchdown after that kick, making the score 20-17 with a little over six minutes in the game. Enter Larry Brown with his key interception of Neil O'Donnell's pass. Emmitt took the ball over the goal line for his second score of the day. The game ended with the score of 27-17. The Steelers controlled the clock for much of the second half, yet I feel we dominated more than the score suggests.

Number Three – Super Bowl XXX

The bigger our lead, the more the opposition tends to throw the ball-and thus, because of my unique position as a nickel back, the more I get to play. I was thrilled that we played a game that seemed to give us such an advantage over the Steelers. It was reminiscent of the Atlanta Super Bowl for me, in terms of playing time.

I recall one particular play later in the game where the powerful Steeler running back, Bam Morris, headed my direction. I squared off, hitting him straight on at full speed. It felt like time was suspended for a moment as neither of us were moving forward or backward. He wasn't gaining on me, but I wasn't bringing him down either. Eventually I could sense him trying to move sideways, in an attempt to break free of my hold. What an incredible rush of exhilaration swept over me as I won our little battle, finally bringing him to the ground!

Therein lies another distinction for me in Super Bowl XXX. It's one thing to be in a Super Bowl. It's another feeling to say you played in a Super Bowl. But it is something different yet to say you made plays in a Super Bowl.

The locker room was electric! I tried to take it all in, savoring every sweet moment of victory. My eye wandered around the clubhouse, focusing on several of our coaches who seemed unusually ecstatic about this victory. I saw Mike Zimmer, our defensive backs coach. It was pretty obvious by his smile that this was his first Super Bowl victory. The same smile was planted on our offensive coordinator's face, Ernie Zampese. What a thrill!

How could anyone ever forget Jerry kissing Barry!

I also noticed a special look of satisfaction in the face of Dave Campo. This was the first year he had been elevated to the position of defensive coordinator. I couldn't help but think that this was quite an accomplishment for him.

After the trophy presentation and all the hoopla in the locker room calmed down I was looking for one thing. Where was that helicopter of Jerry's and was there a seat in it for me?

27 - The Show Goes On!

My time as a Cowboy player did come to an end after 15 seasons. The press finally got it right. I wouldn't make the team for the 1998 season. I felt like I still had the ability and heart to continue playing. Instead new Head Coach Chan Gailey gave me the opportunity to coach and if they needed me during the season, I would be called up. It didn't happen and I continued as a coach for five more years.

When Shoot For The STAR was first released I was still on the team and we had yet to win Super Bowl XXX. I was living my dream. Now, more than 15 years later I can look back and see my life as a player in the National Football League like a highlight reel. During the rest of the book I will take you back to the Glory Days and give you some of the insight into why I think the Cowboys were able to overcome adversity in the Eighties to become one of the most beloved team of the Nineties. I give you my take on players that made the Cowboys great. I will share with you my observations about the fortunes, both good and bad, of the Cowboys.

As a Cowboy, I was able to play for three great coaches that helped shape me as a man through their inspiration, example and friendship. It is they type of leadership that is found in championship coaches today. It was in an era where teams were family, and even though winning was the goal, winning as a family was the prize.

In today's game of free-agency, teams have to be rebuilt every year. Few long term contracts are handed out and players staying in the league for more than five years is rare, let alone staying with the same team. I was lucky to have played for the Cowboys. I was lucky to have great coaches and very lucky to have Jerry Jones as an owner. Sure there are a few things that I think could have been done better, but I wouldn't change a thing because I was the luckiest of all to have played for the Cowboys when the saying was "Once a Cowboy, Always a Cowboy."

The rest of the book is written to bring our many fans up to date on the life Denise and I dreamed of beyond the NFL. You might think that winning three Super Bowl rings, being an All Pro and winning all kinds of awards as a player would be hard to top. While it was certainly a great time in my life, the blessings that have resulted because of my success on the field and my faith in Christ has been incredibly fulfilling.

I wasn't ready to give up playing for the Cowboys. In my heart I know that if Barry Switzer had still been the coach, I would have probably played a couple more years. I was mentally and physically prepared to do so. It broke my heart when faced with the ultimatum. I had made the team over and over with the attitude that at any time, either injury or a coach's decision could take me out of the game, just like all of the great players I had seen come and go.

After all the meetings and the ultimatum was given to me to retire or continue as a coach, I was down. It was a dark a gloomy day in my life. The press had been predicting it throughout my career and I defied odds and proved them wrong. Now, faced with the decision of trying to get on with another team or starting my coaching career, I was angry. It took me back to the Hershel Walker trade and how down I was after learning that Jimmy Johnson had traded for a boatload of defensive players and my job was on the bubble. Only this was different. I had a whole house full of kids that needed me and moving them from Dallas was not something I wanted.

Like so many times in the past, I prayed and put it into Gods hands. Then I found a vacant office in the Cowboy's practice facility and called my Dad. My voice was harsh and cracking when I told him about the decision. Even as a man in his late thirties that had been so blessed, I was near tears. With a strong clear voice he once again gave me strength.

"Billy, the Cowboys gave you the chance to live your dreams. You climbed the mountain and stayed on top longer than most. Now is the time to start living your other dreams. You have a whole house full of young boys to coach and inspire. You have the opportunity to give back what so many coaches have given you. Now get your ass up and do what you have done since you were a little boy playing for the Headhunters. Bring it under control and *Be the BEST*." The phone clicked.

I got up and even though I was not called up to play that year, I gave my all to coaching. What I found was pure joy in watching my players develop and make great plays. Even more satisfying, I started coaching the Bates boys and that has given me as much pleasure and satisfaction as playing on Super Bowl teams.

Staying on the sidelines during the next six years in the NFL was a change. Although I wanted to be on the field, this was the closest thing to playing. I learned to love the game from a different perspective, not as a player, but as a motivator. Football is a brutal sport and can only be played with passion. Jerry Jones and the Cowboys family were second only to my own family. Once again, I am living the dream.

The Bates boys are great football players. I can say that because I am their father. Beyond being tough as nails on the gridiron, they are great young men who strive to always give their best. They have the passion I brought to the game with the great heart and clear head of their mother.

At this writing they are finding their own way in the football world. It has been my privilege to be able to coach and watch them as they have found success. Two have been on State Championship teams. The younger two have helped build a winning program at a new high school in Florida. It has been amazing watching them Shoot for their STARS.

Graham is nearing completion of his college career at Arkansas State. Where he goes from here is wide open. He has gotten a solid education and played some great football in a top notch program.

Hunter continues to play at Northwestern since he was redshirted a year. It has not always been a smooth road for either of them, but their ability to overcome adversity is outstanding. The coaches are looking for some great things from him.

Tanner made the decision to go to a new high school and helped lay the foundation for a winning program at Ponte Vedra High School. His passion for the game and nose for the football led his team as they overcame the painful years of a new program. He has taken that passion into his education and will graduate from Full Sail University with a career in sound and music recording in front of him.

Dillon is the youngest and already the biggest of the Bates boys. Having successful older brothers and a Dad that played, has set the bar high for him. He has exceeded expectations by becoming a starting linebacker for the Ponte Vedra Sharks during his freshman year and playing on a District Championship team his sophomore year. I can see that he has the expectations to be even better than his brothers and me.

I now know the joy my own Dad felt when watching me throughout my career. Even though we lost my Dad to cancer this year he got to the see the success of his grandsons. My love for him was great and I can see and feel the love of my own sons as they succeed in life.

Brianna is still my little princess and one the boys biggest fan, sitting next to her Mother and Grandmother Momo. It has been hard to get to Friday night games, travel to the older boy's college games and hit a few Cowboys games in the mix. She loves her brothers and still brings the little girl out in a house full of smelly football players. She is a blessing who brings balance to the family.

28 - After All These Years

"The only thing constant is change" were words my Dad gave me when I was young. During my years as a Cowboy, the only constant I had was me. We had gone through front office, ownership and coaching changes and through all of this I felt every day that my job was on the line. It is the nature of the game. People come and people go but what remained constant was the STAR on the side of my helmet.

I have often been asked to compare and contrast Coaches' Tom Landry, Jimmy Johnson and Barry Switzer. I have thought long and hard about each coaching style and their effects on me and the players around me. Being a Head Coach in the NFL has to be one of the hardest jobs. Like a General or an *Admiral* they have to make tough choices that affect people's lives on a daily basis. They can't get too close to players because a decision they make could put them out of a job or trade him to another team. Although they kept an arm's length relationship I felt a special bond with each of them.

Coach Landry gained admission into the Pro Football Hall of Fame with a style and manner that is seldom seen in coaches today. I admired him from the time I first started to play football in the 1960s at age seven. His winning ways took the Cowboys to the top where they are still recognized as America's Team. The culture he instituted is still prevalent in the Cowboy's organization. His football tactics including the flex defense and multiple set offenses are still successful today.

When I got the invitation from the Cowboys to come to camp, I was thrilled at the thought of playing for them. I knew my work was cut out for me. Before I got there I had a game plan for making the team. I would do everything and anything that I needed to do to prove myself to Coach Landry. He had played defensive back for the Giants in the 1950s and was even a player-coach before coaching full time. If I was going to make the team I would have to prove to him my value as a player and a coach. It was my plan to not only play at the highest level my body would allow me, but to raise the level of those around me so that as a team we were better and the individual pieces. How else was an un-drafted rookie going to make the team? After fifteen years in the league, I figure my game plan must have worked. Coach Landry saw something in me that he wanted on his team.

Today when coaching my boys, not just my own sons but all the boys I coach, I instill in them the importance of being a leader. Coach Landry taught me to not only be a leader on but off the field. The confidence he placed in me spurred me on. I did not want to let him down. If I made a wrong read, wasn't prepared or made a silly mistake he would catch it in the film room. Those sessions could be brutal.

Coach Landry could watch a film and see all eleven players reactions and even if one player made a mistake, he would catch it. Those valuable film sessions taught me how to look and plan for our games. He would focus on what we did best and make it better. His expectations were such that if a player continually made mistakes, he would soon be playing in another helmet. I wanted to keep the STAR on the side of my head, so I heeded every word.

In today's game a Head Coach, in most cases, is the General on the sideline, making all of the on the field decisions well before the game starts. Offensive, Defensive and Special Teams coaches spend hours watching films and scheming for opponents. The Head Coach blesses them and then watches the plans being implemented on the field. Some Head Coaches still act in the roll of Coordinator. They all have input during the games and their word is final. Still in most cases it is up to the Coordinators to call the plays. Coach Landry had an amazing ability to coach all phases of the game. He was both the offensive and defensive coordinator.

Coach Landry was different. His practices were scheduled different. During the season Tuesday was our day off. On Wednesday he would sit with the offense and put in the game plan, watch films and prepare the team to practice. They knew what to do in practice and under his watchful eye the offense would run the plays until they had the timing down. Then they would line up and we would scrimmage under game conditions against our defense which would emulate our opponent's defense. It was starters against starters and we made it a point to play hard on every down.

Thursdays were our day with Coach Landry. Just like the offense, he would put in the game plan and watch films. He demanded close attention or you would be called out. When it was time to take the field, we all knew what was expected. He would internalize the practice and then make changes to personnel if a player wasn't getting the job done. Thursdays were our long day. Not only did we focus on defense, we worked on special teams play. I took the special teams practice even more serious; since that is the reason I believe he chose me to be a Cowboy.

All throughout my career, me and Darrell Johnson on our own account and along with our other special teams' players would stay after the grueling Thursday practices, order pizzas and then review game films of our upcoming opponent. We would spend hours looking for that one little thing that might swing the game our way. It was a staple in Coach Landry's philosophy that if we were prepared, we would have the confidence to succeed when the opportunity arose. Because of this we were able to swing the momentum to the Cowboys on many occasions. We became known for our great special teams play.

Coach Landry motivated us by holding us accountable to the team, coaches and fans. He told us over and over that "To reach our goal of winning we have to plan how we will accomplish it and stick with the plan."

Coach Johnson was quite the character as a coach. He could be funny, serious and downright nasty in the same paragraph. I planned to impress him with my style of play and the work ethic it took to maintain my abilities. I came to play full out on every play, of every day of practice.

When Coach Johnson took over the team after the 1988 season, we were not a cohesive team. Quite frankly, we had problems and weren't winning. I was miserable, the coaches were miserable, the other players were miserable and the fans were miserable. It was time for a change. We needed enthusiasm.

I will talk about Jerry Jones later, but let me say now; he is truly a class act. He got resistance when he bought the team. Players and fans thought that this self-made, self-promoting billionaire would ruin the Cowboy culture. He was exactly what we needed and he brought in a Head Coach that was exactly who we needed.

Jimmy was brash. He came in real cocky and had all the answers. We were a team of veterans and had our share of success. Here was this college coach with a lot of confidence coming in to tell us how to play the pro game. Not only that, he was replacing a legend. Coach Landry was loved by the people of Dallas. Even when the Cowboys didn't win and they were yelling for change, he was still a pillar.

I have to give it to Jimmy. He is as tough as they come. He is a smart coach who knows how to win. He was determined to break us down and make us into a team of winners. Losing fifteen games in that first year was agonizing. It was especially hard on the veterans. The push back was serious. We had our ways of doing things and Jimmy had his. When the two clashed, there were sparks, fire and explosions. If Jerry Jones could fire the coach of America's Team, then no one was safe. Not even the ball boys.

In 1989 the Cowboys were in our sixth year of being mediocre team. With only ten wins in the last two years, we were the laughing stock of the league. This serious decline was about to be painfully stopped when Jimmy made the Hershel Walker trade. I hated to see Hershel go. He had become a friend. I had gotten over being run over by him in college and he had extended a hand of friendship to me. He was even that triplets first birthday party. The ripple effects of trading Hershel were felt throughout the team. We immediately had five new players on the team. It would later dwindle to four after Darrin Nelson refused to report and was traded. I wondered myself if I would end up on the streets to make room for one of the new guys. They had to make room on the roster and I was one of those "expendable players" as the press would occasionally say. I was now only a part-time linebacker specializing in the nickel and leading the special teams.

The trade was made in the middle of the week and announced on Thursday. Jimmy had his fill of losing and the only way to make significant changes was a block buster trade. It was the biggest trade in the history of the NFL with thirteen players and draft picks trading teams. It was unheard of and it was especially unheard of because we were already into the season. Most trades take place after the season or right before the season starts.

I recall that we didn't see Jimmy much at practice that week. I thought that was real strange. Coach Landry would seldom say anything to anyone in practice. He would save it for the film room. Jimmy was completely the opposite. He would be on the field coaching. Believe me, you either did it his way or he would find someone immediately to take your spot. I appreciated the directness of his approach. If he wanted me to drop my right foot and turn my shoulders to cover the flat that is exactly what I would do. I always felt he had a magnifying glass on me because I was probably the most expendable player on the team, or at least I thought so at the time.

Jimmy wasn't on the field because he was dealing away our best running back. The cackle in the locker room was that he was also looking to trade Michael Irvin. I had friends all over the league that had passed through my career at Tennessee and with the Cowboys who asked me what was going on. Jimmy liked to negotiate through the media. When it was found out that Hershel and Michael were on the trade block, the media went wild with speculation. There was talk of trading Michael to Oakland. That was the one that got me. I practiced against these guys every day and knew even then, with Troy so early in his career, that he and Michael had something special.

Hershel was our top back. He had size and speed and I personally can attest to his strength. The Giants, Browns and Falcons had all showed interest in acquiring Hershel. This is where Jimmy wanted them. It was all over the press. Then he was contacted by the Vikings and gave them a shot. He knew that if he could get the teams into an auction, the Cowboys would end up with a better deal.

I think that Jimmy and Jerry both dreamed this scenario up and now it was playing into their hands. Jerry had made his billions prospecting for oil and gas. He knows how to make a deal and it has been proven over the years that he certainly knows how to take a risk. Jerry's push of the Cowboys back to the Super Bowl started with step one, hiring Jimmy Johnson. Step two was getting the talent the fastest way possible, hence the block buster trade.

I had come off the field a little later than normal after the Thursday practice that week. I had stayed to watch Troy and Michael work on their timing. Steve Walsh was our starting quarterback and Troy was anxiously waiting his turn. We had just spent over an hour in the skeleton drill where they were throwing against the simulated defense of the 49ers who we would play that next Sunday. I needed a little lift. Everyone knew Hershel wouldn't be on the team in short order. Even though, he came out like a true professional and practiced, except today. The trade was here, so let it happen were my feelings. Just get it over with.

It was then that Troy took a three step drop, pushed off his back foot and put the ball on a bullet path toward the outstretched hands of Michael. It was like magic. Troy's drop was perfect, his footwork fast and clean. When his back foot planted there was no hesitation as his motion came forward and his arm flashed. The incredible speed of the release was immediately overshadowed by the tight flight of the spiraling ball to a spot where only Michael Irvin could catch it. I looked around and I wasn't the only one watching.

I had seen thousands of out patterns over the years, and this one was perfect. Michaels wide smile and high pitched holler brought everyone's attention when he caught the ball. Instantly, his right foot hit the ground and he was cutting up the field. I knew of no cornerback in the league that could cover that route, with that type of timing.

If they tried to jump the route, then what Michael and Troy did next would sting them deep. Running exactly the same speed and tempo, Michael cut to the outside. He would judge to see if the corner was too close and if so, on his third step, he would turn up field where Troy would have thrown the ball over his inside shoulder with just a little loft.

The distasteful losing, the trade talk, the fear of losing my position all left for a few moments that afternoon. Watching these two young men sharpening their skills made me excited for our future. At that time I didn't know who would be coming in to run the football but I felt great about the abilities of these two. I felt confident that we were going to take this team upward what I didn't know was that the trade would eventually bring us Emmitt Smith.

We got shellacked that weekend 31-14 by the 49ers. The turmoil of the trade had taken our focus off of the ballgame. Steve Young and Jerry Rice cleaned up on us. The two of them were fabulous together. But what Jimmy and Jerry were about to unleash on the league would match their success.

On that cool October afternoon, I could only dream about the future and it reached up and slapped me hard. The parking lot was full of cars. That only meant one thing to me as I walked into the locker room; Questions from reporters. What did I hear? When did they announce it? Who were they going to replace on the roster? I felt it was probably going to be me. I wondered if I could sneak around the side of the building and make it out of there without going through the gauntlet. Instead I charged ahead.

Walking into the locker room door I could hear the chatter. Questions being fired off. Players were sitting back on their stools at their lockers and the reporters were milling about looking for anyone to talk to. I heard it and I know almost everyone heard it. "Bates" Nearly everyone stopped and the room quieted. I could feel their stares as I made my way across the room to my locker. About half way across, the chatter continued. I wondered if they knew something I didn't. Peeling my uniform, I was able to avoid the reporters.

They would usually give us space until we got our practice equipment off and if we didn't smell too bad from the sweat, they would start asking questions. I was able to make it into the shower and relished the hot water hoping that the longer I stayed in the shower, the fewer questions I would be asked. Besides, it was Thursday night and I was looking forward to our informal pizza party where we would scheme our specialty team game plan.

A towel draped around me, I headed for my locker, trying not to attract attention. Keeping my eyes down I stepped across the middle of the wide open locker room and when I looked up, there was Brad Sham. Without saying a word he handed me a piece of paper. I stopped and looked down at it. Brad is the voice of the Cowboys and a wonderful friend. What he handed me was a list of names and positions. I looked at him and he nodded. "That's the list of players. He also got eight draft picks." I was amazed at the number of players but what concerned me most and I am sure the reason Brad brought me the list was the positions of the players that were traded for. Looking down again I saw the names of Jesse Solomon and David Howard. Both were linebackers. Also on the list were two more defensive players; cornerback Issac Holt and defensive end Alex Stewart.

Brad stood firm beside me as I took in the news. I adjusted my eyes and looked back down at the paper in disbelief. Four defensive players I thought. I am the one defensive player that is expendable and they not only bring in four players on the defensive side of the ball, two of them are linebackers. My head just about exploded. I had worked so hard to make this team and this piece of paper appeared to be my death warrant. Looking at Brad, he too knew it wasn't good news for me. As much as he liked me and as good of a friend that he was, this bit of the news was especially hard for him. He had been through thick and thin with the Cowboys and seen a lot of good quality people come and go.

It is times like these when I have learned not to panic. I sure wanted to. I looked at Brad and he gave me a pat then turned and walked away. I crushed and threw the paper in my locker. I could barely get dressed. I kept thinking about those names and what it meant to me and I would get lost in putting my pants on. My heart was breaking. I didn't have to worry about avoiding the press. They avoided me like the plague.

I left the locker room and headed down the hallway to the meeting rooms. The special team players were the ones on the bubble. They were coming and going so fast that we had to really focus to make sure we were prepared and everybody knew what to do and when to be on the field.

I had to get alone for a while and think about this. I had asked for the films to be put in one of the larger film rooms because tonight we were inviting in several of the other special teams players and instead of pizza, we were going to have barbeque. I entered to the smell of mesquite roasted ribs and brisket. I was glad to have something to take the pressure off my mind. I carried on the meeting in stride. No one mentioned the trade and we focused as best we could on the upcoming game with the 49ers.

I had insisted on getting a cell phone. Back then, they either put it in your car or you carried it in a bag. I had seen some of our player's phones and figured it was a good idea to have one, say with the triplets and all. It was really an excuse to get one. Tonight I would need it.

First, let me take you back to my rookie year. I made the team and boy was I happy to be in Dallas. I also needed a place to stay. With a nice healthy paycheck, I could buy a place and then when I finally got Denise to marry me, we would have our home ready. There were a couple of Cowboys who were partners in a condominium complex. It was near the training facility, so it was perfect. I rolled in and signed up for one of the top of the line condos they had to offer. It was beautiful. What I didn't know was that the Cowboys were about to relocate the training facility across town to Valley Ranch, about an hour and a half away. Needless to say, they laughed all the way to the bank and I had a heck of a commute back and forth to practice. We were in an apartment at Valley Ranch before the season was over.

On this night I looked forward to getting home to Denise and the babies. My mind was reeling. I was mad. I was hurt. I was confused and I was insecure. When I got in my car I said a prayer asking for the Lord to guide me in his way and not mine. I still had a lump in my throat and my heart was beating too fast. Finally I pulled off the Interstate and just sat there for a minute. I needed to call my Dad. He would know what to do. He always gave me great advice and I depended on him more than anyone would ever know. He was a rock.

I pulled the bag phone up onto the seat and dialed the phone. I could see Dad sitting in his chair watching the news. I looked down and it was 9:30 Dallas time, so Knoxville would be an hour later. He picked up the phone and gave me his warm "Hi Billy" greeting. Just his voice alone helped deflate the pressure mounting in my head. He already knew about the trade. It had been on the news and ESPN.

"I thought you might call" he said a matter of factly.

"I didn't want to bother you Dad. It's just…." I started.

"I know son. You work so hard for something and then it is jerked away. Let me tell you something son. I have watched you for your whole life and I have always admired how confident you have been" he said.

I couldn't say a word. I felt ashamed because he was right. I was always confident because I knew that I could outwork anybody. I was confident because I got results. Now I was coming home with my tail between my legs because I felt my career might be coming to quick end.

"I knew one day you would come to me and tell me you were no longer a Cowboy. I prepared all kinds of things in my mind to tell you, things that might help you. What I am about to tell you, you already know. It was told to you by Coach Pruett years ago. Son, 'when the going gets tough, the tough get going' " he said with strength in his voice. Then the receiver clicked. He was gone.

In that moment I put it all behind me. I was a Cowboy and living my dream so they were going to have to pry my helmet from my cold dead hands if they were going to get rid of me. I am not saying that the next two months were easy. They were in no means easy. I had babies to keep me company in the middle of the night when I wasn't sleeping. There is nothing like a baby, or two or even three lying on your chest to take your mind off your problems.

Jerry and Jimmy were all over the TV. Some commentators thought they were crazy to give up on Walker and yet they couldn't disagree that the quality of players they received and the number of draft picks could be game changers for the Cowboys. I even heard my name mentioned as a possible casualty of the trade. Sure, I knew it was me, a couple of rookies and one of our linemen who had a nagging injury that may have to go. On those long nights I took solace in knowing I had the right team on my side.

Those few weeks were painful both on and off the field. As a matter of fact, the whole rest of the season was a nightmare. Jimmy was experimenting with different personnel groups and I felt fortunate to maintain my position in the nickel defense. I had to keep the pace and continue to outwork everyone. Our next game was against Kansas City. They had also seen some lean times but with Marty Schottenheimer at the helm, they were righting the ship and would eventually end the nineties with one of the best winning records of any team in the NFL. On this Sunday we were going into Arrowhead, a mass of red screaming fans that take their Chiefs seriously.

During our early warm ups I was fielding punts from Mike Saxon. We usually give the punters one side of the field and let them boom away. It was a cool morning so they were really getting the balls up high. During this time of warm ups is when I would usually sneak a few peaks at the other team to see who and how they were fielding their kicks. I would love nothing more than to cause a fumble today. I felt like I needed to impress Jimmy more so he would keep me around.

Sneaking that peak sent a chill down my back. There, on the fifty yard line, not more than ten yards away stood Christian Okoye fielding punts. Christian was a runningback known at the Nigerian Nightmare. He was huge standing 6'3' and weighing 260 pounds. He was in his sweats, which were two sizes too small and looked like he was in full pads. He would catch the ball with soft hands and lower his shoulder up field. Turning around he would jog back and then launch the ball back toward the punter in a high tight spiral. The Chiefs punter was booming the ball nearly sixty yards in the air and Christian was throwing them back that far with a flick of the wrist.

There was no way I wanted to hit this man at full speed or vice versa. It was rumored he ran a 4.4 with all that muscle. Fortunately they did not put him back on the returns even though he looked like he could handle it. That afternoon he did take our defense apart on the ground. He ran the ball 33 times for 170 yards and two touchdowns. We gave up 423 yards on defense. We tried to come back in the fourth quarter. At least we didn't give up and the Chiefs knew they were in a fight as we finished the game with two fourth quarter touchdowns. Since they were running so much, I very seldom made it on the field in the nickel defense. We moved on to the next game, still looking for a win.

Jimmy found a lot of good play in the Kansas City game. He handed out some good compliments and most important, I was safe for another week. Jimmy was looking close at everybody, not just me. I was pleasantly surprised to find myself on the team when we played the Redskins in a Sunday night game at RFK Stadium two weeks later. We were still painfully looking for a win. I was looking for a way to keep my job. There was still a lot of speculation in the air and my name kept surfacing. It was tearing my guts out. This is not what I bargained for when dreaming of playing for the Cowboys. As you can tell I hate losing. Even if I am playing horse in the driveway, I play to win.

We were facing a Super Bowl MVP in Doug Williams. He could beat us with a rocket arm and if we covered tight, he would run. We had to get to him fast and throw him off his first receiver. That meant the first 1.7 seconds we had to cover tight then commit to stop him on the run. He was big and strong and when he took off he was like a gazelle. I loved it because it I could leave the full all out rush to Jim Jeffcoat and Ed Too Tall Jones and play the nickel like it is designed. It left me wide open to fly around causing havoc. They contained him in the pocket and even though he threw for 296 yards, none of the catches went for a touchdown. We absolutely shut down Ernst Byner and their rushing game to just 50 yards.

I was really anxious about the game since I felt I was on the bubble. I quietly thanked the schedule makers for putting us against the Redskins on that Sunday. I decided to have fun and "play" my game. We had been pressing so hard to win that we lost the fun and were creating way too much pressure both physically and mentally. I still knew that I had to do something special to stand out and keep my job. That's when I made one of the most important plays of my career.

I was causing havoc. Our film studies had pinned down the consistencies in the Redskins offense. Coaches Dave Wannstedt and Dave Campo were at the top of their game and had us positioned perfectly to stop nearly every play. It was late in the third quarter and we were tied after the Redskin's Chip Lohmiller matched Roger Rezak's first half field goal. I had been in on a number of tackles and had caused Williams to go to his second receiver a number of times with coverage. After we stalled on our next drive, Saxon pushed them back with an outstanding punt. Then Williams kick started the Redskins and they reacted as he threw some great passes with pinpoint accuracy. He pushed them out to midfield and we had to stop them. They kept pushing converted two more third downs. Then the "play" that changed the game happened for me.

My read had me dropping back at a forty-five degree angle and then covering the deep flat. My gut told me that the receiver would break it off short. I was into my second step to the flat when I saw Ed Too Tall Jones hand fly up into the air. I knew the ball was on the way. My moment was approaching and I was at full sprint at an angle to cut in front of the receiver. I didn't see the ball until it was over the line. The total distance of the ball in the air was around 30 yards. I had seen Williams throw some fast ball strikes for three quarters and this was a fast ball. I was taught to catch a ball by watching the front point where the four seams come together. This ball was traveling so hard and spinning so fast that I only saw a blur as I put my hands up together. The velocity nearly knocked me down but the familiar feel of the leather slapping into my hands burned like catching a shooting star. It was mine and I was fully extended without actually diving.

I caught my momentum and put my foot into the ground. If I was going to intercept it, I had better do something with it. I used the momentum to change direction and maintain a good deal of speed. Two steps later I was heading toward our goal line. This is exactly what I was looking for to impress Jimmy and keep my job. That little jewel was tucked under my arm and I was going to make the most of it. I took it back to our 42 yard line before I got tripped up. I still think to this day that if I hadn't been laughing so hard I would have taken it to the house.

The play was on all the highlight reels. ESPN and all of the Dallas Stations led with it. Jimmy loved the press and Jerry knew how important it was to have highlights like this to stimulate the fan base. I was in the right place at the right time. A couple of plays later we broke the tie with a Paul Palmer run from 35 yards out. Three fourth quarter stops and a field goal by Saxon sealed the deal and we had a taste of winning again. We celebrated and I was one of the last Cowboys to ever mess with Jimmy's hair. I thought for sure he was going to cut me every time Dale Hansen at Channel 8 used the clip in their Cowboys pre-game promotions. The changes that next week didn't affect my position on the team. Changes were made though. The Redskins game was the last Steve Walsh started for the Cowboys. Jimmy had shaken the cup again and what spilled out was a decision that would change the Cowboys. Aikman had beaten out Walsh for the starting position. We had only won one game, but Jimmy was adamant in this decision. He was going to go with his number one pick, Troy Aikman. He had used the quarterback controversy to draw attention to something besides the dismal record. Whether on purpose or not, the distraction worked and the media took a liking to Troy. It had to be agonizing for Jimmy since Steve Walsh was his quarterback at Miami and they were proven winners.

I need to stop here about Jimmy and give a quick shout out to Tim Tebow. Tim played at Nease High School near Jacksonville Florida, the same one that my son's Graham and Hunter played at. Tim has proven himself at every level. For all of those who challenge his future I say bunk. He has jumped into the fire and won the Bronco's starting job and just like gold, the furnace has to get really hot before it becomes pure gold. Troy Aikman jumped into the fire and won the job at Dallas and his first year he was 0-11. Time will tell if Timmy will succeed. Knowing both of these men I can draw one conclusion about them that makes them winners. They expect nothing less. Sometimes the expectation or confidence can overshadow the joy of winning, but having spent my career and knowing thousands of players and coaches in the NFL, the winners win because they expect to win. Timmy is as tough as a rock both physically and mentally. He will do anything it takes to be a winner because he has a purpose and a platform.

I can say with confidence that my prediction is Timmy will continue to win. The way he plays the game is refreshing and most of all he shows his faith and gives glory to the Lord for putting him into a position share it. Timmy is a winner because he "expects" to win.

Now back to that horrible 1-15 season. The next week we traveled to Sun Devil Stadium to take on the Cardinals. Troy lit it up, throwing for 379 yards and two touchdowns in a game we were leading into the fourth quarter. Then Ernie Jones, a second year receiver, caught three balls for

139 yards and two touchdowns. Although we lost, we felt we were getting closer.

Everyone was still on pins and needles about their jobs, especially the defense. The new players had come in and were learning the system. I tried to help in every way I could, knowing that at any time, it may be over for me. I did the only thing I could and did my job every day to the best of my ability. I had Jimmy's favor for the moment and I wasn't going to give it up.

The last game of the season was memorable. We lost big time to the Packers and what was memorable to me was that Troy must have gotten sacked 12 times in the game. Jimmy left him out there and he was getting killed. The toughness he showed and his ability to get back up after being hit full speed by the Packers blitzing was incredible. I have stood on the sidelines and witnessed spectacular individual feats all my life. On that day, I witnessed the birth of a Hall of Fame Quarterback.

Jimmy loved to use the media to negotiate and motivate. That is why I think he has done such a great job in the NFL pregame and highlight shows. He knows the game and understands the psyche of the players and coaches. He has mastered the ability to look straight into the camera and convincingly share is point of view. He is terribly entertaining because he has so many friends in the league that are more than happy to share their thoughts and information with him.

The great trade was negotiated with the help of the media. Coach Landry very seldom granted the access and TV time that Jimmy craved. I think he mastered it quickly in his first year with a survivor mentality. By drawing attention away from the on-field performance, he was granted the time to tear down the remnants of the previous four fruitless Cowboys campaigns and build back a team based on a solid foundation of players he personally picked. His taste for speed was well noted. He was moving the Cowboys from the Smash Mouth football to Speed Ball.

There had been a lot of speculation late in the season that the Cowboys were playing to get the Number 1 draft pick. It just wasn't true. Jimmy is a winner and expected to win every game. I saw the pain on his face when we lost. It was the same steely eyes but instead of his pearly whites outlined by his dimples, his pursed lips said it all. He hated it.

When I look back now I realize just how much I hated losing. At the time I hated what was happening to the team and because Jimmy was shaking things up I knew the losing ways were going out the door. If only I could hold on and prove I was a winner too. The anxiety was incredible. Now, after all these years I can really admire what he did for the Cowboys.

With the wholehearted backing of a new Owner, he broke us down like a wild horse and brought us back by teaching us to function as a team. His history in the college game required him to rebuild the team every year due to graduations. Jimmy did what he did best.

At Miami his leadership had led to a National Championship team. He built the team from the bottom up. He was definitely the coach for the Cowboys task. The results were phenomenal with two Super Bowl wins and retaking the title of America's Team. At the time it was excruciating. Had it not been for the birth of the triplets, good words from my Dad and the undying support and love of Denise, my days as a Cowboy would have probably ended. Now it is apparent that the actions taken by Jimmy led me from playing on bottom of the rung teams to the top of the mountain championship team.

Jimmy made the Cowboys team better by setting the expectation (there is that expectation word again) of winning for the team. The first time I met him after he was hired; he flashed me a smile and heartily shook my hand. I could see he was sizing me up so I was standing tall and squeezed his hand so he would remember. I couldn't help but feel that National Championship ring on his right hand. I felt the weight of it when I squeezed. It was hard not to notice. He looked me square in the eye and in a hushed voice he convincingly said "We have a lot of hard work to do." I agreed and left the room with an appreciation for him. Others didn't like his showboat presence and cocky attitude. It fired me up.

Coach Landry limited himself in the spotlight preferring to let the players and the play on the field define the team. Jimmy wanted to define the team and then challenge us to step up and live the expectation. (there is that expectation word again) To be a Head Coach in the NFL you have to be made of steel with a Teflon coating. When Jimmy came to the league he added a trumpet to the mix and he loved to play it. The media would get wrapped up in the trumpet playing and Jimmy was able to use them to motivate our team and fans to reach his expectations.

During our week before Super Bowl XXVII in 1992 he was playing the media tune and they were singing in harmony. Dad and Mom came out to the game and we were able to spend time in the southern California rain. During their visit Dad said,

"Coach Johnson is really going out on a limb" referring to the attitude Jimmy was portraying in his interviews.

I quickly answered "Yea, he's going out on a limb for us."

We went on to win the Super Bowl, even though I was injured, I was still part of the team. I was grateful that Jimmy recognized my value and included me. Sometimes injured players are cast aside. Recuperation from an injury can be as much mental as physical. His faith in me recuperated my psyche and inspired me to keep the pace of my workouts and recovery.

During training camp of our second season under Jimmy I knew I was still on the bubble. I knew Jimmy kept a close eye on everything the media chose to air. In my mind I was sure that he taped all ESPN shows and would watch them with the same voracity as game films. He had traded for two linebackers with the Hershel Walker deal and drafted three others. The writing was on the wall and I took heed.

In the NFL it's all about your last play. Jimmy was very enthusiastic on the practice field, especially when there were cameras around. He was an intense coach who knew his business from top to bottom. There wasn't a move or action on the field that he didn't know. Eugene Lockhart said it best "He makes you believe in him." Jimmy was all about fundamentals and enthusiasm.

During his second season as the Head Coach, we had just finished a particularly hard practice during training camp. An overcast sky had held the temperature down so the coaches decided to keep the team out for more sprints. The cameras were rolling and Jimmy was pushing us. After the final sprint I stayed out and tried to cool myself in the shade with an ice pack on my knee.

Sitting near the training room entrance was a Reporter. He had a camera set up and was waiting for Jimmy to come out. Jimmy made him wait while he too cooled down and changed shirts. He was always such a cool character. From where I was sitting around the corner I could hear their conversation.

Jimmy would engage reporters before he started answering questions and get a feel for the answers before going on camera. He was telling the reporter how hard working the team was. He said how impressed he was in our work ethic with player's effort in the weight room. He talked about how the veterans were leading and he was expecting success with the team. Then the camera started to roll. I jumped up and tossed the ice pack to the ground.

You will remember earlier in the book I talked about being in the best shape of my life after my knee injury. Well, I was buff and I walked behind Jimmy in view of the camera to a set of chin up bars. I started to do chin ups. I continued in my best form, listening to the questions and keeping a rhythm. Soon I was over 50 chin-ups and Jimmy was still talking. When he finally took a breath, I dropped down, flexed and started doing push-ups.

The next answer took several minutes and I had to keep perfect form because of the camera. When it was over I popped up and jogged into the locker room. I didn't see the interview until nearly twenty years later on an ESPN special. I was sure Jimmy saw it on the day it premiered. Jimmy was in a class by himself. I am fortunate to call him a friend.

The 1993 season became unsettled before camp started. Jimmy and Jerry were on TV together announcing they had come to a parting of the ways. It was a total shock to the players as well as the media and fans. These guys were college roommates and by all appearances they were enjoying the limelight of winning two Super Bowls. No one knew it was coming. and we had no idea.

Jimmy was a restless guy. He had come to the Cowboys with the goal of winning the Super Bowl and had done it twice. I still don't know if it was a squabble over money. Maybe Jimmy was restless. Some thought he was burned out from the grind of coaching. I believe that he had reached his pinnacle as a coach and was ready for another challenge. Now every week he gets to talk about the issues and problems of every team in the league, but doesn't have to actually fix them. He is now challenged by a group of knuckleheads on FOX NFL Sunday. I don't believe there is anyone who knows more about NFL football than Jimmy Johnson. If the job of Commissioner ever becomes available, he would be a great one.

I did have a big beef with Jimmy over Plan B Free Agency. The agreement allowed the league to protect only 37 players, making them unable to sign with other teams. Even though I was a committed Cowboy, the thought of making more money naturally excited me. I knew the Vikings were interested and the thought of doubling or tripling my paycheck was attractive, especially with five little ones who would need braces and college educations.

My agent was told that I wouldn't be protected and I was starting to make plans. Then came February of 1989 and the eleventh hour. I don't remember the exact date, but Denise and I were home and in bed, anticipating a new contract negotiation. Jimmy called and let me know that I was being protected. I was mad and didn't sleep that night. Here was my chance to cash in like all of the other Free Agents and it was snatched out from under me at the final hour.

When I look back, I realize I would have missed the best years of my career, three Super Bowls and a whole lot of great times in Dallas. I am also flattered that Jimmy thought enough of me to make sure I stayed a Cowboy.

At that moment in time, I felt betrayed. Now I look at the three Super Bowl trophies in my office and wear the rings with pride. Thank you Jimmy.

There was a new Sheriff in Town. Right after the announcement that Jimmy had left, Barry Switzer was on the scene. I had never met Barry but his record as a college coach was nothing short of amazing. I was curious to get to know him. I had learned to trust Jerry's decisions. Who could argue with two consecutive Super Bowls.

Barry walked into a hornets nest. Players were changing teams all over the league with Plan B. Everyone was looking for a better paycheck and we were losing players too. Fortunately Jerry had built an organization that could withstand losing players, and still win. Like I said earlier, the team that Jimmy had coached to two Super Bowls had 60% new players for Super Bowl XXX. Again, it was a grueling process with the changeover.

The better I got to know Barry, the more I liked him. He was a players coach and a great motivator. He was one of the smartest tacticians I have been around. He was always selling players to do their best.

Barry's childhood was a mess. His father was taken away to jail right in front of him at an early age. He grew up on the wrong side of the tracks. My Dad also grew up in a poor area. I know how hard he worked to make his way out of poverty and knowing Barry had a similar upbringing made me respect him even more.

Barry also played football at Arkansas, just like Jimmy and Jerry. He had pulled himself up through football and got a college education. The brotherhood of coaches accepted him as of Frank Broyles protégé. I sensed something familiar with him the first time I met him.

Right before training camp I was able to spend some time with Barry. We talked very little about the team. Mostly we talked about our past and families and got to know each other. The more time I spent with him made me realize why he was such a success in the college ranks. He was unlike Jimmy in many ways, choosing to talk open and frank with his players in the moment. He hid nothing and with me, I knew exactly where I stood.

Barry came in and went right to work evaluating players. By the time we went to camp he knew what he was looking for to make the World Champions better. It became apparent that he wanted players that played with the same passion in which he coached. It was a requirement. It was his requirement along with size, speed and football fundamentals. He was looking to find all four in each player at every position. I know for a fact that he valued heart most of all. Why else would he have kept a 33 year-old, slow undersized linebacker?

Barry was bound and determined to get the right players and the right chemistry on the team. He gave us all the opportunity to compete for the job. The cream rose and I believe that our team his first year was better than any of the previous two. The loss to the 49ers in the playoffs was the culmination of a lot of factors. Barry took the heat and like the man that he was, he stood up for us as a team.

Barry was bound and determined to make us even better. He wasn't finished putting his touches on the Cowboys. He wanted a cornerback who could shut down the 49ers passing attack because he knew it was impossible to win the Super Bowl unless we got through them. That missing piece was Deion Sanders.

Our roster was full of high paid players and getting him in under contract would be the trick. Jerry Jones, the deal maker, entered the game and soon the talented Deion was wearing a STAR. It came with the added bonus of rocking the 49ers.

We had it all. A quarterback named Aikman who I still consider the best I ever saw. Believe me, I stood on the other side of the line from some of the best and Troy was the real deal. The most courageous runningback I ever witnessed carry the ball. Not the biggest, not the fastest but absolutely the best. Michael Irvin had turned into a football hungry player. He wanted the ball and when he got it, magic happened. They were the big guns, but each will tell you that it took the whole team to win the Championships.

Barry made sure they were surrounded by the best players money could buy and Jerry had no problem writing the checks. I have mentioned a lot of players throughout this book but I would be remiss if I didn't mention these Super Bowl XXX teammates.

We had a stellar defense anchored by funny man Charles Haley. Charles was near the end of his career but we wouldn't let him go without winning one more Silver Football with us. He was a great teammate that kept things loose in the locker room. Although he made his mark on the field, his locker room antics cracked us up.

Russell Maryland came to the team because of the Hershel Walker trade. Throw in Leon Lett, Darren Woodson, Darrin Smith and Tony Tolbert on the Defense.

Mark Tuinei, Larry Allen, Erik Williams, Derreck Kennard, and Nate Newton blasted the holes for Emmitt and protected Troy. Jay Novacek was the best tight end in the game. When Troy wasn't throwing to Jay or Michael, he had Kevin William and out of the backfield Daryl Johnston.

Barry spent the 1995 season tuning up the team to make a playoff run. By the time the playoffs came, we were tuned up and confident. He enjoyed winning and the team expected it. The confidence of our team entering the game was almost scary. We didn't want to be too over confident. Barry made sure we were ready and win the Super Bowl we did.

Having played for such different coaches gave me exposure to different coaching styles. I like to think that when I started coaching, I brought the best of each of them to my players. If I could give each of them just a little of the best that was given me, my success as a coach would be felt for years to come.

I still get the question "Who was the best coach you played for?" It generally comes from someone wanting to know who I thought was the best between Tom Landry, Jimmy Johnson and Barry Switzer. I have tried to stay out of that trap because each of them gave their best.

The question I like to answer is "Who had the most impact on my life?" He wasn't a high paid professional coach, or a dedicated college coaching icon. He was Ken Sparks and if you have read this far into the book, you know how he impacted my life. Thank you Ken.

29 - Dan Bates

It was 1957, my dad, Dan Bates had married my mother, Peggy Jane Graham. Within two months after graduating from the University of Tennessee, he enlisted in the Navy and was soon in Officers Candidate School in Newport Rhode Island.

My true Hero

In order to know a man, I think it is important to know where he comes from. During my life, some of the best men I have known have been the ones who had to overcome adversity in order to succeed. Well, that was my dad. He grew up in one of the poorest counties in the country. His parents had to work multiple jobs just to make ends meet and they still lived in a house in the poorest part of the county. The house was set up on blocks, and they raised chickens underneath it. Dad was in charge of climbing into the crawlspace and gathering the eggs.

As a young man, he had to work to help support his family after the depression and World War II. His dream was to attend the University of Tennessee. All of the jobs delivering newspapers, painting houses, digging ditches and working on the surrounding farms all paid off when he was accepted.

He had caught the eye of my mother in high school. She wrote in her diary that "He was tall dark and handsome and had ladies eyeing his good looks." She went on to write in the family history "He had a keen mind and was very analytical, was good in math, organized things well, was well mannered, industrious, and aggressive and had high goals." She was a good judge of character proven by their nearly 55 years of marriage.

Like I said it was 1957 and Dad had been accepted into Officer Candidate School in Newport. Commander S.H. Manown wrote to my Dad; "You have completed one of the most rigorous and intensified courses existing anywhere in our service schools of the United States Armed Forces. It is with great pleasure and pride that I offer you my sincere congratulations. We have given you an insight into what the Navy will demand of you as an officer. The enthusiasm with which you have assumed these responsibilities has won the confidence and praise of the entire staff and leaves us with no doubt of your ability to meet the problems which you will face as an officer."

Dad worked hard in OC School. It was tough schooling and the only way to graduate was to put in the extra time and effort to make it through. He did it with flying colors. There was a sign that posted in their study hall. The hall was a long narrow hallway with two rows of picnic tables down the sides. It said:

"We Have Not yet Begun to Study. If you can't make it, Don't fake it."

The tables would be piled full of books, everything from electricity to ordinance.

Dad did so well his assignment was the USS Intrepid. The famous World War II carrier had been refitted as an attack carrier and he was commissioned and assigned to her for the largest peacetime naval exercise of that era, NATO's Operation Strikeback. They were actually playing war games to intercept hostile enemies in the Atlantic. After he left the Navy, the Intrepid became a museum in New York Harbor. It is now called the Intrepid Sea-Space-Air Museum and has been named a National Historic Landmark. Every time I fly to New York I sit next to the window so I can see that beautiful ship. When I get the chance, I visit and stand on the bridge where my Dad stood watch so many years ago.

Dad carried his Naval training with him the rest of his life. He was sharp, direct and demanded discipline. His hard work paid off when he retired from Exxon where he had held several high level sales and marketing positions. He was well known in our community of Farragut for being the President of the Booster Club which built the football stadium and in several local organizations for giving his time.

What does my Dad's life have to do with me being an All Pro, National Football League Player? You might think it is the discipline or drive he required of me. You might think it was his example of hard work. Well, maybe to some extent those were beneficial to my development. What my Dad gave me was the "Expectation" of being a winner. He was a winner in life because he expected it. It was the way he taught me to think.

30 - New STARS

Since I was a little kid I dreamed big. Coach Sparks drilled it into us to dream big. I would sit and look at my Dad's yearbook and see him in his basketball uniform and dream about playing basketball. I worked hard to live my dreams and have been fortunate to see many of them come true. When I met my dream gal I had to work hard to get her too. Together we have lived a phenomenal life. She has shared my dreams and I am a lucky man to have her by my side. Through the thick and thin, she has always been there. My love for her grows every day.

Denise and I dreamed of having a big family, living in a beautiful home in a community of caring people with great schools for our kids. After coaching 5 years for the Cowboys with Chan Gailey and Dave Campo, I reunited with my good friend, former Jacksonville Jaguars Head Coach Jack Del Rio. Jack was a linebacker for the Cowboys and we both played special teams.

When we were playing in Dallas several of players had gotten together and pledged that whomever became a Head Coach first would hire the others on his staff. Jack got his shot in Jacksonville when they fired Tom Coughlin. He called and ask me join his staff. Jack didn't have to convince me to leave Dallas and take the position.

Jacksonville is a wonderful city. It has beautiful beaches on the Atlantic Ocean, a lot of fishing and incredible golf courses. The one that attracted me the most was Sawgrass. The PGA is located in Ponte Vedra Beach and the Players Championship is played at Sawgrass. My love for golf, which is a game my mother taught me, and the mild temperature of a beach community were all inviting.

Previous to the offer, we had spent quite a bit of time in the Jacksonville area. We had several football camps at the University of North Florida and would bring in Troy, Emmitt and other teamates. I would bring the family for beach time and I got in some great golf with one of my best friends Gary Verble.

It would mean moving my family from the only home they knew, away from our friends and away from the Cowboys family. It was tough but

Denise made it easy. She knew I still had STARS to chase. It would also give me a little more time with the boys as they continued to play sports.

It was an exciting time for the Bates family. Denise made it quite the adventure for the kids. They had surprises always just around the corner. As long as they had each other, they were fine. We were the Bates family and we banded together to get through the move.

We knew what we were leaving behind. The adventure was in front of us and we certainly didn't know what to expect. It was exciting, yet sorrowful. When I finally got a chance to talk with Jerry Jones, he shook my hand, looked me right in the eye with the widest smile on his face and said "Once a Cowboy, Always a Cowboy."

Denise had the toughest job with the kids. Moving them to a new school in a new community was tough. I was focused on football so she made the arrangements and we moved to the beach community of Ponte Vedra. As much as we loved Dallas, I had dreams of staying in football and this was the best route. Besides, Ponte Vedra boasts some of the finest golf courses in the world.

I didn't stay with the Jaguars long because my other business interests required more attention. This also gave me the ability to go from an 80 hour work week to a 40 hour week and the great benefit of being able to coach my sons in high school. I kinda did the reverse in my coaching career, starting in the NFL and ending up with a gang of boys on the high school gridiron.

We had a house full of boys and one beautiful daughter. Brianna has a strong personality like her mother and growing up with four boys in the house made her solid. She figured out the psyche of boys early on and she is able to use it to her advantage. She was my little princess but if the boys backed her into a corner, she could hold her own. In turn, she didn't have many problems with other boys because her brothers were always there for her. I am sure she is tired of me saying boys are bad, except your brothers of course.

I admire my little girl who is now attending the University of Florida as an English major. She wants to write and now has a highly successful blog about cooking. Her, Denise and Momo, Denise's mother, are the boys biggest fans. With two Division 1 and a high school player in the household, she finds herself in the stands a lot.

Even with a lot of the focus being on the boys, she was able to carve out her own life. She is delightful, fun loving and respectful. Ask anyone who has tried and they will tell you it is really hard to get accepted at Florida. Brianna got the grades and worked to get the other intangibles such as community service and volunteer activities to gain admission. I very much look forward to watching her as she continues to grow, has a successful writing career, family and lives her dreams.

The boys. Graham and Hunter are big brothers to Tanner and Dillon. I have been fortunate enough to coach all four in sports but most amazing is that I have been able to coach them in high school football. I thought it would be a tough decision to leave the NFL and believe that one day I may return, but for now, I am living the dream. When I look around at the parents and how they have so willingly entrusted their sons to our coaches, it can evoke a lot of great memories about my coaches. The faith and trust that parents put into coaches is amazing. It is seen at the great sports programs that have grown throughout our nation.

My first coach was my Dad. He was also quite a basketball player and told me that the main thing a coach should do with his players is to "take good young men and make them better." That is my mission with my sons and the boys on their teams. When it came my time to give back, coaching my sons has been a highlight in my life. Most coaches are volunteers that pass along what they have been taught by their coaches. High School football coaches can be the most important people in the lives of our young men and can have the greatest impact on their future. They don't do it for the money because it is just not there. It takes dedication and resolve combined with grit to push, pull and inspire players to give their all on the practice field and be prepared for greatness on the playing field.

Craig Howard was the Head Coach at Nease High School. I hit it off with Craig and soon he asked and I heartily accepted the coaching job for the freshman team at Nease when Graham and Hunter were there. It is the same school Tim Tebow attended and they were building a first class football program. I had coached the boys on their teams in Dallas, but my time then had to be focused as player and coach in the NFL. Now was the time for me to stretch my abilities and convey the game of football to my boys. They loved the game of football and being able to share my knowledge with them was another dream come true.

Graham and Hunter, even though they were premature babies, had grown into strong fast athletes. Their love for the game showed with their passion both on and off the field. I was able to show them techniques, fundamentals and the thinking part of the game early. What I couldn't give them is passion for the game. They both had that passion. Maybe it came because they saw how hard I worked, the Super Bowl wins and the awards I received. Some think it was the burning desire to achieve that both Denise and I had instilled in them. I truly believe that it was because they had to fight for their lives from the moment they were born. In the beginning, every breath was a struggle because their little lungs were not fully developed. From the very start they learned to overcome the odds. While I was stretching myself to be the best I could be and play in the NFL, they were showing me how much they wanted to live. They were my little buddies who spent long nights in my arms and put my life into perspective.

Coaching the boys has been one of the most enjoyable experiences in my life. It was tough on them because everyone expected them to be the best. I could drill the fundamentals and get them in top physical shape, but I couldn't play for them. They had to step up and play with passion. It didn't surprise me that they were leaders on the field. Just like the winners I had played with and for throughout my career they set their own expectations and lived up to them.

Football has always given me the gift of good friends. Over the years there have been many teammates and coaches that I still consider my best friends. I was told by my Dad that "Years after playing the game, you won't remember all the scores or all the great plays you made. What you will remember are the friendships you made and the admiration for your coaches." It still rings true today and I feel fortunate to be blessed by those relationships.

Coaching their freshman team was a lot tougher than I expected. I had been coaching highly trained and experienced athletes and sometimes when I talked about certain plays and defensive coverage's, these boys looked at me with blank stares. I was quickly informed by Graham and Hunter that I had to go back to the basics. Nobody knew what I talking about.

That Nease freshman team went on to an undefeated season. I learned more from them than I could ever give back to them. Graham was a real yes sir, no sir player. I told him what to do and he did it without question. Hunter was just the opposite. Whenever I told him to do something, he wanted to know why. He questioned everything. Even though they were triplets, they still had their own personalities.

During that freshman year Graham was playing receiver and Hunter was the safety. The team went undefeated and we were thrilled when Hunter got called up to catch punts for the varsity.

Their sophomore season at Nease found both Graham and Hunter on the Varsity team. They worked hard during the summer and were growing stronger and faster. I was a proud Dad. Nease had turned into a

powerhouse in the state of Florida and here were my boys right in the middle of it.

The teams consisted not only of the boys that worked hard and believed they could win, but of their parents, schoolmates, teachers, coaches, boosters and the community. It was fun to be a part of something special.

During their sophomore season, Graham was on the offense catching balls from Tim Tebow.

Graham catches a Tim Tebow Touchdown

He did a great job and during the next three years the Nease Panthers went to the State Championship game. They won it when Graham and Hunter were sophomores.

Graham moved back to the other side of the ball. He was a 6' tall corner and built right for getting the attention of the college scouts. They had seen him catch the ball for Tebow and now were back to see him on the defensive side of the ball.

Hunter continued to be the thinker on the field. He was able to position himself to make plays because he stayed a step ahead of the opposing coaches. We had spent a lot of time in the film room and he soaked it in. Tendencies, keys and big playmakers were sought out and he always seemed to be in the play.

Hunter turns the corner on a punt return

Graham and Hunter started getting noticed by college coaches during their sophomore season because of their all-out play and the championship caliber program. It certainly didn't hurt to have a top rated player like Tim Tebow on the team. He was being recruited by all of the major programs.

The scouting turned into full blown recruiting the following year. We wanted the best for the boys and they stepped up in the classroom and on the field. Most important for any parent who has an athlete that is being recruited is to first make a list of the schools your athlete wants to attend for the right reasons. We put education first. It was quite an experience having two boys and Brianna looking at schools at the same time. Needless to say it was a hectic time around the Bates household. Once they were able to name the schools, remember it must be their decision, we were able to really get into the fun part of visiting schools.

Northwestern was the first to offer the boys, both of them, scholarships. Denise and I were elated. To have the boys at the same school would sure make it easier to get to their games on Saturday after coaching Tanner and Dillon on Friday night. It was too good to be true.

The boys applied for entrance and we thought everything was moving along on schedule. The entrance requirements for Northwestern are extremely high. They had signed their commitment letters and were getting set to become college freshmen. Then we found out late that Graham's

SAT score was just a few points short and he would have to retake it. He jumped right on it and moved it up, but by then they had offered the scholarship to another player.

We were scrambling. Because it was so late, most of the scholarships were gone. We spent a lot of time on the phone and one of the schools that had been in his top five, Arkansas State were elated that he was available. All of the sudden we had four boys playing on four teams in three different parts of the country. Denise said "Hold on for a spectacular ride!" It has been nothing less than remarkable.

Brianna had her own moves on the field

Brianna was focused on going to Florida. Although there are many great schools in Florida and we wanted to make sure her decision was the right one for her so we visited several. Before she finally decided to become a Gator. Her experience has been great there and she has impressed us with her dedication to the school work while having a first-class college experience.

Tanner is an incredibly natural athlete. Being a couple of years younger than the older boys he had to strive hard to keep up with them. He dug real deep to stay out from the shadows of his older brothers. His love

323

and attention is focused on the arts and music is his passion. He also loved playing football and when it came time to move up to high school football, I didn't know if he would have the same passion for the game. I didn't want to make the mistake of forcing him to play so the decision was totally up to him.

Nease High School was outgrowing its campus and it was decided that a new high school would be built in Ponte Vedra. When they split the school, Tanner had the option of attending either. He decided to go to the new school. Dillon would soon be following him. When they started football workouts I didn't know if he would play. It would be a struggle because the team didn't have one senior player and most of Nease's players stayed with their program.

Tanner makes headlines

I was pleasantly pleased when Tanner announced he would play at Ponte Vedra. The decision was a hard one, since they would be playing seasoned teams with only a junior and sophomore team.

I had met the new Head Coach Mike Loyd. He was a former NFL quarterback who had coached Northeastern Oklahoma to the National Championship (91-95) with a winning percentage of .870. He had since

been coaching championship high school teams in Oklahoma. Over the years he has put nearly two hundred players in Division One schools and numerous others in small college programs.

He had the credentials but what I was really impressed with was he had the intangibles and was up for the challenge. Although he was highly sought after by schools in Florida and Oklahoma he came to Ponte Vedra and dedicated himself to building a winning program. He knew it would be hard work and convinced the boys that if they followed him they could become winners.

Tanner really liked him and bought in to the program. It would give him the chance to be on the ground floor of building the program out from under the shadows of Graham and Hunter.

Coach Loyd reminds me of the best coaches I had the privilege of playing for. He is cool, calm and collected and the boys looked up to him as a leader. I appreciate that he is a man of faith and he shares it with the boys. He reminded me of Coach Sparks who had given me so much inspiration and guidance as a high school football player and I couldn't ask for a better coach for Tanner and Dillon.

Tanner thrived as a player and leader for the Ponte Vedra Sharks. Even though their record against some of the toughest teams in the area wasn't great, the team played every down and never gave up. Coach Loyd welcomed me on the staff as a volunteer coach and I jumped at it. Owning my own businesses allowed the time, although not as much as I would have liked, to spend coaching.

When Tanner stepped on the field, he wasn't the biggest or fastest. What he had was heart and an incredible nose for the football. He played cornerback and his knack for reading and reacting to the plays in front of him put him in position to make great plays. When he made a play, it was full out. He knew his assignments and his coverage was excellent. He had worked hard to hone his skills and playing football with his big brothers required him to be scrappy.

The Sharks were playing Creekside High School in Jacksonville during his senior year. Tanner was being tested in coverage and had made several good plays on the ball early in the game, not allowing a completion on his side of the field. In the second half Creekside started running the ball more. On a wide sweep he came up hard and just as the big back turned the corner, Tanner flew into his mid-section with a picture perfect tackle. Sometime during the hit a finger got into his facemask and poked his right eye. When he got to the sideline he had a bloody black eye. After a trip to the Emergency Room and some stitches, his eye was OK.

The next day we flew to Arkansas State to watch Graham play. He wore the black eye like a badge of honor. Pound for pound he was the toughest kid on the team. Me, I was living the dream.

When it came time for Tanner to decide on what school he would attend there weren't a lot of colleges scouting him. That was just fine with Tanner. He is focused on his music and fortunately Full Sail University is in nearby Orlando. He was hooked on his first visit there. They had all of the latest digital audio and film equipment and it would allow him to fully exploit his love for music.

Just like Brianna, he has made his way with good grades and passion for his future in audio recording. When he explains it to me I get lost in the technical aspects but see the confidence, determination and growth of my son. Many doors are beginning to open for him in the industry. I am amazed at his accomplishments and the way he has tackled his education.

Dillon is our youngest son. The bar his brothers have set is high and the prospects for Dillon are growing. Being the youngest in a football family, he has stepped up to the task. Not many kids get the chance to play varsity football as a freshman, let alone start like he did.

Sophomore Dillon,
a 101 tackle season

Dillon has always been one of the bigger and better athletes in his class. He was over six feet tall as an eighth grader and demanded the attention of the varsity coaches when he arrived on the practice field his freshman year at over 6'3" and weighing 195 pounds. Just like the other boys he has the heart of a football player.

Under Coach Mike Loyd the Sharks have become a good football team. Their workout shirts have "TEAM MATTERS MOST" printed on the back. On the front they say, "We work ours off in the Spring so we can kick yours in the Fall." His teams are some of the hardest working boys in the weight room, on the field and in the classroom that I have ever seen. Their record started to show it during Dillon's freshman season. They were competitive in nearly every ball game and ended the season with a 6-4 record. In three short years Coach Loyd had built a team that goes beyond being respectful. They are good. The boys have come together as a team. There is no finger pointing or harsh words between them as they all work together and have learned how to win. The parents, families, coaches, administration and community have come together to support them in their journey.

Coach Loyd has turned down more lucrative coaching jobs to continue to lead the Sharks. The boys understand his commitment to them and believe he will lead them to new heights. He has publicly said many times that this is the best group of players he has ever coached.

I can see the level of expectation (there is that word again) that he has for the team, coaches and families. They have fought through many hard losses and are now enjoying the fruits of their work.

They gladly go in for off-season training and before school early morning work-outs. They are a cohesive unit. It takes me back to my glory days with the Cowboys and I am enjoying it immensely.

Dillon is a linebacker in the Sharks 3-4 defense. With his height he can see what is happening in front of him and reacts quickly. As a freshman he was one of the top tacklers on the team and intercepted two passes, one for a pick-six touchdown.

Dillon has the combined size and speed of his older brothers with a nose for the ball like Tanner. As he continues to grow and fill out he is surely to be one of the biggest Bates boys yet. His physique reminds me of my Dad, tall and strong.

The Sharks started Dillon's sophomore season with high expectations. The expectations weren't from the press or opposing coaches, they were set by the boys themselves. Their goal was to win the District Championship and make the Florida State playoffs. They surpassed that goal and advanced to the Regional Championship game. During the season they have had to show their character by playing from behind in four games.

Dillon has become a better football player every game. He expects, and everyone on his team expects to win. They started the season against one of the toughest state ranked teams in Florida. Bartram Trail plays in a higher division and had a veteran team taking the field. Their quarterback,

Nathan Peterman, had committed to play for the Vols, so I know he was going to be a force to be reckoned with. Their offensive line had played together for two years and had a couple of Division One prospects with good size and skills. The quarterback had a couple of outstanding receivers that were also Division One prospects with amazing speed and great hands. When he wasn't throwing he was handing off to one of the best backs in the area and son of a former NFL running back .

The Sharks kept the game close, keeping pace with the hot handed Peterman by matching the Bears two scoring drives with two 80 yard drives of their own. Then a couple of missed opportunities and penalties allowed the Bartram Trail team to capitalize and extend their lead.

Even in the loss the opposing coach, Darrell Sutherland gave them high praise for their effort by saying "There is absolutely no quit in that team. They play hard to the end." Even in the loss the Sharks were poised and the coaches were able to take a lot of positives from the game.

I was especially impressed with our special teams who had a blocked punt and our kicker Kyle Frederico, an early signee with Rutgers University, who booted a 42 yard field goal that got called back because of a penalty. Special teams started to make a big difference in our games. By the time the regular season ended, they had blocked nine punts.

The Sharks went on to win the District, accomplishing their preseason goal and then won two Florida State playoff games for a record of 11-2. Their new goal is to win the State Championship.

The city of Ponte Vedra got behind the team. The Regional Championship game was played in Wakulla, Florida. It was a four hour bus ride and the Sharks had almost as many fans in the stands as the host team War Eagles.

Although it was a close game and the defense played strong, a tough running attack by the War Eagles chewed up the clock. In the end the Sharks were driving for a tying score when a turnover stopped them. They had gone beyond their expectations and by going to the Regional Final, were only a couple of games short of the State Championship.

The excitement continues to build for the Sharks and the youngest Bates boy.

31 - Miracles and Family

Hershel Walker and I met on the college gridiron, two gladiators whose lives crossed paths in many different ways during our careers and beyond. Hershel was a bright spot in my first years as a Cowboy. He was there during the downward spiral we experienced in the mid-eighties. That big ol smile of his never dulled. He was one of the greatest athletes I ever met, played against, played with and got run over by.

Because he got me involved in the March of Dimes, the miracle drug Surfactant was made available to my children. It was truly a miracle.

As a way of giving back to the March of Dimes, Denise and I have committed to give a portion of the proceeds from the sale of this book to the Dallas March of Dimes in honor of our children. We are grateful for the wonderful gift of life they gave us.

I had my own
Cheering Section

Earlier in the book I wrote about Jerry Jones and what he meant to me and our family. He is definitely a class act. Cowboys Stadium is an incredible facility. There is no stadium in the world that matches it. Jerry made sure every detail was to the benefit of the fans and players.

329

Like so many owners in the NFL, Jerry knows that he just manages the team. It is the fans who own the team. They put their hard earned money toward seats, jerseys and popcorn. Without them, why would Jerry spend a billion dollars on Cowboys Stadium?

He is dedicated to the Cowboys beyond what anyone can imagine. Not the organization that he owns but the players he manages. During my final year as a Cowboy, NFL Films came in to do a special on me. I had been in the league for 15 years and had been through it all, going from the bottom of the league to the top.

Along with me they interviewed Joe Avezzano and Moose Johnson. They had footage with me and Coach Landry from early in my career. I told them about the Free Agent experience becoming a Cowboy. They even got me yelling "Bad to the bone!"

Billy Davis called my family the "rabbit family" because of the kids. Then they interviewed Jerry Jones. What he said touched my heart. He got it. He understood why I worked so hard every day.

Jerry Jones said *"The game, the dedication that it takes, You give yourself up. You do the things that you weren't made to do. Those are the kind of things our fans think of when they think of Bill Bates. He's a big part of the tradition of the Dallas Cowboys."*

Jerry has always gone out of his way to make me a part of the Cowboys and Jones family. To him, it is all about family.

I began my career as a long shot. Every day was a long shot for me to survive in the league. After a career of playing more than 200 games over fifteen years, I can honestly say that I honored that STAR every time I took the field.

I shot for the STAR and I am living my dream.
How about you?

Cowboys Years

BILL BATES   DALLAS COWBOYS

★ ★ ★ ★ ★ ★ ★ ★

Tom Landry Legend Award

1985 Mackey Award

ALL MADDEN AWARD

Bob Lilly Awards

BATES BOYS

Coaching Hunter and Graham 's
Preston Wood Baptist

*From Freshman summer
camp*

To State Championship rings

Graham at Arkansas State

Dillon as a Ponte Vedra Shark

Coach Mike Loyd with Dillon

Family

A true Football Mama

A Cowboy Family

BILL BATES
SAFETY
1983-1997

Bill Bates Biography

PROFESSIONAL: A member of the 1992, 1993 and 1995 Super Bowl Champions team, Bill has been a long time favorite of Cowboys fans. He was named the winner of the Bob Lilly Award four years in a row, from 1990 - 1994. This award is selected by a vote of the fans and annually goes to the Cowboy player who displays leadership and character on and off the field. The 1993 season had seen him return from a disabling knee injury that prematurely ended his 1992 season.

After the 1993 season Bill was selected by his teammates to receive the Ed Block Courage Award for successfully overcoming his injury. In 1995, Bill was named by the fans and his team-mates the "Unsung Hero" award, which is given to one player from each NFL team. He has also been the recipient of the Dallas All Sports Association Courage Award. Bill was selected to the All-Madden Team for twelve years in a row and made the roster of the Madden-Summerall "ALL DALLAS COWBOY TEAM" and the Madden Hall of Fame.

Bates named the Cowboys three Super Bowl victories as the most memorable moments of his playing career. He was a part of championship teams in 1992, 1993, and 1995 as Dallas cemented its place as the team of the 90s. But one of his favorite memories involves the famed coif of his former coach. "There was that time when we defeated the Redskins in Washington, around the time when Jimmy Johnson first came to Dallas," Bates recalled. "At the end of the game I rubbed his head - not on purpose - which appeared to be sprayed down with hair spray and everyone was getting on him about it. For years after that, the clip where I rubbed his head was used as the opening to a sports show- fortunately that didn't end my career."

When Bates retired following the 1997 season, he tied the club record for service with 15 seasons in Dallas. In that time he amassed 217 games played (second in team history), over 700 tackles and 14 interceptions.

Bates joined the Cowboys again as a special teams/defensive assistant coach in 1998 under then-head coach Chan Gailey. He was defensive backs coach and defensive nickel package/special team's assistant with coach Campo until 2003 when he became the Special Teams coach for the Jacksonville Jaguars.

While Bates has many great memories and stories from his time in the NFL, he has always been a family man first and foremost. When he and his wife Denise had triplets in 1989, he gained a new perspective on raising kids. "Having as many kids as I did made me want to really look out for the community," he said. It was these blessings plus the births of Tanner in 1991 and Dillon in 1995 that motivated the founding of the Bill Bates Foundation for Children. The foundation helps distribute funds to other organizations dedicated to helping kids. Bates was named the "Best Dad in Dallas" in 1994 for his ability to juggle his football career and fatherhood.

Bates currently is working to create a safer environment for football players through the production of air-cooled shoulder pads and the Temperature Management System (TMS). These pads were designed by researchers at the University of Florida who also created the Gatorade sports beverages. The TMS acts as a players' personal air conditioner and lowers the temperature of a players' body, thus reducing the chances of a heat stroke caused by dehydration. When the shoulder pads are hooked up to the cooling unit, cool air passes over areas of the player's shoulders and back. The Dallas Cowboys, Houston Texans, Green Bay Packers, Jacksonville Jaguars and the Indianapolis Colts are among the NFL teams that have already adopted the new air-cooled shoulder pads. As well, the Florida Gators.

As an inspirational team leader, Bill exemplified the qualities of perseverance and dedication every time he stepped onto the field. Prior to the 1990 season, Jimmy Johnson tabbed Bill as the Cowboys' special team's captain.

Also, as Barry Switzer took over he made sure his role would remain the same and he held that position for the remainder of his career. In 1995, his leadership and intelligence helped the Dallas special teams become one of the NFL's very best.

He was a very visible member of the Dallas nickel defense at middle linebacker position. His last minute interception at Chicago's Soldier Field preserved Dallas' 17 - 13 win in the team's triumphant return to the playoffs after a six year absence, and will surely go down as one of the big plays in the rebuilding of the Dallas Cowboys.

Bates was one of only a handful of Dallas players who had previous post season experience as a Cowboy. One of the NFL's true success stories, Bill has been overcoming the odds his entire career, starting in 1983 when he made the team as a long shot free agent rookie and coached by head coach Tom Landry and secondary coach Gene Stallings.

Bill immediately became a visible figure on the field with his ferocious special teams play. It was Bates' notoriety that helped propel the NFL into adding a spot on the Pro-Bowl teams for special team's. In 1984, he became the first NFC player so honored.

COLLEGE: Bill was a four year starting safety at Tennessee. He was named second-team All-Southeastern Conference his junior and senior seasons. Recently he was awarded a position on the 100 Year All Tennessee Team and induction to the Greater Knoxville Sports Hall of Fame. Bates developed a reputation as the Vol's hardest hitter and surest tackler. He intercepted nine passes and recovered six fumbles in his career.

PERSONAL: William Frederick Bates was born and raised in Knoxville, TN where he starred in football, basketball and as a sprinter on the track team at Farragut High School. He was all-state in football and basketball. Bill and his wife Denise have five children, triplets, Graham (Arkansas State playing football), Brianna (University of Florida) and Hunter (Northwestern playing football), Tanner and Dillon.

Bill served as the Chairperson for the March of Dimes "Blue Jeans for Babies" campaign for healthier babies and Bank One "Spirit of Christmas" campaign which provides gifts for abused and needy children. Bill was the spokesperson for the Children's Advocacy Center golf tournament and he helped start the Wednesday's child golf tournament in Dallas benefiting homeless children. He continued his celebrity chair for the 26th year of the tournament.

Bill stared with Michael Irvin and Joe Avezanno in the show 4th and Long on Spike TV. The show gave a contract with the Dallas Cowboys to Jesse Holly. Jesse made the team in 2009 and he continues to make his mark on special teams with the team.

He has also donated his time and energy to various other charitable organizations including: United Way, Children's Medical Center, Scottish Rite Hospital, FCA, Campus Crusade and Young Life.

Bill has started his own organization to benefit children. The Bill Bates Foundation For Children and The Bill Bates High School Football Classic were created to raise money for worthwhile organizations that help children.

After 15 years as a NFL player and 6 years as a coach in the League (5 for the Cowboys and 1 with the Jaguars), Bill is enjoying life out of the NFL. He coached his triplet boy's football team in Jacksonville at Nease High School winning the 2005 Florida High School 4A State Championship (Heisman Trophy Winner Timmy Tebow) and runner up in 2006 and 2007. He coached Tanner for 2 years at Ponte Vedra High. Most recently he coached Dillon as the Ponte Vedra Sharks won their District Championship and two State Playoffs games.

Also, he was the Head Coach for team Texas in the college All Star game, Texas vs the Nation in 2010 and 2011. The Texas team defeated the National team, 36-17 in 2010. 2011 they won again with a dramatic goal line stand on the last play of the game.

Bill is involved in a number of businesses which include Austin Custom Homes, Patio Scapes, Temperature Management Systems (air cooled football shoulder pads) Planet High School. The Bates' now reside in Ponte Vedra Beach, Florida where they are raising and coaching their family.

45993697R00194

Made in the USA
San Bernardino, CA
22 February 2017